The Florida Manatee

UNIVERSITY PRESS OF FLORIDA

Florida A&M University, Tallahassee
Florida Atlantic University, Boca Raton
Florida Gulf Coast University, Ft. Myers
Florida International University, Miami
Florida State University, Tallahassee
University of Central Florida, Orlando
University of Florida, Gainesville
University of North Florida, Jacksonville
University of South Florida, Tampa
University of West Florida, Pensacola

The Florida
Manatee
Biology and
Conservation

Roger L. Reep and Robert K. Bonde

UNIVERSITY PRESS OF FLORIDA

Gainesville • Tallahassee • Tampa • Boca Raton
Pensacola • Orlando • Miami • Jacksonville • Ft. Myers

Copyright 2006 by Roger L. Reep and Robert K. Bonde
Printed in the United States of America on acid-free paper

11 10 09 08 07 06   6 5 4 3 2 1

Library of Congress Cataloging-in-Publication Data
Reep, Roger.
The Florida Manatee / Roger L. Reep and
Robert K. Bonde.
p. cm.
Includes bibliographical references.
ISBN 0-8130-2949-x (alk. paper)
1. West Indian manatee—Florida.
I. Bonde, Robert K. II. Title.
QL737.S63R44   2006
599.dc22   2005058578

The University Press of Florida is the scholarly publishing
agency for the State University System of Florida, comprising
Florida A&M University, Florida Atlantic University, Florida
Gulf Coast University, Florida International University,
Florida State University, University of Central Florida,
University of Florida, University of North Florida, University
of South Florida, and University of West Florida.

University Press of Florida
15 Northwest 15th Street
Gainesville, FL 32611-2079
http://www.upf.com

599.55

This book is dedicated to the proposition
that it only takes a few people to change
the world, and you are one of them. For
those who rise to the challenge, may you
seek the middle ground of harmony in
the midst of harsh realities.

Contents

Foreword

Manatees first captured my interest 25 years ago. At that time there was very little in the scientific literature about these unusual mammals, and they were generally unknown to the public. My interest was stimulated by discovering Joseph C. Moore's 1956 account of manatee behavior based on recognition of individuals by patterns of scars from propellers. At the same time, my friends and colleagues Galen Rathbun and Bob Brownell had begun to build up the Sirenia Project within the U.S. Fish and Wildlife Service in Gainesville. The Sirenia Project and its many cooperators aimed to increase scientific knowledge of manatees, dugongs, and their habitats through long-term research. This new emphasis was mandated and funded by the Marine Mammal Protection Act of 1972, landmark ecosystem-based legislation signed by President Richard M. Nixon. Additional impetus for research on manatees, particularly that aimed at management, came shortly thereafter through the Endangered Species Act of 1973, the flagship environmental legislation also from the Nixon era and subsequently emulated by nations throughout the world. Approximately 25 years ago the State of Florida added their mandate through the Florida Manatee Sanctuary Act.

Within a year my interest coincided with this set of mandates and transported me to Gainesville to join the team at the Sirenia Project. Days after arriving I found myself side by side with Bob Bonde and Cathy Beck, conducting a necropsy on a dead manatee calf they had brought from the coast to the "manatee graveyard" in the live-oak woods southwest of town. At the time, I didn't really grasp the spectacularly unique aspects of manatee anatomy. With repetition of necropsies (an all-too-familiar procedure for many manatee biologists, but one that forms the basis for much manatee research) I came to appreciate how much manatees could teach us even from their carcasses. Then in the early 1980s a then-new faculty member at the College of Veterinary Medicine at the University of Florida introduced himself and expressed an interest in obtaining samples from some of these cases for research on questions about manatee neuroanatomy. Roger Reep had grown up in Florida and had maintained a nearly lifelong curiosity about these animals. The ensuing years saw much collaboration. I recall extensive sessions on campus brainstorming with Roger about relationships among manatee neuroanatomy, behavioral ecology, and life history, and traveling with him to explore Amazonian manatee habitat in eastern Ecuador. I also have fond memories of flying through clear morning skies with Bob, searching for manatees as we passed over mirror-calm lagoons bordered by tropical forest on our expedition to the Bocas del Toro region with Fundacion Panama. These and other collaborations were driven by a sense of curiosity, interest, and adventure (accented during the Panama trip by heightened political tensions from the Noriega regime and a nagging uncertainty about how the kids playing with our 55-gallon drums of airplane fuel at the Bocas airstrip might have compromised our safety). There is uniqueness to manatee research, and it comes out in this book. Although I have left this field, Roger and Bob have stayed the course and continue to carry out research and to teach and train others.

Although now only from afar, I am still interested in manatees and manatee research. If you have read to this point, you are too. Keep reading. Roger and Bob have tried to reach the interested layperson with accounts of some of the newest findings in manatee research without overburdening technical detail and have accompanied these with some superb illustrations. They also provide direct attribution to many of the individual researchers, which gives a humanized flavor of "who did what" and helps put the course of manatee research in a chronological perspective. The emphasis is on Florida, and the book documents and explains some of the often difficult-to-grasp aspects of manatee biology, environment, and the biopolitics surrounding the intersection of science and management in an increasingly litigious society that has developed since the landmark legislation of the early 1970s. More importantly, the book will lead you through the biological background into a number of fascinating areas emphasized in recent research that Roger and Bob have sometimes been in the thick of, ranging from explanations of the microorganisms that cause manatee die-offs during red tide blooms, to methods of captive rehabilitation, to descriptions of complicated long-distance migrations. Particularly interesting are the topics that touch on the speculative and tantalizing aspects of the evolution of manatee anatomy, behavior, life history, and perceptual biology. The latter includes voyages from the cells at the bases of manatee hairs to specialized regions of the brain that are critical to the existence of these mammals.

Like the enormous feeding capacity of manatees, there is much to digest here for both the general audience and the scientist. Laypersons can find reference to technical papers that provide more detail if they so desire. Scientists and specialists may see places that provoke contention, but that's part of the way science works: if an explanation seems incomplete, more research is stimulated, and the depth of understanding grows. This, too, is one of the interesting overall aims of the book: to provide a chronicle that uses manatees and people in Florida as an example of the pathways down which scientific research progresses. Start turning the pages, and enjoy the journey.

Thomas J. O'Shea, Ph.D.
U.S. Geological Survey
Fort Collins Science Center
Fort Collins, Colorado

Preface and Acknowledgments

Like Don Quixote, we are all tilting at windmills. Sometimes we even aim at the same one. When that happens, we have the opportunity to achieve something that helps to unite humankind. The recent history of manatees in Florida is inextricably linked to its human population, most obviously through common use of waterways. It is quite unique and rewarding to have a large, wild animal living in the canals and waterways just outside the windows of our homes. But as intriguing as this is, it often has its costs. Encounters between humans and manatees have been positive and negative, from awe-inspiring, direct underwater contacts between divers and 1,000-pound animals to speedboaters inflicting on manatees the mortal wounds made by watercraft impacts. General awareness of environmental issues has increased dramatically in the last 25 years as exemplified by the case of manatees in Florida. In the following chapters we discuss the manatee's evolutionary history, lifestyle, population dynamics, feeding and movement patterns, unique nervous system features, and sensory abilities. We also discuss the threats posed by people and the precarious situation challenging the manatee in the 21st century. We review the medical treatment of sick and injured manatees, which has witnessed remarkable advances in recent years, and end with a look at some recent technological innovations that are helping us to better understand the habits of these Florida natives, which in turn may help reduce lethal impacts by boats.

A loosely knit community of dedicated individuals has devoted careers or available spare time in research, management, public relations, education, fieldwork, and fundraising related to the preservation and understanding of Florida manatees. It is our hope that by sharing some of their stories we may help them draw closer together in the realization of a common dream: the peaceful coexistence of manatees and people in Florida.

Many individuals contributed in a variety of ways to this book. We especially wish to acknowledge Bruce Ackerman, Gordon Bauer, Cathy Beck, Joe Cheatwood, Kari Clifton, Chip Deutsch, Daryl Domning, Ed Gerstein, Laura Gerstein, Woodie Hartman, Rachel Henriques, Iske Larkin, Mark Lowe, Rick McKenzie, Chris Marshall, Tom O'Shea, Meghan Pitchford, Tom Pitchford, Buddy Powell, Adrienne Reep, Dudley Reep, Jim Reid, John Reynolds, Butch Rommel, Sarah Scruggs, Maggie Stoll, Mark Sweat, Gabe Trinity, Scott Wright, and several anonymous reviewers. A special thanks to our editors, Ken Scott and John Byram.

Florida Manatee Traits

Population and habitat

- Evolved about five million years ago from Caribbean stock
- First appeared in Florida over one million years ago
- Present estimated minimum population 3,300
- Listed as endangered under federal Endangered Species Act; also protected under Marine Mammal Protection Act
- Adapted for tropics to subtropics; Florida at northern extreme of range
- Marine and freshwater distribution, coinciding with coastal grass beds and rivers
- Preferred water depth of 1–4 m
- No natural predators
- Low genetic diversity
- Little intermingling between East and West Coast populations
- 30 percent of annual mortality from anthropogenic causes

Life history

- Sexual maturity at two to five years of age
- Mating herds and scramble polygyny
- Long gestation time, about 12–14 months
- Single offspring, twinning rare
- Newborns 18–45 kg and about 1.2 m long
- 1.5- to 2.5-year dependency period
- Calves suckle from axillary teats
- Underwater suckling three to five minutes every one to two hours around the clock
- Long period of early learning
- Mother-calf bond main social unit
- No territoriality or aggression
- 2.5- to 3.0-year calving interval
- Maximum age more than 50 years

Feeding

- Obligate aquatic herbivory
- Abundant food resources
- Snout deflection consistent with generalist feeding strategy
- 5–10 percent of body weight consumed per day from wide variety (approximately 60) of plant species
- Feeding period four to eight hours per day
- Prehensile use of perioral bristles during feeding
- Long gut transit time, about seven days
- Hindgut fermentation as in horses
- Continual tooth replacement ("marching molars")

Anatomy and physiology

- Large body size (adults average 400–550 kg and 2.7–3.0 m)
- Females usually larger and heavier than males
- Low metabolic rate; susceptibility to cold stress
- Densely mineralized bone; may aid buoyancy control
- Two-part diaphragm, oriented longitudinally
- Elongated lungs
- Internal testes with vascular cooling
- Paddle shaped tail
- Three to four fingernails on pectoral flippers
- Gray-brown skin with numerous pits; skin sloughed often

Behavior and brain

- Slow movements, 0–25 km/h (0–16 mph)
- Seasonal migration for thermoregulation
- Warm-water sites sought in winter
- Freshwater sought in marine/estuarine environments
- Site fidelity on seasonal basis
- 10-minute breathing intervals when resting
- Low encephalization quotient
- Smooth cerebral cortex surface
- Reduced visual, olfactory, and taste systems
- Expanded sensory hair system
- Tactile exploration using oral disk
- Nuzzling behavior
- Hearing best at 10–18 kHz
- Vocalizations rare; chirps and squeaks

The Florida Manatee

Figure 1.1. Manatee and diver at Crystal River. (Reproduced by permission, © Francois Fournier and Joe Cheatwood.)

1 Manatees in Florida

One morning

On a clear cold winter morning the silence in the water is broken by the sound of an approaching motor boat. It grows louder as it approaches a group of sleeping manatees. Such noise is becoming more and more common these days. One manatee, Piety, briefly takes note, but continues resting in the warm spring waters of the sanctuary with her young calf. She is old and used to this habitual activity, now part of the manatee life. Her calf, however, does not understand and curiosity arouses his attention. He wants to investigate, and mom wants to sleep.

When the boaters toss their anchor into the water, several manatees nearby are startled. Soon, though, they settle down and continue their business of resting and cavorting (plate 1). The manatees can hear the excited voices of the people on the boat. They talk of how this will be an awesome experience and are almost overly jubilant in their anticipation of a dive with wild manatees.

One of the divers remembers reading that manatees are gentle. But in the clear water they look large, ominous, and threatening (fig. 1.1). He is somewhat concerned that if he were to get into the water, the manatee might bite him or bump him or hurt him. But his curiosity gets the better of him, and he dons his mask, fins, and snorkel and slowly enters the water. To him, the water feels cold.

To Piety's calf the water is warm. It is good to wake up in warm spring waters, as the temperature in the Gulf of Mexico is very cold. Last night, mom took him down the river so she could feed. He occasionally eats plants but prefers mom's milk. The calf usually accompanies her on feeding trips at night when boats are not as numerous. Night is a good time, and the calf likes to travel in the calm, quiet, dark waters. He feels safe with his mother.

The diver tries to focus in the water. Everything's clear up close, but distances are cloudy, sort of like swimming in fog. The calf turns his attention to the boat that now has a swimmer in the water. He hurries over to this novel object, an object that is awkward and spends too much time near the surface. The surface is a place the calf has been trained to associate with peril. Within seconds the diver and manatee meet. Eyes transfixed on one another in mutual interest—it's love at first sight!

If this is a good interaction both will leave contented. But too often people let their emotions get the better of them, and they chase the manatees (plate 2). Our diver learns that if he remains silent and lets the manatee discover him first, then the animal will be much more relaxed. He also knows, as does the manatee, that divers cannot go into the sanctuary. The sanctuary is a safe zone; people must respect that.

Manatees today

Manatees are unusual mammals as many Floridians can attest. Their rotund appearance, slow movements, simple social structure, and curiosity toward humans make them appear to be relaxed and contented, even good humored. Viewed biologically, based on scientific studies made over the past 30 years, these same traits are the result of plentiful food sources, a large digestive tract, slow metabolism, and a lack of predators. Aggressive tendencies appear at mating times when herds of males follow a single female and jostle vigorously for the position next to her. Manatee social structure is fairly simple, with the cow-calf bond representing the most enduring form of relationship. Winter aggregations of large numbers of manatees probably represent opportunistic gatherings in warm-water areas that are primarily nonsocial in nature, but much remains to be learned about patterns of vocal communication and social interactions in these settings. An extended period of early care by the mother affords the young calf opportunities to learn survival skills: where to go to find nutritious grass beds on which to graze, freshwater to drink, and warm water during the winter. Millions of years of evolution have shaped manatees to this lifestyle, including their particular blend of sensory and motor abilities centered around feeding activities and finding their way in turbid water.

The early history of people and manatees in Florida revolved around hunting.[1] Florida manatees appear to have originated from Caribbean stock that migrated northward within the last 12,000 years, following the most recent glaciation.[2] Based upon archeological findings, native Floridians were catching and eating manatees as early as 8,000 B.C. Pipes carved in the shape of manatees were apparently used for ceremonial purposes, indicating a general cultural familiarity with these animals.[3] As recently as the twentieth century, the Seminole Indians hunted manatees for food and oil and used their bones for tools.[4] This long history of hunting probably kept manatees from becoming extremely abundant, but hunting pressure does not appear to have been severe enough to threaten Florida manatees with extinction.[5] This stands in contrast to the plight of manatees in South America where they were hunted commercially. The English viewed all of Florida as a manatee sanctuary in the 1700s, and the State of Florida enacted legal protection for manatees in 1893, including fines and prison sentences for offenders. Still, throughout this period, manatees were often taken illegally by hunters and fishermen throughout their range in Florida. This scattered hunting continued during the 1930s and 1940s when meat was scarce due to conditions arising from the Great Depression and World War II.[6] Based on a comprehensive survey of historical documents, O'Shea concluded that both the distribution and abundance of manatees in Florida were probably fairly stable until recently.[7] They enjoyed a nearly ideal niche: plenty of food, lots of territory to explore, and no natural predators until humans entered the picture.

General public awareness of manatees in Florida increased in the mid-twentieth century as the human population increased and pleasure boating became more prevalent. The development of concentrated housing and the addition of power plants in coastal areas like Crystal River, Tampa Bay, Fort Myers, Miami, Riviera Beach, and Brevard County brought people into contact with winter aggregations of manatees at industrial warm-water sites. Manatees also may have become more numerous in Florida around this time, as they expanded their range northward and discovered new sources of warm water.[8] As recently as 1951, Charlotte Harbor was considered to be the northern winter limit for Gulf coast manatees.[9] Efforts to strengthen legal protection for manatees, initiated in the late 1970s, were partly stimulated by apparent increases in manatee mortality and injury due to collisions with boats.

Continued increase of Florida's human population has intensified this problem, as the activities of boaters, divers, and manatees overlap in the aquatic
environment. Various public agencies, private groups, and scientists are
searching for ways to lessen harmful interactions between boats and manatees. These efforts include the establishment of manatee sanctuaries off limits
to boaters and divers, slow speed zones for boaters, educational initiatives, and
technological approaches that alert boaters to the presence of manatees in
specific areas or use warning devices on boats to alert manatees to the presence of boats in their vicinity. Many Floridians enjoy boating, and debates
about the best approach to manatee protection are often energetic. Some
manatee advocates favor increasing marine patrols and levying greater fines
for speeding, while some boating groups argue that manatees are now plentiful enough that they no longer require protection. We explore these issues
throughout the remainder of this book. Much like the question of how to
manage statewide water distribution for human consumption, the essential
fact is that Florida's increasing human population brings with it inherent
challenges and problems. To a biologist, the plight of manatees in Florida is a
case of limited resources that must be protected wisely if humans and manatees are to coexist. The trick is finding the right balance.

The evolution of manatees represents a unique branch of mammalian history, including four-legged terrestrial ancestors that lived 50 million years ago
and 25-foot-long Steller's sea cows that were present in the North Pacific as
recently as the eighteenth century. In chapter 2 we examine the combination
of ecological variables that may have encouraged the transition from terrestrial to aquatic herbivory among sirenians and discuss evidence that in prehu-
man times there was a much greater diversity of sirenian species than today,
due to a greater abundance and diversity of aquatic vegetation.

Much of what we know about the biology of present-day manatees has
been discovered in the past 30 years. In chapter 3 we discuss the variety of unusual anatomical and physiological adaptations that characterize Florida
manatees. These include specialized facial bristles, muscles, and teeth for
feeding on aquatic plants; a highly modified digestive system that bears some
similarity to that of horses; high density bones that appear to have evolved in
connection with maintenance of neutral buoyancy in the water; and novel
lungs and diaphragm. The low metabolic rate of manatees is an adaptation to

being an aquatic herbivore. It limits their ability to keep warm in cooler water and also drives seasonal migrations to warm water sites, including industrial effluents from power plants. This raises a host of ethical issues for manatee welfare related to the consequences of impending power plant closures.

The acknowledgment that Florida manatees are endangered resulted from decisions made without the wealth of knowledge that has been gained in recent years. In chapter 4 we present the history of conservation efforts related to manatees and delve into the politics surrounding management decisions that affect manatees. In order to make intelligent decisions about the status of an endangered population, it is crucial to determine whether the population is stable, declining, or flourishing. Sometimes the age structure of the population and how it changes are enlightening in this regard. The degree of genetic diversity throughout the population is also highly relevant. These factors determine how well the population will withstand challenges such as hurricanes, red tide outbreaks, and viral infections. The population status of Florida manatees is dealt with in greater detail in chapter 5, which discusses various efforts to assess population trends in Florida manatees. The need to seek warm water in the winter months typifies Florida manatees that live at the northern extreme of the worldwide latitudinal range for manatees. Thus, seasonal movements are common and largely predictable on a group basis. However, individual manatees display a wide variety of movement patterns throughout the year. Some are homebodies and others are wanderers. In chapter 6 we discuss where manatees go and how radio tracking technology is used to gain this knowledge.

The nervous system contains the biological machinery that defines the range of sensory, motor, and cognitive capacities for a species. Manatee brains exhibit many unusual features, and these are explored in chapter 7, which discusses our knowledge of manatee brain traits and their evolution and the unique type of "intelligence" that manatees may possess.[10] Currently, intensive work is focused on the sensory capabilities of manatees because these abilities represent their interface with our world. For example, the body surface of manatees has very sparsely distributed hair, not thick enough to provide warmth. Because it has been found to be of a specialized sensory type, like the whiskers of mice, seals, and cats, we are presented with the intriguing possibility that manatee body hair represents a distributed system of detectors used to monitor water movements associated with other animals, currents, tides, and signal features of the underwater environment. Such a system could also play a role in the navigational ability of manatees. In chapter 8 we take a close look at this unusual hair system, unique among mammals as far as we know. Along the same lines, the manatee nervous system evinces a wide array of unusual features apparently connected with the animals' need to subsist most of the time in rather murky aquatic environments (although most of the manatee photographs we see are taken in very clear spring water). Reduced visual capacity appears to be compensated by increases in hearing and tactile sensation. Our expanding knowledge of manatee sensory systems and perceptual abilities is being used in the design of technology that aims to minimize harmful encounters between manatees and boats.

One of the responsibilities taken on by manatee biologists and veterinarians is the rescue and rehabilitation of sick or injured manatees, including newborn calves that have been orphaned or abandoned. Sadly, cruel or ignorant people sometimes deliberately harass manatees, tying them with ropes to drag behind their boats or intentionally hitting them with watercraft.[11] Rehabilitation efforts represent cooperative endeavors that often yield new insights into the care and medical treatment of manatees, including anesthesia, surgical procedure, blood chemistry, cold stress, and immunology. Chapter 9 treats these topics as well as the criteria that are considered when releasing captive animals back into the wild environment.

We are now faced with decisions about how we are going to successfully coexist with manatees. The pertinent issues reflect more general questions about the appropriate relationship between Floridians and their natural environment. Can we answer these questions in constructive ways by working through existing political and legal channels? Where is the common ground when diverse interest groups come to the table? What are the most important considerations when dealing with issues such as boat speed zones and the establishment of sanctuaries? How do we ensure that all voices and points of view are heard and considered fairly? What new approaches can we develop? Chapter 10 presents a road map for the future.

2 Origins

Evolutionary history

Manatees belong to a sirenian lineage that can be traced back about 50 million years. One of the earliest known sirenians was a creature called *Pezosiren portelli*, a pig-sized animal identified from fossil skeletal remains recovered from Jamaica (fig. 2.1).[1] *Pezosiren* had four limbs and possessed features diagnostic for the order Sirenia, including an elongated rostrum (snout and jaw), enlarged nasal cavities located toward the rear of the snout, dense bone, and other specialized skeletal features. This ancient sirenian apparently split its time between land and water like today's hippos, eating plants in both environments; it represents a true intermediate form in the transition from life on land to the total return to water by later sirenians. Inferred from skeletal remains, the structural design of its joints, limbs, and neck support system suggest that *Pezosiren* walked on land like terrestrial mammals of similar size; other features (changed position of the nasal cavities, lack of nasal sinuses, and dense ribs) are aquatic specializations also seen in living sirenians. Unlike today's manatees, which use a paddle-shaped tail to generate propulsive force to move through the water, *Pezosiren* probably moved a lot like an otter, lengthening its body in combination with thrusting movements of the hind limbs.

Daryl Domning is the world's expert on sirenian evolution and has been for over 30 years. He grew up collecting bones around Biloxi, Mississippi, and became acquainted with sirenian fossils as a youth on family trips to Florida. After studying geology and biology at Tulane University he went to the University of California, Berkeley, to do research on North Pacific sirenians. In the mid-1970s Daryl spent time in Brazil working with Amazonian manatees. He took a job at Howard University in Washington, D.C., in the late 1970s, teaching anatomy to medical and dental students, and he has been there ever

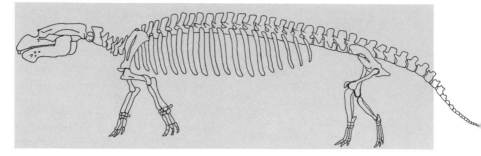

Figure 2.1. Artist's rendition of the skeleton of the ancestral sirenian, *Pezosiren*, dating from about 50 million years ago. (After D. Domning 2001a, fig. 1, 626, courtesy of Nature Publishing Group.)

since. As seems fitting for a paleontologist, his office is in the oldest building in the medical school complex. In his lab are trays of fossil sirenian bones, many on loan from the Smithsonian's National Museum of Natural History where he does much of his work. Some of these specimens have been collected by amateur enthusiasts.

Over 35 species of sirenians are known to have existed at some time over the last 50 million years, but only four species in two families (Trichechidae and Dugongidae) exist today.[2] Three are members of the manatee lineage and one is of the dugong lineage. Although three of these four living species are manatees, most sirenian fossils are from the dugong lineage, whose sole remaining species lives in coastal areas of the Indian Ocean, Red Sea, and Persian Gulf and in coastal waters of Australia, Indonesia, and Southeast Asia. Manatees in their current form are a relatively recent offshoot, having evolved in the Caribbean region about two million years ago. The evolutionary relationships among sirenians are not completely known, but sirenians probably originated in the Old World together with the ancestors of elephants, then migrated to the New World where their known fossil record actually begins, dating to about 50 million years ago. Although fossil sirenians have been found worldwide, Florida and the Caribbean are the only locations known to harbor specimens in every epoch from 50 million years ago until now. It is likely that many fossil sirenian discoveries are yet to be made even in this area, where about two new fossil species are discovered every year. Who knows what finds lie undiscovered in poorly explored areas like Arabia and Africa?

In order to make sense of the relationships among the known fossil sirenians, Domning analyzed the attributes of fossil sirenians and constructed a family tree (fig. 2.2).[3] He did this by examining the distribution of "character states" for each species and then used a computer program to analyze the resulting matrix of numbers. In theory, a character is any feature that can be observed. But because we are talking about fossils, the characters are all skeletal—things like tooth structure, shape and angle of the jaw, and position of the nostrils. For practical reasons, most characters are "bipolar," considered to exist in one of two states: 0 or 1. For example, a tooth that is curved (1) or not (0). Other characters are scored as present or absent, such as a particular portion of a skull bone. And some characters are considered to have three possible states, as in the length of the zygomatic portion of the maxillary bone: long (0), shortened (1), shortened and transformed (2). Domning used 62 such characters and made a table of their status in 36 species of sirenians, including those living today. The computer program then analyzed this table of numbers and grouped species that share a large number of derived (evolutionarily advanced) characters, generating a series of trees that represent possible relationships among the species. Based on the known ages of some fossils or on other considerations, it is sometimes possible to decide which character states are primitive—widespread among early species—versus derived—more recent specializations limited to subsets of species. This information can be used to evaluate the validity of the various trees that are generated. Domning's results indicated that there are four families within the order Sirenia: Prorastomidae, Protosirenidae, Dugongidae, and Trichechidae. The prorastomids and protosirens are the earliest groups; the four-limbed *Pezosiren* mentioned earlier is a prorastomid. Manatees belong to the trichechids, which probably arose from the dugong or protosiren lineage 25–40 million years ago. The time of origin is unclear due to the scarcity of early trichechid fossils.

In all vertebrates, the structure and arrangement of teeth relates directly to their function, and teeth probably played a major role in the recent evolutionary history of manatees and dugongs. Modern manatees replace their teeth in a conveyer belt fashion. As front teeth become worn from abrasion they fall out and are replaced by rear teeth marching forward at a rate of about 1 mm per month. Specialized regions at the rear of each upper and lower jaw continually produce new teeth throughout the manatee's life. Dugongids have no such arrangement, but their teeth wear more slowly because the aquatic plants they eat are much less abrasive than those fed on by manatees. The Steller's sea cow that lived in the north Pacific Ocean until hunted to extinction in the 1700s had no teeth at all. Its diet of algae did not require them, but its rough palate, also characteristic of other sirenians, was probably useful in the mechanical breakdown of algae.

If sirenian evolution is so richly represented by fossils in the Caribbean, why are dugongs now found only in the Indian and Pacific oceans, whereas manatees are only present in the Atlantic? A plausible scenario for the evolution of manatees has been constructed by Domning through consideration of changes over time in geology, aquatic plants and their abundance and distribution, and anatomical specializations for feeding that are evident in skeletal remains.[4] For many humans living in modern times when few of us hunt or forage for subsistence, it is easy to forget how important feeding adaptations

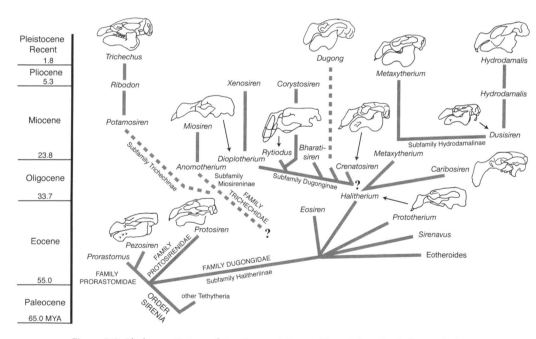

Figure 2.2. Phylogenetic tree of sirenian evolution, with variations in skull morphology indicated for some taxa. (Illustration courtesy of Gabe Trinity and Daryl Domning.)

have been in the evolution of different lineages. Being an herbivore is vastly different from being a carnivore or an omnivore; a walrus that relies on sucking mollusks out of their shells as its main food source requires anatomical modifications radically different from those of a seal that chases and catches fish. This emphasis on feeding adaptations does not simply reflect the fact that teeth and jaws are one of the features that can be easily analyzed in fossil remains; it also reflects the crucial link between feeding success, survival, and range of geographic distribution.

Around 50 million years ago, the earliest sirenians, prorastomids like *Pezosiren portelli*, were wandering around on four legs between terrestrial and aquatic habitats, probably spending most of their time in the water. Prorastomids had straight, narrow snouts like some browsing terrestrial ungulates of today, suggesting that they engaged in selective browsing of aquatic plants. Protosirenids were also quadrupeds, but their skeletons suggest that they spent little if any time on land.[5] They had a broader snout that was downturned, evidence that they fed by grazing on underwater meadows.[6] Early sirenians had incisors, canines, premolars, and molars; today's Florida manatees have only molars. Fossil sirenians exhibit variation in the breadth of the jaws, presence or absence of tusks (enlarged incisor teeth) and their size, and the degree to which the upper jaw is turned downward. In living sirenians the extent to which the snout region is downturned indicates the location in the water column of the plants they eat. Present-day dugongs have very broad, downturned snouts and are exclusively bottom feeders; Amazonian manatees whose snouts are much less downturned often feed on floating meadows; Florida manatees lie in the middle, feeding primarily on the bottom but also at the surface. The tusks seen in many dugongid fossils were probably used in digging up rhizomes, the buried stems of plants that contain stored nutrients; larger tusks would have been advantageous for digging up larger rhizomes.

By the Oligocene (approximately 30 million years ago), the prorastomids and protosirenids were extinct, but there was a diversity of dugongid species in the Caribbean, each of which exhibited a different combination of jaws, teeth, and tusks. This suggests that each species was adapted for feeding on a different subset of the available marine plants, which were also much more diverse than today. This specialized adaptation, called niche partitioning, promotes the coexistence of species in the same geographical region by reducing their competition for the same food resources. Trichechids were apparently confined to freshwater and estuarine habitats at this time. The flourishing of dugongids over many millions of years is reflected in the abundance of their fossils that continue to be found in Florida.

The next phase of sirenian evolution appears to have been influenced by major geological events. Around 12 million years ago a large inland sea covered much of what was to become the Amazon basin (fig. 2.3). This sea appears to have had three outlets: one to the north, one to the south, and one in the same location as the mouth of today's Amazon River.[7] As the Andes Mountains uplifted and sea levels dropped, the outlets to the north and south were closed. By the end of the Pliocene (about two million years ago), dugongids had apparently died out in the Caribbean. Domning has suggested that the uplifting of the Andes Mountains about four million years ago triggered a flow of nutrients and sediment into the Amazon basin, which in turn promoted the dominance of aquatic grasses that were higher in silica content and therefore more abrasive to teeth.[8] The trichechid *Ribodon*, ancestor to the modern manatees, had evolved horizontal tooth replacement, which allowed it to thrive on these more abrasive grasses. The onset of continental glaciation probably extended this trend to other coastal areas by lowering sea levels and increasing erosion and cooling. These and other climatological factors likely led to a reduction in the diversity and abundance of the Caribbean marine sea

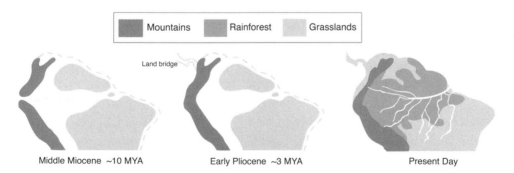

Figure 2.3. Amazonian geography over time. Uplift of the Andes changed the shape of the Amazon River basin. Note the appearance of the Panama land bridge. (Illustration by Gabe Trinity.)

grasses on which dugongids had become specialized. In addition, because dugongids had not evolved horizontal tooth replacement, their teeth wore down rapidly on the coarser sea grasses. This may have contributed to their extinction in the Caribbean and the Amazon basin.

The Andean uplift also sealed off the inland Amazonian basin from the Pacific. Manatees trapped in this region evolved small, complexly crowned teeth and a reduced downward snout deflection, adaptations for feeding on the large floating freshwater grass meadows. This group became the Amazonian manatee, *Trichechus inunguis*. West Indian manatees on the Atlantic coast of South America developed broader, more downturned snouts than those of the Amazonian manatees, allowing them to feed on underwater plants as well as those at the surface; they went on to become the Florida and Antillean subspecies *T. manatus latirostris* and *T. manatus manatus*. The West African manatee *T. senegalensis* appears to have evolved from the West Indian manatee when it dispersed to Africa around 1.5 million years ago. This dispersal was probably facilitated by ocean currents. The oldest *T. manatus* fossil found in Florida is about 1.3 million years old. However, this is not a fossil of the modern Florida subspecies *T. manatus latirostris*. Based upon genetic evidence, modern Florida manatees appear to have originated from Caribbean stock that migrated northward within the last 12,000 years, following the most recent glaciation.[9]

Feeding behavior

Feeding strategies play a major role in animal evolution generally, and this is reflected in the diversity of sensory and motor specializations for obtaining and consuming food resources. For example, the spectacular diversity of beaks among Darwin's Galapagos Islands finches is associated in part with their breaking open and feeding on nuts and seeds of particular sizes and hardness. We have discussed the importance of feeding adaptations to sirenian evolution, both with respect to the exploitation by all sirenians of aquatic vegetation as their sole food source—a niche free of competition from other mammals—and with regard to the ascent of manatees and the demise of dugongs in the Caribbean region due in part to the development of horizontal tooth replacement by manatees. When we examine more closely the particular ways in which manatees have become adapted to feed exclusively on aquatic plants, we begin to appreciate the degree of anatomical and physiological specialization that is possible when natural selection has millions of years to operate on a taxonomic lineage possessing an adequate range of genetic variation and plasticity.

Not only are sirenians unique among mammals in utilizing aquatic plants as their sole food source, they also exhibit corresponding anatomical specializations associated with their feeding behavior. When a manatee feeds, the lips and jaws are in constant repetitive motion. The flippers are not usually used to grab plants; rather, they hang by the manatee's sides while the upper lips are protruded and long stout bristles on the lips are used like fingers to tear off portions of the plants and bring them into the mouth. This manner of feeding, and the use of modified facial hair to grasp objects, is unique to sirenians. During his time in Brazil, Daryl Domning collected teeth shed by captive manatees and found that the rate of tooth replacement varies according to what type of plants manatees are eating. Those that require more chewing or cause greater abrasion lead to more rapid tooth replacement.

The facial region of manatees is fleshy and contains an abundance of hair, packed about thirty times denser than that on the rest of the body where it is very sparsely distributed (fig. 2.4).[10] The lips contain long stiff hairs called bristles by James Murie, a nineteenth-century anatomist and pathologist who produced detailed and beautifully illustrated descriptions of manatee anatomy.[11] There are about 220 perioral bristles per face, organized into four patches on each upper lip and two on the lower lips (fig. 2.5).[12] Each patch contains bristles having a specific length and stiffness. The largest upper lip bristles are similar in many respects to the whiskers of mice, dogs, and other mammals. The remainder of the face has hair rather than bristles. Compared to our faces, the manatee face exhibits an expanded region between the upper lip and nostrils. This region is called the oral disk, and it contains "bristle-like hairs" intermediate in stiffness between hairs and perioral bristles. The bristle-like hairs are used as tactile "feelers" when manatees investigate novel objects (see chapter 8).

The use of the perioral bristles in feeding was described by several English scientists in the late 1800s. In 1875 Chapman described manatees as fanning food into their mouths using bristles situated on their upper and lower lips. In

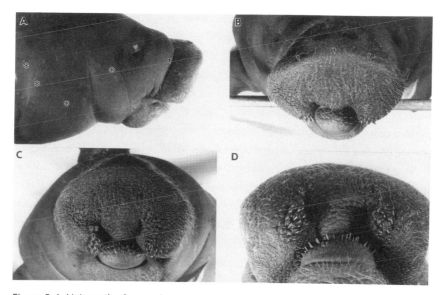

Figure 2.4. Hair on the face and body of the manatee, from several perspectives. In panel A, asterisks indicate some of the papillae associated with hair follicles on the body; v points to the eye; arrowhead designates the postnasal crease that divides the muzzle from the rest of the face. Arrowheads in panel B demarcate the orofacial ridge. U2 in panel C indicates the location of the largest perioral bristles. U1 in panel D indicates the U1 field of perioral bristles. (From Reep et al. 1998: 261; illustration courtesy of the Society for Marine Mammalogy.)

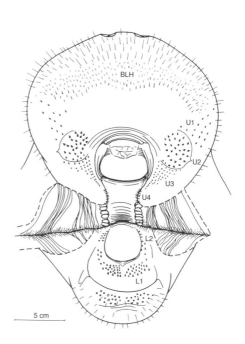

Figure 2.5. Hair on the manatee face, including groups of thick bristles on the upper lips (U1–U4) and lower lips (L1–L2). Bristle-like hairs (BLH) are present on the oral disk. (Drawing by Laura Line.)

1877 Garrod described the overall effect as being similar to that of a caterpillar feeding upon a leaf. In 1880 Murie described manatees as having "great mobility and special use of the inner circumscribed bristle-clad portions of the upper lip." In recent years, Chris Marshall, a marine mammal biologist at Texas A&M University, has made extensive investigations of manatee and dugong feeding. Here's what he found about how the feeding cycle works.[13] As a manatee approaches a bed of underwater plants, it performs a "flare response" consisting of activation of muscles that expand and flatten the snout region (interestingly, it often closes its eyes as well). This flaring also causes the large upper lip perioral bristles to protrude outward from their usual relaxed position inside folds of skin. The muscles used in the flare response are the same ones we use to make facial expressions of various kinds. As the upper part of the manatee face undergoes the flare response, the lower jaw drops down to open the mouth. Next, the upper lip bristles move synchronously in a sweeping fashion toward each other as they gather plants and bring them to the mouth. As the lower jaw closes, its perioral bristles evert and push the plants further into the oral cavity.[14] Dugongs have a similar arrangement, but the oral disk is larger and the bristles operate somewhat differently. In contrast to manatees, when dugongs feed, the upper bristles sweep outward and back so that food is brought into either side of the mouth in a pattern of movement similar to a swimmer's breast stroke. Synchronous movement is usually seen during contact with plants or other objects like boat anchor lines, but Chris observed that manatees are capable of using each side independently. This occurs when an animal is attempting to dislodge an object that is stuck or when it reverses the direction of one bristle field in order to expel apparently distasteful vegetation.[15] Once food is brought into the oral cavity, the palate acts as an accessory grinding surface (fig. 2.6).[16]

The use of whiskers to grab things is called "oripulation" to indicate manipulation by the mouth, because true "manipulation" refers to the manus, or hand. Other mammals use vibrissae to detect tactile cues but not for oripulation. Many pinnipeds employ "whisking" movements of their vibrissae for more directed tactile exploration and social displays. For example, California sea lions (*Zalophus californianus*) possess extremely mobile vibrissae that can be rotated from the resting position along the side of the head to extend almost directly forward from the muzzle.[17] The manatee snout is like a

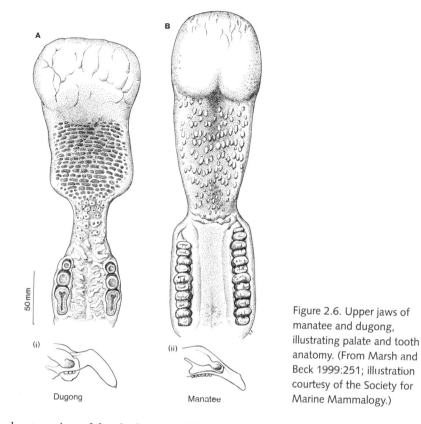

Figure 2.6. Upper jaws of manatee and dugong, illustrating palate and tooth anatomy. (From Marsh and Beck 1999:251; illustration courtesy of the Society for Marine Mammalogy.)

short version of the elephant trunk both structurally and in the way it is used. Both are examples of "muscular hydrostats," as are tongues and squid tentacles.[18] These all consist of groups of muscles that can perform movements including elongation, shortening, and twisting without the structural support of skeletal elements. This range of diversity among mammalian vibrissae and snouts exemplifies the degree to which different species exhibit specializations that serve their particular ways of making a living. Furthermore, it illustrates the dramatic range of variety that is produced by natural selection acting on anatomical potential over a long period of time.

3 The Manatee Lifestyle

Manatees seem unusual to most people who encounter them for the first time. This feeling only becomes stronger as one becomes more familiar with their behavioral traits and anatomical and physiological characteristics and how these differ from those of other marine mammals. For example, along with all sirenians, Florida manatees never leave the water, and they actively feed exclusively on plants. In contrast, pinnipeds (seals, sea lions, and walruses) regularly haul out onto land to rest and breed and to feed on mollusks, krill, and fish rather than plants. Cetaceans live exclusively in the water like sirenians, but they eat a variety of food items ranging from plankton to seals.

Like all species, Florida manatees have evolved to fit within the constraints of their environment. Many aspects of their anatomy, physiology, and behavior represent adaptations for feeding, reproduction, and navigation in the shallow water habitats along the coast of Florida. Their role as aquatic herbivores is tied closely to body shape and size, metabolic rate, and digestive system function. These factors, then, influence other important aspects of their lifestyle, including lack of predation, movement patterns, thermoregulation, and even reproduction and social behaviors. The adaptations represented by the collection of all these traits define what it means to be a Florida manatee. Because every species represents an experiment by nature over an extended period of time, special cases define the range of evolutionary outcomes that are possible. Therefore, to learn about manatees is also to witness the results of 50 million years of mammalian history. Some of the main traits that define life as a Florida manatee, treated in greater detail throughout this book, are summarized in the list "Florida Manatee Traits" immediately following the preface.

There are many ways for species to be successful. At one end of the spectrum are those that live in environments subject to rapidly changing conditions: tenuous food resources, high predation, unstable climate, or all of these. These species often succeed by investing in numbers—breeding frequently, having large litters, and spending little time caring for the young. Such species, which include many rodents, are characterized by small body size and short life spans. At the other extreme are species like manatees that live in relatively stable environments with plentiful food resources. These species breed less frequently, have one or two offspring at a time, and invest significant time in caring for and protecting the young. They tend to be large bodied, thus being less subject to predation, and are longer lived. Naturally, there are many intermediate conditions and variations on these extremes. In fact, over long periods of time even a trait as seemingly fundamental as reproductive strategy may become altered in response to changing environmental conditions.[1]

Manatee form

The architectural phrase "form follows function" also applies to the bodies of animals. Like other mammals, manatees breathe air, are warm blooded, have hair on their bodies, give birth to live young, and produce milk for their babies. But being a marine mammal also requires many adaptations for life in the water. Through the action of natural selection over millions of years, manatee bodies have become streamlined, affording little resistance to water flow (fig. 3.1). The neck has melded with the rest of the body. There are no external ear flaps; they are not functional in the water and would only cause excessive drag. Hind limbs were not necessary for a fully aquatic existence. The tail has become flattened into a spatula-like paddle, very effective for propulsion. Having less resistance in the water allows for easier travel, involving less expenditure of energy—important for an animal with a low metabolic rate. Manatees propel themselves through the water with up and down undulations of their broad tails, which they tilt like a rudder for turning. They often use the tips of their flippers to "walk" along the bottom in shallow water. Nostrils are located at the top and tip of the snout making it easier to breathe at the surface. Collectively, these and a host of other specialized adaptive features are unique to manatees. Dugongs share most of these traits as well. Consequently, manatees and dugongs are classified taxonomically as belonging to the order Sirenia. Differences between mammalian orders are large compared to the differences between species or families. Superficial resemblances among the three primary groups of aquatic mammals—cetaceans, pinnipeds, and sirenians—are examples of convergent evolution due to the action of natural selection to produce adaptations to life in water and do not reflect true relatedness, as each of these groups belongs to a different mammalian order.

In contrast to convergent evolution in unrelated orders, taxonomic relatedness may be evident by the retention of traits not found in other lineages, even if the relatives in question have diverged for millions of years. In this regard, it is intriguing that sirenians share some unusual features with elephants, their most closely related mammalian counterparts. Manatees and dugongs have a prehensile snout that allows them to manipulate objects in the

Figure 3.1. Five members of the order Sirenia, four of which still exist. (Adapted by Carol Dizack from an illustration by Pieter Folkens, © 1989).

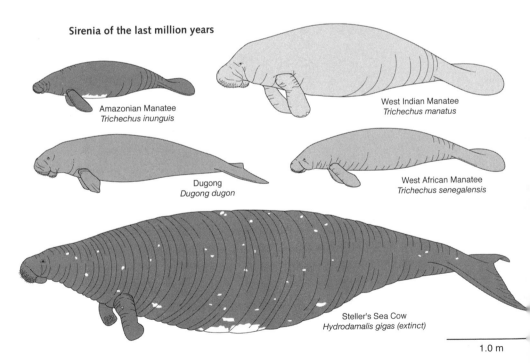

Sirenia of the last million years

Amazonian Manatee
Trichechus inunguis

West Indian Manatee
Trichechus manatus

Dugong
Dugong dugon

West African Manatee
Trichechus senegalensis

Steller's Sea Cow
Hydrodamalis gigas (extinct)

1.0 m

water (plate 3). This highly functional biological tool serves primarily for grasping vegetation and bringing it into the mouth. The snout's tactile function appears to be similar to that of the tip of the elephant's long trunk. The hairs on the body are sparse and are actually sensory organs that help detect vibrations in the water. Manatees have molariform teeth only and lack canines and incisors. This makes them efficient at chewing vegetation. Similar to elephants and hyraxes (their other closest relative), teeth are slowly replaced as they wear down by new teeth behind them. Moving at a slow rate of about 1–2 mm per month (similar to what orthodontists can do to reposition human teeth mechanically using braces), newly generated manatee teeth continually march forward in the left and right tooth rows of the upper and lower jaws. Old teeth fall out when they reach the front of the row. This gives the manatee a lifetime of unlimited tooth production—very practical for feeding on vegetation that often contains large amounts of abrasive material. Unlike manatees, elephants and hyraxes have a finite supply of replacement teeth, and this is thought to limit their lifespan. Interestingly, dugongs never developed tooth replacement. It is possible that manatees "rediscovered" a capability for tooth replacement that was latent in their genetic heritage and, in the process, modified it. Developmental geneticists and evolutionary biologists now possess tools of molecular biology that will allow us to determine the plausibility of this scenario.

Like elephants, manatees have very thick skin—sometimes over 2.5 cm (1") thick. The thin outer epidermis is gray and possesses numerous shallow pits, giving it a pebbly appearance. Their thick dermis helps protect manatees when they rub against rough, jagged objects in the water like branches and limestone outcroppings. The skin also has phenomenal, but not well understood, healing abilities that allow manatees to withstand incredible lesions that penetrate the thick underlying dermis to expose muscles and associated deep structures (plate 4).

There are three to four nails on each flipper of a Florida manatee (nails are absent in Amazonian manatees). Hairs about 3–5 cm in length are sparsely distributed over the body. Barnacles often grow on manatees that spend long periods of time in marine environments. (The same three species of barnacles found on manatees are also seen on green sea turtles;[2] other marine mammals carry other species of barnacles.) Sloughing of patches of epidermis is common, and coloration is also influenced by epiphytes (algae) and other biota that opportunistically occupy the surface of the manatee. Scar tissue is often white and persists for many years or decades, making it possible for scientists to identify individual manatees.

The skin may also have other properties that help manatees regulate body temperature. Sending the blood through vessels located near the body surface can help these tropical animals release body heat during warm months. Conversely, in the winter, manatees are often observed exposing their backs above the water surface to the warming rays of the sun. Physiologically, manatees are tropical animals not well suited for life at relatively cold temperatures that can occur in Florida. Here, manatees are larger than their counterparts elsewhere in the tropics. This may help them deal with temperature extremes, because larger mammals lose internally generated heat less readily to the environment than do smaller mammals. The relationship between size and heat loss is magnified in water. As anyone who has been swimming in cold water can testify, heat is lost more readily in water than in air. The internal body temperature of Florida manatees at rest is 36°C (96.8°F), and they begin to display signs of cold stress with prolonged exposure to water less than 20°C (68°F).[3]

Manatee bones are very dense and solid. During the economic depression of the 1930s, manatee bone was used by artisans in the United States to make carvings similar to scrimshaw engraved on whale teeth. According to our Mexican colleague Benjamin Morales, this craft is still practiced in some places in Mexico. The weight of their dense bone works like ballast, helping manatees easily descend to ocean, river, or spring bottoms. (Similarly, when human swimmers enter the water, they need weight belts to help them submerge.) Dense bone, together with other adaptations related to the lungs, allows manatees to easily obtain neutral buoyancy in the water column, making resting, foraging, and swimming much easier.

Aquatic herbivory

Florida manatees are known as generalists with respect to their feeding habits, because they utilize over 60 species of freshwater and marine vegetation. This includes plants located on the bottom, floating at the surface, and growing on banks (fig. 3.2).[4] It is curious that so few species of animals graze on sea grasses;

they include manatees, sea turtles, some birds, sea urchins, and snails. Low availability of nitrogen compounds (proteins), cell wall components that are difficult to digest, and the presence of toxins are factors that may limit more widespread utilization of sea grasses as food.[5] Abundance of aquatic vegetation and lack of predation have probably been major determinants in the evolution of the rather sedentary lifestyle observed in Florida manatees. Manatees spend four to eight hours per day feeding and normally consume a volume of plants corresponding to 5–10 percent of their body weights per day—not a trivial amount for a 500–kg animal![6] Manatees use certain strategies in their feeding behavior that appear to be related to preferences based on taste or

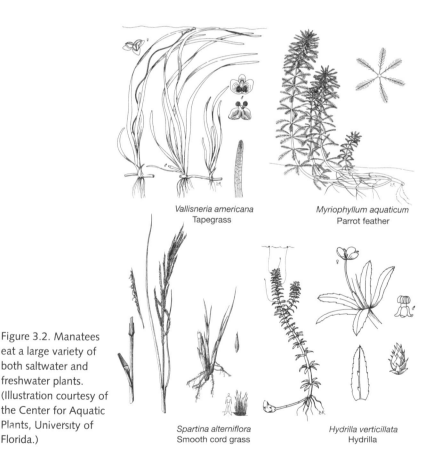

Vallisneria americana
Tapegrass

Myriophyllum aquaticum
Parrot feather

Figure 3.2. Manatees eat a large variety of both saltwater and freshwater plants. (Illustration courtesy of the Center for Aquatic Plants, University of Florida.)

Spartina alterniflora
Smooth cord grass

Hydrilla verticillata
Hydrilla

nutrition, but this is not known for certain. Some marine plants have significantly more protein than similar amounts of freshwater vegetation depending on the time of year; other nutrients like carbohydrates vary seasonally as well.[7] Manatees are suspected on some occasions of traveling long distances just to fill their stomachs with more nutritious sea grass rather than foraging on more abundant local freshwater plants. When in Crystal River in the winter, manatees occasionally leave the freshwater system on feeding bouts that take them downriver into the salt water where they readily locate and feed on *Ruppia*, or widgeon grass, a common sea grass in the area. Whether these movements by manatees are exclusively aimed at finding *Ruppia* is not known.

By grazing selectively on underwater plants, manatees help promote a high level of productivity in sea grass communities and affect succession, the change over time in the type and abundance of aquatic vegetation.[8] Their grazing can also influence nutrient content and digestibility by altering the proportion of new growth and changing the patterns of use by other primary consumers.[9] The nutritive value of sea grass varies with plant part, age of the plant, and season of the year.[10] Protein is highest in fresh green leaves. Chemical compounds known as phenols and flavones are naturally occurring in some sea grasses and represent potential toxins.[11] Manatees prefer to feed on new growth, which is highest in nutritional value,[12] thus effectively avoiding high fiber and lignin that would reduce digestive efficiency. Their strategy seems to be to keep the gut full at all times. Thus, their nutrient intake is limited only by the time needed for digestion, not the rate of food consumption. In a healthy adult, the digestive tract plus its contents accounts for about 15 percent of total body weight.[13] Some of the gut contents consist of parasites: nematode worms in the stomach and trematode worms in the small and large intestines.[14] In today's environment, manatees also routinely ingest foreign objects that sometimes kill them—items such as plastic bags, fish hooks, and pieces of rope.[15]

Sea grass beds provide much more than food for manatees. They are the nursery grounds for numerous species of fish, shellfish, and other wildlife. They filter suspended materials from the water and stabilize the bottom. However, the sufficient light penetration required by sea grasses to grow and flourish may be compromised by increased turbidity resulting from dredging, storm-water runoff, or boating.[16] Nutrient loading from storm-water runoff can also be deleterious because it promotes algal blooms that can reduce the light reaching deeper plants. In addition, some algae are epiphytes that attach directly to the leaves of sea grasses. Light penetration is the single most important factor affecting sea grass growth and survival.[17] Declines, therefore, often occur at the deep margins of sea grass beds. Sea grass recolonization is slow, often taking years—a fact that can be easily appreciated from aerial views of sea grass beds damaged by boat groundings or trails cut by swirling propellers.

Hurricanes and other intense storms occur regularly along the Florida coast and can disrupt manatee life in several ways.[18] Storm surges can cause significant seawater intrusion into brackish and freshwater habitat, raising salinity and thus negatively affecting plant life. High energy waves and strong currents may uproot sea grass beds and disorient manatees. Additionally, storm disturbance may lead to significant cooling of surface water, causing manatees to leave previously suitable habitat. Cooling is of greatest concern due to the potentially catastrophic impact of a winter storm on an aggregation of manatees at a warm water refuge. Under such conditions, a significant number of manatees could die from cold stress. This would present a problem for recovery of the Florida manatee population because of its relatively small size, low reproductive rate, and genetic homogeneity. Hurricanes, winter storms, and exposure to toxic red tides all represent catastrophic events that can lead to rapid population decline, greatly increasing the likelihood of manatee extinction.[19]

Manatee digestion and metabolic rate

The manatee digestive system (plate 5) is similar in structure to that of the horse: both are hindgut fermenters with lengthy sections of intestines to process their food. However, manatees exhibit a combination of unusual traits rarely seen in other mammals. One of these, called the accessory digestive gland (or cardiac gland), is associated with the stomach. This gland produces hydrochloric acid, digestive enzymes, and mucus. In other species, the cells that do this are located throughout much of the stomach lining. Isolating these cells in a separate gland may protect them from the abrasive effects of ingested sand.[20] The duodenum, that portion of the small intestine located just below the stomach, contains large outpockets that appear to serve as storage sites for ingested food arriving from the stomach. It appears that food passes rather quickly through the small intestine and collects in the large intestine. At the junction of the small and large intestines, the enlarged, muscularized, paired cecum is a major site of volatile fatty acid production and absorption and of cellulose digestion by microorganisms.[21] In contrast to humans, manatees absorb most of their nutrients in the large rather than the small intestine. Manatees also consume a relatively low quality food source, meaning that it is high in fiber, low in protein, and low in caloric value. They appear to maximize the efficiency with which they extract nutrients by utilizing an extremely slow gut transit time for ingested food. In an early study, Mark Lomolino and Katherine Ewel measured passage rates of manatees by changing the diet of captive manatees from lettuce (*Lactuca lactuca*) to water hyacinth (*Eichhornia crassipes*) and noting the color change of the feces.[22] The researchers calculated a transit time of 146 hours (about six days), which seemed extremely long considering that the horse, another hindgut fermenter, has a transit time of just 28–38 hours. By comparison, ruminants like cows and buffalos process food in 70–95 hours and elephants in 21–46 hours. To investigate this issue further, Iske Larkin undertook a study of manatee gut transit time using colored corn.[23] The corn was ground from the corncob into small pieces and had the appearance of grits. It was fed to the manatees in gel cubes, and fecal samples were collected each day until corn was found in the feces. This delay was defined as the transit time. Once corn was identified in the feces, feeding of the marker was halted to measure the time necessary for the total amount of marker fed to pass through the gastrointestinal tract. This delay was defined as the retention time. From four captive manatees monitored at Miami Seaquarium, transit time averaged seven days and retention time averaged eight days, periods comparable to the long transit time reported in the earlier study. The use of two different colors—red corn on days one through three and blue corn on days four through six—indicated that no mixing occurred within the gut, thus suggesting that digesta travels through the tract as a bolus. Species that appear to come within the same range of gut transit time as manatees are highly specialized herbivores and include the koala, the three-toed sloth, and the two-toed sloth.[24]

Manatees are very efficient at digesting cellulose compared to other herbivores, including the horse, and this is probably attributable to their slow gut passage time, large body size, and the lower lignin content of aquatic versus terrestrial vegetation.[25] Thus, manatee digestive function combines the slow passage time and high efficiency typical of ruminants with the hindgut fermentation seen in nonruminants. This appears to be possible because aquatic vegetation has lower fiber content than terrestrial vegetation. So why aren't manatees ruminants? Manatees and other sirenians presumably inherited their digestive tract anatomy from their terrestrial ancestors. This kind of question illustrates one of the central dilemmas in evolutionary biology: how to know whether a trait is the result of change due to natural selection or whether developmental constraints have narrowed, or even prevented, the range of such change.

Manatees possess six to eight cheek teeth (molars) in each jaw quadrant. As described earlier, the bone between adjacent tooth sockets continuously breaks down and reforms so that all the teeth move forward at a rate of 1–2 mm a month. The teeth are continuously replaced from the rear as the front ones fall out (plate 5, detail).[26] This mechanism apparently evolved in conjunction with the appearance of abrasive sea grasses and allowed manatees to thrive as conditions changed in the Caribbean basin during the Pliocene and Pleistocene.[27] Additionally, located in front of the teeth on the roof of the mouth is a roughly textured structure called the horny plate that helps manatees manipulate and pulverize ingested plants.[28]

Manatees have an exceedingly low metabolic rate compared to other mammals of similar size, and this may be related to what they eat.[29] Brian McNab, a physiologist at the University of Florida, has argued that diet and food habits play a significant determining role in the evolution of basal metabolic rate among animals generally.[30] Energetics in turn constrain other aspects of an organism's lifestyle. The Florida manatee's tropical origins appear to be reflected in its adaptation to warm environments. An animal's thermoneutral zone is that range of temperatures in which it does not need to use active metabolism to keep warm at the low end or to throw off excessive heat at the high end. For Florida manatees, the lower end of the thermoneutral zone is 20–23°C (68–74°F),[31] in contrast to 8–15°C for bottlenose dolphins, sea otters, and sea lions.[32] This corresponds to the observed low tolerance of manatees for cold water, so that they actively seek out warm water locales in the winter months. Adults are able to respond to brief, moderate cold (19–20°C) by increasing their metabolism; younger animals, however, are apparently unable to do so.[33] Perhaps because of their tropical origins, manatees did not evolve robust anatomical and physiological adaptations to prolonged cold water, and their metabolic rate is not able to compensate adequately under those conditions. Thyroid hormones directly influence metabolic processes. In manatees, these hormones are within the range of values reported for other marine and terrestrial mammals, suggesting that the low metabolic rate of manatees is not due to reduced thyroid hormone levels.[34] During periods of reduced food consumption or fasting, thyroid hormone levels increase and appear to drive the oxidation of fat stores to provide water and energy needs.[35] At present, we don't know if the very low metabolic rate observed in manatees is due to an inherent limitation imposed by the food they eat as appears to be the case for sloths.

Biologists have long wondered whether or not manatees require freshwater to drink. Manatees regularly visit freshwater sites after spending time grazing in sea grass meadows. This suggests at least a preference for regular freshwater intake, although they can also spend prolonged periods in salt water. Studies by Rudy Ortiz, working with Graham Worthy at Texas A&M University, demonstrated that manatees adapt to freshwater and saltwater environments by regulating the balance of electrolytes in their blood.[36] This enables them to tolerate periods of reduced availability of freshwater. Although the plants eaten by manatees are 60–95 percent water and thus comprise a significant water source, marine sea grasses contain more salt than freshwater grasses.[37] The anatomy of the manatee kidney suggests an ability to concentrate urine (and thus conserve water) that would be useful in the saltwater environment.[38] Captive manatees fed only on saltier sea grasses and denied access to freshwater eventually refuse to eat sea grass, suggesting that they do require regular access to freshwater.[39]

Living in water

Because manatees usually feed underwater for several hours per day at depths ranging from 1–3 m, they have a need to control their degree of buoyancy as well as the horizontal position of their body. Both of these needs represent potential expenditures of energy when maintained over long periods. As we have seen, manatees have a low metabolic rate; so they would benefit from adaptations that conserve energy. In manatees these adaptations involve the skeleton, lungs, diaphragm, and skin.

Most mammals tend to float with the head end of the body higher than the legs due to the anterior location of the lungs and the weight of the hind limbs.[40] This can present problems for swimming, where the most efficient body position is horizontal. Fast swimmers, like cetaceans and pinnipeds, can get around this problem by using flippers, fins, and flukes as hydrofoils to control body position.[41] By contrast, excluding brief bursts of speed, manatees are slow swimmers and must rely on other methods for positioning. The loss of hind limbs is advantageous in this regard, as it shifts the center of gravity forward, thus producing a more horizontal body position in the water. Similarly, having most of the body's weight located in the middle region of the body maximizes maneuverability. Manatees accomplish this by having most of their skeletal weight concentrated in the very dense ribs.[42] The ribs increase in size and density during growth, comprising 36 percent of total skeletal weight in calves and 60 percent in adults, so that the center of gravity shifts from the front to the middle of the body. Consequently, young manatee calves tend to float head up, whereas older individuals are more horizontal.[43]

Some body materials like bone and muscle are denser than water and thus promote sinking or negative buoyancy. But fat is less dense than water and promotes floating or positive buoyancy. By adjusting the relative amounts of these materials, a body may be made more or less buoyant. As a mammal dives, its buoyancy decreases because of pressure-induced reduction in lung volume. Buoyancy is also influenced by body density, such that lower density animals achieve negative buoyancy at deeper depths. Deep-diving cetaceans and pinnipeds have low body density, mostly due to low bone density and generous fat deposits. This causes them to become negatively buoyant at depths of 20–80 m. By contrast, manatees become negatively buoyant at much shallower depths, partly because of their dense rib bones but also because their thick, dense skin is nearly devoid of fat.[44] Unlike the skin of cetaceans and pinnipeds, manatee skin is denser than water. The large, elongated lungs of manatees provide a positive buoyancy counterbalance that allows for comfortable surfacing when they need to breathe.

We know that we are more buoyant in salt water than in freshwater. When we put on wet suits and enter the water, we need to add lead weights to help our bodies achieve neutral buoyancy. When we go into salt water, we may have to add an extra 1–2 kg of weight in some cases. In captivity, manatees that are moved from saltwater systems and placed in freshwater may initially have difficulty coming to the surface to breathe. They struggle, grab a breath, and then immediately plummet to the bottom. It may take a couple of days for them to adjust their body chemistry to completely reach neutral buoyancy.

A flexible aquatic existence requires the ability to change buoyancies depending on the need to breathe, dive to the bottom, or cruise horizontally while feeding. This may be done using air. The lungs, when inflated, promote buoyancy, as does the large volume of gas usually present in the gut of a healthy manatee. How might lung volume be precisely regulated by a submerged manatee to maintain horizontal body position? The lungs of manatees are elongated and flattened and extend along the spine for the length of

Figure 3.3. Manatee internal anatomy is illustrated in this artist's rendition. The longitudinal diaphragm is shaded. Finger bones are visible within the flipper. (Illustration by Gabe Trinity. From the cover of *Anatomical Record* 259, no. 1, reproduced by permission of Wiley-Liss, Inc.)

the rib cage.[45] The diaphragm is also longitudinally oriented in manatees (fig. 3.3), rather than transversely oriented as in most mammals.[46] Each side of the diaphragm constitutes a hemidiaphragm that has multiple attachments to the vertebrae on that side. Each hemidiaphragm is capable of independent, compartmentalized muscular contractions capable of adjusting the volume of the pleural cavity, providing for precise control of buoyancy and body position.[47] Intestinal gas also represents a significant factor in buoyancy control. Constipated manatees are often unable to dive, but following treatment with a laxative they emit large volumes of gas and regain their buoyancy control and diving ability.[48] In healthy manatees, controlled flatulence through the action of the diaphragm on intestinal gas volume may contribute to buoyancy control.[49] Thus, the major factors controlling manatee body position in the water appear to be the ballast and stable center of gravity provided by dense ribs together with the buoyancy offered by elongated lungs and the precise regulation of air volume by the two hemidiaphragms.

The ability of manatees to regulate their buoyancy enables them to position themselves accurately underwater when engaging in behaviors like feeding. It also allows them easy access to the surface to breathe. Unfortunately, manatees usually breathe with their nostrils only just above the water's surface, which often makes them invisible to boaters and thus vulnerable to collisions that result in injury or even death—so much so that manatees in Florida are endangered. Without our intervention to reduce manatee mortality in their natural habitat, recovery of the species will be difficult.

4 Endangered!

Manatees in Florida

Manatees evolved in a seemingly ideal niche. As generalist aquatic herbivores with no apparent natural predators, they have been free to evolve into an incredible and unusual marine mammal. Today, however, manatees are threatened by the possibility of accelerated extinction. At the northern limit of the species range, Florida manatees face exposure to seasonal cold stress and harm caused by human activity, most notably boat collisions and development-driven habitat reduction. Within the last century, numerous environmental changes have occurred so rapidly that many species, including the manatee, have had little time to adjust. Although our Florida manatee appears to be an adaptable subspecies, it takes generations for selective processes to affect a species' ability to adapt to relatively rapid changes. Threats to manatee survival continue to increase, and each year deaths involving human contact account for more casualties. Collisions with watercraft are the primary cause of human-contact-related manatee mortality (figs. 4.1, 4.2), but other preventable deaths result from entrapment in water control structures (lock gates and flood dams), entanglement in fishing gear, ingestion of hooks, drowning in nets, poaching, and vandalism (fig. 4.3). This is not a list to be proud of, but managers have used this information in an effort to reduce such senseless deaths.

When Woodie Hartman, a graduate student from Cornell University, slipped into the Crystal River for the first time in 1967 he was enthralled by the mysterious manatee. Woodie's advisor, well-known mammalogist James Layne, had given him the choice of working on wild hogs in the hot pinewoods far from the coast, or on manatees, which at the time were only understood in vague terms. Hartman chose wisely and became the first person to do a comprehensive study of manatee behavior and life history. At his first sight of manatees in the clear water—a thrashing mating herd of many animals—he jumped right back in the boat so scared was he by their chaotic activity. Later, Woodie borrowed a Kodak Brownie camera with a homemade underwater camera housing from the local dive shop owner and began taking photos of manatees during his daily observations. Early on, he encountered Buddy Powell, a local teenager cruising around in a Boston Whaler left to him by his grandmother. Buddy's boat was much faster than Woodie's slow chugging flat bottom with its small motor, and Buddy's father was willing to buy gas! Buddy knew the territory, had the right accent, and was also intrigued by manatees. They began a fruitful collaboration that involved interviewing locals, doing aerial surveys, and getting in the water to observe the animals. As a result of these studies, Woodie came to suspect that manatees weren't very common around Crystal River until the mid-1960s.

Today swimmers continue to be impressed with these fascinating creatures. Hartman's initial manatee encounters differed from those of present-day swimmers in that only a few manatees used Crystal River during the late 1960s—63 manatees to be exact and no more than three dozen at any one time.[1] Today, the number of manatees using Crystal River exceeds 400, and some of the same individuals that Hartman recognized in 1968 can still be found. It is generally agreed that more manatees live in Florida today than historic accounts indicate. At the same time, many more people live in Florida than ever before, and our activities pose an increasingly greater potential threat to manatees' long-term survival. Therefore, there is an ever more urgent need for sanctuaries and laws to protect these animals and their essential habitat. Hartman and Powell tried to get Citrus County to establish a manatee refuge at Crystal River in the late 1960s, but the county was concerned about possible negative economic impacts. The state also rejected this early initiative. How ironic that swimming with manatees is now one of the most popular activities in Crystal River and contributes substantially to the local economy! In fact, the dive shop owner who lent Woodie the Kodak quit the business around 1972 because the number of divers was getting out of hand— around 1,000 a year then compared to over 100,000 today.

In chapter 2 we discussed how the sirenian lineage has evolved. Ancestors of our present-day manatees and dugongs have come and gone, but this pro-

Figure 4.1. Manatees are difficult to see at the water's surface, and often all that is visible are circular ripples termed "footprints." (Photograph by U.S. Geological Survey.)

Figure 4.2. Watercraft collisions are the leading cause of human-related manatee deaths and account for 25 percent of all reported manatee deaths in Florida. (Photograph by U.S. Geological Survey.)

cess unfolded over many millions of years. Today, we are experiencing rapid extinction of many species, primarily due to the technological advances that are changing our planet. In the mid-1700s Georg Wilhelm Steller, a surgeon and naturalist on an expedition to the Bering Sea, documented the decimation of a magnificent creature related to the manatee, Steller's sea cow.[2] Within a span of about 30 years, the existence of that species was erased by hunters.[3] This calamity illustrates the fragile stability of all the species on Earth and our need for a strong will and a steadfast commitment to protect these creatures and our other valuable natural resources.

Indigenous peoples have hunted manatees and dugongs for thousands of years.[4] Bones excavated from burial grounds and kitchen middens attest to the practice of manatee hunting among Indians throughout the Caribbean, Central America, and South America. Early explorers visited coastal ports and stocked up on manatee meat reserves for their long voyages at sea. Some of them came to be called "buccaneers"—a word derived from the French word "boucan" meaning "the place to cure meat."[5] Thus, there is a direct connection between manatees and the term buccaneer. In 1900s Brazil, manatees were killed for their skins at an alarming rate of approximately 4,000 to 7,000 animals per year over a 20-year period.[6] This culling of wild animals from virgin populations in the Amazon basin illustrates the potential impact people can have in this fragile ecosystem.

Protection

Although manatees have been protected by law in Florida since 1893, it was not until recently that manatees were adequately protected by federal legislation in Florida and elsewhere in their range. The effort to protect manatees conflicted with previous attitudes about the use of natural resources. In the 1600s a papal decree was issued claiming that manatees were actually fish, so that Catholics could eat the meat on Fridays.[7] In 1907, the state of Florida strengthened its laws to levy fines for killing or harassing manatees. Enforcement was very difficult to accomplish, however, as it has been in several other countries throughout the manatee's range. Even today this issue plagues the conservation efforts of many countries. Recent recognition and advancements by international organizations such as the World Conservation Union, the World Wildlife Fund, the Wildlife Conservation Society, the Wildlife Trust, Sirenian International, and Save the Manatee Club have provided incentives to establish educational programs about sirenians, while encouraging ecotourism as an alternative to exploitation. Through these programs, people are educated about the intrinsic value of wildlife and how it fits into the ecosystem as a whole. As a result, they often begin to realize that most species are better left as part of the environment, rather than exploited to extinction to fill the coffers or the stew pot.

Today's laws in the U.S. have evolved from several sources. Federal legislation including the Marine Mammal Protection Act of 1972 and the Endangered Species Act of 1973, and subsequent amendments, provided clout and ample protection in Florida as well as the rest of the United States.[8] These acts helped to pave the way for the recovery efforts that followed. In 1978, state laws were strengthened once again with the Florida Manatee Sanctuary Act. This act afforded protection for habitat that was identified as being important to manatees. Collectively, these federal and state regulations are strict, and significant effort is made to implement and enforce them based on the best available scientific data.

The primary responsibility under federal laws for the recovery of the Florida manatee falls under the jurisdiction of the U.S. Fish and Wildlife Service (FWS). Back in 1974, the FWS initiated a program to monitor and study the biology of the species with funds authorized by the Marine Mammal Protection Act (MMPA). The MMPA recognized that it was not enough simply to protect animals; their habitat had to be protected as well. The initial program was operated as a field station under the auspices of the National Fish and Wildlife Laboratory of the U.S. Fish and Wildlife Service and included Howard "Duke" Campbell, Blair Irvine, and Buddy Powell. It was later to become known as the Sirenia Project. This handful of researchers was tasked with addressing questions directly related to the biology and the status of manatees and to protection of their habitat. The Jacksonville office of the FWS was responsible for management of Florida's manatee population through regulations and law enforcement, whereas the Sirenia Project was given the responsibility of research on manatee biology. This separation of missions was designed to encourage the collection of objective scientific data and to promote its interpretation free from overt political influence. Present-

Causes of Florida Manatee Mortality: 1974–2004

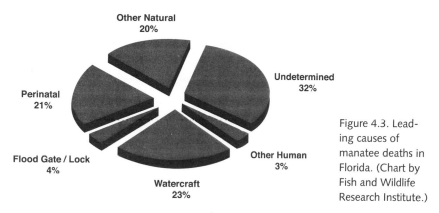

Other Natural
20%

Undetermined
32%

Perinatal
21%

Flood Gate / Lock
4%

Other Human
3%

Watercraft
23%

Figure 4.3. Leading causes of manatee deaths in Florida. (Chart by Fish and Wildlife Research Institute.)

day conflicts involving boat speed zones, estimated numbers of manatees in the state, and efforts to downlist manatees from endangered to threatened clearly illustrate the need for such separation.

First organized under the FWS, the Sirenia Project was in the mid-1990s placed under the jurisdiction of the National Biological Survey and later the U.S. Geological Survey (USGS). The Sirenia Project represented the first organized group dedicated to research on the biology of the Florida manatee. It included pioneers of aerial survey, life history and behavioral research, telemetry, habitat assessment, and carcass recovery to determine causes of death. In 1978, Galen Rathbun became the first Sirenia project leader. Galen was a native Californian who had previously conducted research on elephant shrews in Kenya. He hired Tom O'Shea in 1979 to help expand the program. Tom and Galen had met in Africa, where Tom was doing research on bats. Galen's boss in Washington was Bob Brownell, section chief for Marine Mammal Research of the National Fish and Wildlife Laboratory. In late 1978, Bob Brownell hired Cathy Beck and Bob Bonde to run the carcass salvage program. Brownell had worked on marine mammals in California and elsewhere and knew Cathy and Bob through their work at the Los Angeles County Museum of Natural History where they prepared specimens. Other early researchers included Jane Packard, who did important work on aerial surveys, population modeling, and interactions between manatees and aquatic plants, and Howard Kochman, a biologist with statistical expertise who was given responsibility for the detailed analyses that are so important for interpreting mountains of data. Howard, Cathy, and Bob are still there today. Dan Odell, a marine mammalogist then at the University of Miami, was also instrumental in organizing manatee research and protection around the state and worked closely with the Sirenia Project. Dan would later move to Hubbs-SeaWorld Research Institute to continue his studies on marine mammals. He led the Southeastern Marine Mammal Stranding Network and served as president of the international Society for Marine Mammalogy. During his tenure with the University of Miami, one of his students, John Reynolds, became involved in manatee biology and research. John began conducting behavioral, anatomical, and genetic studies and leading long-term aerial surveys at power plants to document manatee use of these artificial warm-water refugia throughout Florida. John also served as a professor at Eckerd College where he mentored several students in various aspects of marine mammal research. John is presently the chairman of the U.S. Marine Mammal Commission and head of manatee research at Mote Marine Laboratory in Sarasota, Florida.

Back in the late 1970s there were only nine people working full-time on the Sirenia Project. Today that number has dwindled to eight full-time biologists. In contrast, in the 1970s there was only one state employee, Harry Harper, who worked part-time on manatee issues. He was a Florida Marine Patrol officer stationed in Tallahassee. At the same time, behind-the-scenes pioneers worked to advance manatee protection and research. One of these leaders was John Twiss, director of the U.S. Marine Mammal Commission, who was fundamental in helping secure financial and political support for manatees. Also during this period, Pat Rose, an avid conservationist and administrator with the Florida Audubon Society, led an effort to bring the issues related to manatee recovery to the public eye and organized winter aerial surveys of manatees aggregated at power plant warm-water discharges. During this early period, the state continued to increase its efforts as well and hired Pat. Under his direction at the Florida Marine Research Institute (now the Fish and Wildlife Research Institute, FWRI), the state's program started developing in earnest in the early 1980s. The first staff included Brad Weigle, Beth Beeler, and Leslie Ward-Geiger. They were joined in the mid-1980s by Scott Wright and Bruce Ackerman and later, in the 1990s, by Richard Flamm. Notable leaders of the state program have included Pat Rose, Brad Weigle, Buddy Powell, and Elsa

Haubold. Pat later led the state's manatee management activities at the Bureau of Protected Species Management in Tallahassee. He has devoted his life to manatee conservation and was instrumental in the formation of the Save the Manatee Club. Presently, he remains an advocate for manatee issues and works for the Save the Manatee Club as director of government relations. Development of Florida's Save the Manatee Trust Fund in 1990 ensured a reliable source of funding for state-sanctioned projects through sales of manatee license plates and decals, boat registration fees, and voluntary donations. As one can see from this brief history, manatee conservation efforts have expanded and changed over the years. During the infancy of these various federal and state programs, researchers were excited about studying this poorly understood species. That fascination remains today, as there is still a great deal to learn.

Today, manatee protection is very complex and still falls under the direction of the FWS at the federal level with direction and guidance from the Marine Mammal Commission (fig. 4.4). Many players and interested parties co-

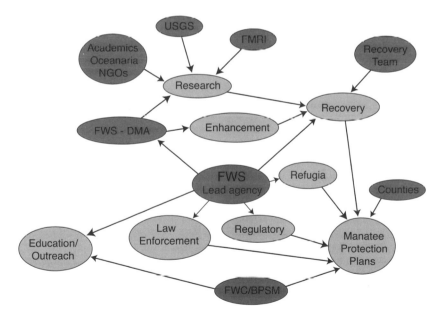

Figure 4.4. Network of researchers, managers, and conservationists that work with the Fish and Wildlife Service on manatee recovery. (Diagram by U.S. Geological Survey.)

ordinate endeavors to adequately protect these animals. Efforts leading to manatee recovery are coordinated by the Florida Manatee Recovery Team of the FWS. This team is composed of several working groups and task forces that address specific components of recovery. For example, there are working groups and subgroups to address regulatory issues, manatee protection, entanglement, water control structures, and interagency/oceanaria management. A population status working group looks at modeling the manatee population to detect trends in growth or decline. A habitat group explores warm-water and food resource concerns for Florida manatees. And, of course, there is a manatee education group that works to inform the public about manatee issues. It is through consultation with these working groups or teams that the FWS obtains advice for implementing its task of protecting the manatee. Today there are close to 50 employees working full-time on manatee issues for the State of Florida. Over the last 20 years the state has assumed much more responsibility for manatee research and management.

The Manatee Recovery Team is a federally constituted group required by the Endangered Species Act and is made up of representatives of several agencies and organizations with vested interests in manatee welfare, regulations, and recovery. This team is responsible for writing the Florida Manatee Recovery Plan. This document guides the FWS in recovery efforts. Additionally, 13 Florida counties are charged with development of Manatee Protection Plans to ensure adequate protection of manatees on a state level within their jurisdictions. At present, recovery efforts encompass four specific objectives: to (1) minimize causes of manatee disturbance, harassment, injury, and mortality; (2) determine and monitor the status of the manatee population; (3) protect, identify, evaluate, and monitor manatee habitats; and (4) facilitate manatee recovery through public awareness and education. Assisting in the recovery effort are several agencies and organizations as well as various stakeholders that deal with law enforcement, permitting, refugia (places where manatees aggregate), outreach, research, and other special-interest issues. This vast and diverse effort is in compliance with federal guidelines as well.

The Save the Manatee Club was founded in 1981 by singer Jimmy Buffet and then governor of Florida Bob Graham. A nonprofit organization headed by Judith Vallee, it has over 40,000 members throughout the world. Its mission is to promote public awareness and education, to sponsor research, rescue, and rehabilitation efforts, and to advocate and take appropriate legal action for manatees and their habitat. Save the Manatee Club participates in various legal and administrative challenges on behalf of its members to defend and otherwise support actions to protect manatees. It acts as a watchdog group to ensure that the laws protecting manatees and their habitat are obeyed and enforced.

Status

Because of protections afforded by state and federal laws and the improved treatment that accompanies increased human awareness, the demeanor of manatees has changed to the point that individual animals now trust human beings. The consequences of this trust become apparent when manatees become lazy and habituated to handouts because generous, well-meaning people offer them food or freshwater. Such activities are against the law because they alter the manatee's natural behavior. The ramifications of similar kinds of interactions between humans and marine mammals have been pointed out in detail by Reynolds and Wells.[9] Well-intentioned exchanges between people and a species always carry a cost, but most of the burden falls on the manatee. A wayward manatee that happened into Crystal River a few hundred years ago probably would have fallen victim to man's harpoon. But only as recently as 40 years ago, Woodie Hartman was there to embrace manatees in a way that would eventually lead to a burgeoning ecotourism industry—people swimming with manatees rather than killing them for food. This transition was only possible in a country where people place moral and ethical values involving wildlife above greed and the enshrinement of self-sufficiency.

Hartman's meager population of 63 manatees in Crystal River in the late 1960s has grown considerably today. The same trend is apparent in other areas sampled using various aerial survey techniques. Today many managers estimate that there are 3,300 to 4,000 manatees in Florida. This number remains a guess, and actually, precision may not be all that necessary. As long as managers can predict with certainty where manatees are and what habitats are important to them, it may not be crucial to know the exact number of individuals. Scientists today realize that population trends are often more important determinants of recovery than the total number of animals. Data collected to predict trends also yields clues about the overall status of the manatee population. The Manatee Population Status Working Group is leading that investigation, and the results can enlighten all concerned parties by increasing our understanding of manatee population dynamics.

It is important to note that there are different groups or subpopulations of manatees in Florida (discussed in detail in the next chapter). The status of the Florida manatee population as a whole may depend on the status of each of these subpopulations. Each group needs to be managed differently, because the manatees in each group have different life history characteristics, employ different strategies in order to succeed in each area, and are subject to different threats. For example, threats from watercraft and red tide exposure are currently greater in southwest Florida than they are in northwest Florida.

Recovery

Recovery is defined as "the improvement in status of a listed species to the point that the listing is no longer appropriate under the criteria set out in the Endangered Species Act." We protect animals from human-related threats to their well-being as best we can, but the clock continues to tick for manatees in Florida. Natural conditions are also at issue as Mother Nature continues to pound manatees with winter cold fronts along the northern limit of their range. The U.S. Fish and Wildlife Service has a detailed recovery plan that outlines specific steps necessary to achieve manatee recovery.[10] Most ongoing and current research and management efforts are mandated by this document. Its first edition, published back in 1981, was touted as one of the best-structured and best-written guides available for any endangered species at that time. Its example has resulted in stronger recovery plans for several other endangered species.

Recently the State of Florida initiated a proposal to downlist the Florida manatee from endangered to threatened status. Based on the very broad and encompassing state criteria, the manatee might even be considered for removal from the state's endangered species list entirely. Regardless of what the state decides to do with manatees, the federal government is charged with the ultimate responsibility of determining their status relative to the criteria written into the Endangered Species Act. These criteria require the secretary of the interior to make decisions on the listing status of manatees based on the best scientific data available, while taking into consideration potential economic impacts. Under the secretary's direction, the FWS approach is to use predictive models that are constructed specifically for the manatee in an effort to assess their current status. Modelers have suggested that even slight changes in a critical factor—number of annual deaths of animals of reproductive age, for example—can have a dramatic impact on future generations of the species.[11] For their part, managers are trying to deal with an apparent increase in the number of reported manatee deaths by reducing threats as much as possible, but often their rationales fall on deaf ears in political arenas.

The FWS Manatee Recovery Facts Sheet states that "Great strides have been made in the protection and recovery of the Florida manatee. It is certainly no longer 'on the brink of extinction.' However, there is much left to be done to secure its future. This will require the cooperation and support of everyone: government, the private sector, and you!" We share these sentiments and encourage everyone to participate in manatee recovery by becoming more aware of their plight and by translating that awareness into responsible action and behavior.

5 How Many Are There?

For people interested in coexisting harmoniously with other animals, the issue of a healthy manatee population seems simple. Certainly we would want to know if the population is in decline and whether or not its critical habitat is in jeopardy due to factors such as reduced food supplies and pollution. Then, if need be, a plan of action could be formulated to do something to improve the situation. But as we shall see, addressing these issues in the real world is actually quite complex, primarily because of scientific and political constraints. Florida is crowded with people, and even those kindly disposed toward manatees engage daily in activities that, when done on a massive scale, can negatively impact manatees or their habitat. Those familiar with other efforts to protect threatened or endangered species, like the spotted owl in the Pacific Northwest, the black-footed ferret in the Great Plains states, or the Florida panther, will recognize that some of the same issues relating to economics and the interplay of cultural habits and environmental values apply to manatees in Florida. However, as Tom O'Shea has emphasized in many forums, there is one big difference. Where Florida manatees are concerned, there are no issues of infringement on the use of private property. All manatee habitat is located on publicly owned waterways. Protection of manatee habitat deprives no loggers or fishermen of their jobs, prevents no farmers from tilling the land or ranchers from grazing their herds in riparian habitats. There is no loss of livestock to threatened predators. In the case of manatees, the primary issue is recreation and the industry that supports it. Should we have fun, go as fast as we want to go, and kill and maim animals or endanger a species in the process?

Why fly?

It was 1968, and Woodie Hartman was terrified of flying, especially with his pilot Grizzly Bear, whose gruff manner and small plane did not inspire confidence. Nevertheless, they flew over Citrus County during the cold snaps of 1968–69 to see how many manatees they could spot. In spite of his fear of flying, Hartman bought an old Piper Cub to continue his survey in 1973. After spending several years studying manatees in Florida waters, Hartman was intensely eager to discover how many manatees were living in the state and where they might be located. His numerous conversations with fishermen and others throughout Florida had yielded a lot of fragmentary and often contradictory information about the location of manatees, but he could not answer these questions based solely on his own observations in the water. It appeared that the only solution was to go flying and find out for himself. Woodie strapped on his football helmet and counted 255 manatees in Florida and southeast Georgia during several flights over a six-week period in the summer of 1973.[1] He christened the plane *Grand Funk Airplane* and was aided by a capable pilot—who got the plane at the end of the study in return for his services—and by two assistants, including James "Buddy" Powell.

On a cold January morning a little over two years later, the engine of another small plane sputtered to life. Blair Irvine was in the passenger's seat as the plane taxied down the runway. Its liftoff marked the beginning of the first intensive statewide manatee survey since Woodie Hartman's initial effort in 1973. During this flight and several others made over a six-day period, Blair and a team of researchers covered much of the known manatee winter aggregation habitat in the state as well as many areas in South Florida within the Everglades National Park. They counted a total of 738 manatees along Florida's coast.[2]

After Irvine's team made its 1976 flights, manatee researchers concluded that there were about 800–1,000 manatees in Florida, and attention turned to other issues largely because of the expense and logistical difficulties associated with aerial surveys of this kind.[3] The spark was rekindled during the 1980s as large aggregations of manatees were observed during the winter to frequent the warm water around power plants throughout the coastal areas of the state. In 1977, aerial surveys were initiated by Pat Rose of Florida Audubon and coordinated by Ross Wilcox and later Winifred Perkins with funding from the Florida Power and Light Company. This lengthy series of surveys was continued by others at Florida Audubon, including Rose McCutcheon, Paul Raymond, Angie McGehee, and others. In 1982 the surveys and their coordination came under the direction of John Reynolds, and the results indicated that these winter aggregations became larger and larger over the decade.[4] By 1989 a total of 1,240 manatees was observed at various sites throughout the state.[5] These surveys continue today under John's expert direction and have logged single counts in excess of 1,400 manatees. Naturally, survey findings have prompted lots of questions. With so many animals seen at warm water sites, surely there were many more manatees scattered around the state. Could it be that manatee numbers were actually on the rise? Had protection efforts finally begun to work? Or, were more efficient and experienced observers partially responsible for count increases? To date, the best aerial survey analyses of winter aggregation sites have been conducted by Craig and Reynolds.[6] Their studies suggest that from 1982 to 1989, there was a 5–7 percent increase in manatee use of aggregation sites along Florida's Atlantic coast. This was followed by a leveling off in use between 1990 and 1993 and then by an increase of 3–6 percent since 1994. By modeling their aggregation site data, they estimated that in 2002 the manatee population along the entire East Coast was about 1,600 individuals.

In the early 1990s Bruce Ackerman of Fish and Wildlife Research Institute (FWRI) coordinated statewide synoptic surveys in response to a statute passed by the Florida state legislature, which mandated "an impartial scientific benchmark census of the manatee population to be conducted annually." The idea behind the synoptic survey was to get a statewide count of manatees during the winter when they are aggregated and thus easiest to find. In 1991, Bruce boarded his plane and along with 15 other aircraft teams supported by nine ground crews flew an extensive statewide synoptic survey that included all known aggregation sites. By putting many people up in airplanes on the same day it is possible to obtain comprehensive coverage of a large portion of the state, while avoiding problems like counting individuals twice because they have moved from one site to another. From 1991–2000, synoptic counts ranged from 1,267–2,639 with lots of variability from one year to the next, much of it caused by changing weather conditions, associated changes in

Plate 1. Though semisocial, manatees are often observed together in investigative, cavorting groups. (Photograph by Clark Wheeler.)

Plate 2. Every year more than 70,000 people come to Crystal River to swim with manatees. To a manatee this can be a bit overwhelming. (Photograph by Clark Wheeler.)

Plate 3. Prehensile lip muscles allow the manatee to grasp objects in a hand-like manner. (Photograph by Clark Wheeler.)

Plate 4. A massive injury to the side of this longtime resident of the Homosassa River. (Photograph by U.S. Geological Survey.)

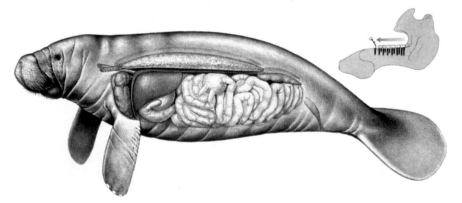

Plate 5. The digestive system of the manatee is large. Tooth progression along the lower jaw is depicted in the detail. (Modified from O'Shea 1994: 69.)

Plate 6. Aerial view of manatees, swimmers, and boats in Crystal River. Manatees appear as elongated light gray objects, boats as rectangles. Boundaries of the sanctuary are marked on the left with rope and buoys. (Photograph by U.S. Geological Survey.)

Plate 7. A manatee calf nurses from its mother's teats, which are located behind each flipper. (Photograph by U.S. Geological Survey.)

Plate 8. Mother and calf bonds are very strong and can last up to two or more years. (Photograph by Clark Wheeler.)

Plate 9. A research team uses long nets to catch wild manatees. (Photograph by U.S. Geological Survey.)

Plate 10. A satellite tag attached to the manatee's tail floats behind him at the water's surface. (Photograph by U.S. Geological Survey.)

Plate 11. Researchers release a tagged wild manatee back into the water in Puerto Rico. (Photograph by U.S. Geological Survey.)

Plate 12. Aerial photo of manatees in the warm water of a power plant discharge in Florida. (Photograph by U.S. Geological Survey.)

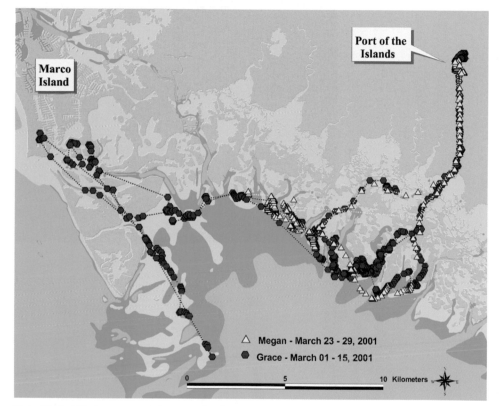

Plate 13. Detailed movements between feeding areas and freshwater sites for two manatees in the Ten Thousand Islands area of southwest Florida obtained using satellite-linked GPS technology. Grass beds shown in green. (Figure by Rachel Henriques and U.S. Geological Survey.)

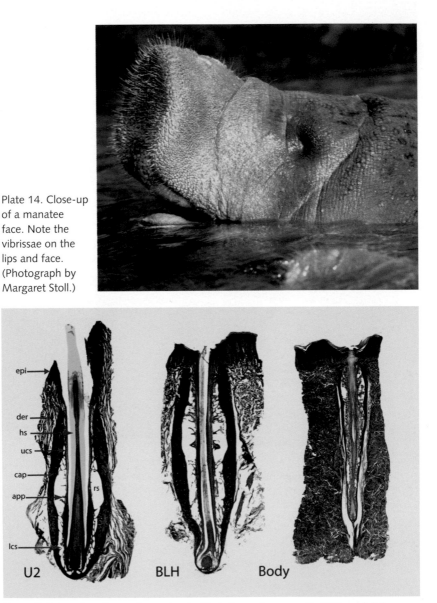

Plate 14. Close-up of a manatee face. Note the vibrissae on the lips and face. (Photograph by Margaret Stoll.)

Plate 15. Internal anatomy of manatee tactile hairs on the upper lip (U2), oral disk (BLH), and body. (From Reep et al. 2001: 6–7 and 2002: 149, courtesy of Karger Press.)

Plate 16. A transportable frame is used to weigh the manatees in Belize. (Photograph by U.S. Geological Survey.)

Plate 17. An educational opportunity with Bob Bonde in the field in Belize. (Photograph by U.S. Geological Survey.)

Plate 18. Researchers ready to release a manatee with the "CritterCam" in Belize. (Photograph by U.S. Geological Survey.)

Plate 19. A lone male rests in the warm, clear waters of Crystal River accompanied by a few fish. (Photograph by Pat Rose.)

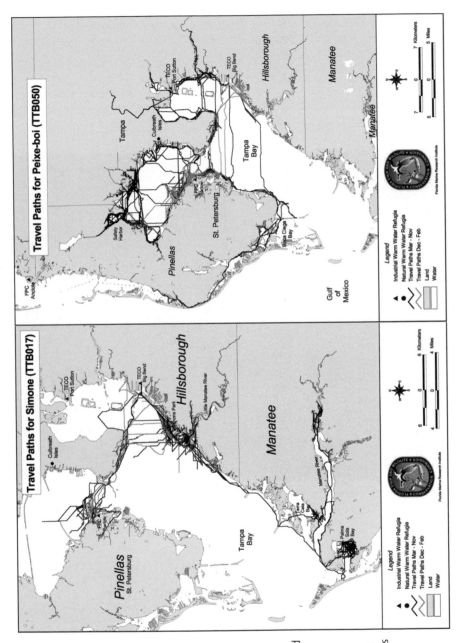

Plate 20. Movement patterns for Peixe-boi and Simone, two manatees who frequent Tampa Bay. (Figure by Alexander Smith and path analysis by Richard Flamm, Wildlife Research Institute.)

water clarity, and occupancy of warm-water sites. Between 2000 and 2001, the count jumped from 2,223 to 3,276 (fig. 5.1).[7] This increase vividly reflects the uncertainty associated with survey numbers, because it is not possible for over 1,000 manatees to have been born in a single year. However, 3,276 may cautiously be taken to represent the minimum estimate for manatee numbers statewide in 2001. Now scientists are concerned with interpreting the synoptic survey results. What do they mean? Researchers agree that there are so many uncontrollable variables involved with these counts that the data are useless for predicting a population number or trends in growth. However, others argue that they are the best data we have to estimate a minimum population of manatees in the southeastern United States. Current and past data on manatee synoptic counts and mortality can be viewed at the FWRI website at http://myfwc.com/manatee/.

Aerial survey methods

The best way to count manatees in clear water or resting at the surface is from the air (plate 6). During distribution surveys researchers climb into an airplane or helicopter (as in the annual synoptic survey) and fly over habitat that

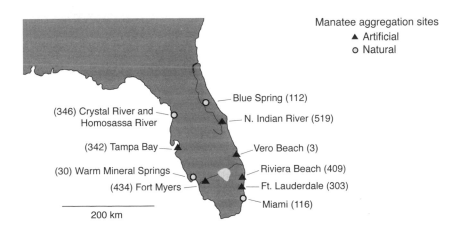

Figure 5.1. Location of large winter aggregation sites in Florida. Numbers represent high counts obtained during the 2001 synoptic survey, when 3,276 manatees were observed. (Map detail by Gabe Trinity.)

contains manatees. They count any manatees they see and record locations on maps and data sheets in order to document seasonal changes in distribution and relative abundance. Whenever researchers fly in order to count manatees, they try to employ a very consistent methodology so that the data will produce statistically valid results.[8] Flight path, cruising speed, altitude, and methods for recording data are standardized for every flight. Though this enhances the reliability of the counts, difficulties still arise when scientists wish to compare counts from different areas. Some sites offer a clear, unobstructed view of the animals below, whereas other areas have very dark, turbid waters. In fact, most manatees living in Florida spend most of their lives in murky water. Weather conditions can also make visibility very difficult. Bright sunny days create glare from the water surface, especially at midday, and the slightest winds can create ripples on the water that obscure objects below the surface.

One of the best methods for establishing trends in counts outside of aggregation sites is through consistent duplication of a specific flight path that winds back and forth in a predetermined, systematic way over a designated body of water. Called a strip-transect survey, this method is more accurate than that described above for distribution surveys. On the other hand, strip-transect surveys are also more costly and time consuming to carry out. Employing this method, the pilot flies at the same optimal altitude and follows an exact flight path. This minimizes observational bias and error, which in turn better enables statisticians to correct for certain variables and compare trends among the data sets.[9] Strip-transect surveying has been utilized in several specific study areas of Florida, most notably Crystal River, the St. Johns River, the Caloosahatchee River, Tampa Bay, Ten Thousand Islands, and the Indian and Banana rivers of Brevard County.[10] In the summers of 1993 and 1994 aerial strip-transects were tested as a method for estimating population sizes in specific locations.

Unlike distribution surveys, transects allow researchers to calculate the actual area searched and extrapolate the population estimate to the entire body of water. This technique works best for areas with uniform characteristics such as depth and water clarity. Portions of the Banana River were chosen to test this technique, including restricted areas administered by NASA. Aerial survey researcher Kari Clifton recalls that "Each day we had to secure permission to enter restricted airspace near the Kennedy Space Center. One day early on in the trials we were hastily told to leave the airspace—they had forgotten to tell us they were launching a weather rocket. We hung around at 200 meters just outside restricted airspace and witnessed the rocket make its departure. Each day thereafter we made it a point to ask NASA air control if there were any rocket launches scheduled that day, often to the dismay and snickers of our colleagues in the background."

An extremely important factor in survey conduct is team and observer experience. In a strip-transect, each plane carries two observers as well as the pilot—the main idea being to reduce observer bias (the chance that animals visible from the aircraft will be overlooked by one observer). The two-observer technique, developed by Helene Marsh of Australia in the course of similar work assessing dugong populations, requires that one observer sit in the backseat of the aircraft. Riding around in a small plane for hours at a time does not make for an easy day on the job. The plane's constant motion, gravitational forces, the wind and cold or heat, the engine noise, and the cramped quarters are all quite taxing. Although the secondary observer sits just behind the primary, the gravitational force he or she experiences as the plane circles is more intense than for the front-seat observer. Surveys are typically flown with the window open to give the front-seat observer a better view of the water near and below the plane. As a result, wind continuously blasts the person in the backseat unless they use their data sheets as a shield or unless the primary observer hangs their head out the window. Kari Clifton reports that "when safely back on the ground, we left the airport with heads buzzing, ears ringing, queasy stomachs, a staggered gait, and a bad case of TB (Tired Butt)."

Bob Bonde flew over 36,000 miles during surveys he conducted in Brevard County in the mid-1980s. "That is more distance than is necessary to fly around the world at the equator," he stated. "I certainly would have preferred to do that and would have collected a lot of frequent flyer miles to boot; however, after all those flights I never saw more than the three airports we landed in for fueling. All the rest of the time we were flying the same methodical flight path, during different times of the year. That data gave me very good information on manatee distribution. However, determining abundance is much more difficult to do."

With data collected from the overall synoptic survey, researchers had hoped to show trends over time and to calculate a minimum base population estimate. This approach is very risky, as Tom O'Shea and his colleagues at the U.S. Geological Survey (USGS) aptly point out.[11] Researchers must exercise care when dealing with simple counts of numbers of manatees during a survey, because results can be more tenuous than those produced by labor-intensive analytical methodologies employing census techniques to express actual trends and abundance within the population. Most managers and the general public do not understand the complexities of using aerial counts to estimate trends in populations. In fact, when reported without qualification, these data can be misleading and actually detrimental to our understanding of cause and effect in population dynamics.[12]

What are the current goals of doing aerial and synoptic surveys of manatees, aside from complying with the mandate from the Florida legislature? To begin with, it is important to know whether the population is increasing or decreasing. Originally it was thought that the most direct way to determine this was by conducting a periodic census where every animal seen is counted. Unfortunately, it isn't possible to see every manatee. Animals move around, necessitating simultaneous counts at various sites throughout the state. Even then, many animals go uncounted because of poor visibility or, among other factors, because they occupy habitat hidden from aerial view. As a result, aerial counts are quite variable even when made within days of each other. In the winter of 1999–2000, for example, 1,629 manatees were counted initially, while ten days later 2,222 were counted. Thus, aerial surveys do not reliably provide accurate estimates of population size. An alternative to counting every manatee is to sample the population—something researchers do when conducting the surveys funded by Florida Power and Light Company. This approach works fairly well for large whales or the manatees' cousins, the dugongs, both of which live in open ocean water, but this strategy is not well suited to surveys along the intricate coastline of Florida with its myriad islands, marshes, and rivers.

Aerial survey data are used by various interest groups to promote their viewpoints. The 1990 mandate by the Florida legislature to conduct an annual census was made in spite of the fact that scientists recognized the impossibility of obtaining an actual population count. In succeeding years, some lobbyists associated with boating interests have jumped on high counts as indicating that the population is stable or increasing and therefore needs no further protection. They have even claimed that low counts are evidence of a conspiracy among conservationists and researchers to make manatees appear more endangered on paper than they are in reality. In any case, a few years of increasing numbers is not the same thing as complete stock recovery; it only suggests that the conditions for survey conduct were good and that the population may be headed in the right direction for recovery. How many manatees would represent a healthy, stable population size? Nobody really knows, but it is important to maintain a safety factor to buffer against infrequent but devastating events like red tide outbreaks, which caused at least 150 manatee deaths in 1996.[13]

Benefits of protected areas

Perhaps the greatest value of aerial surveys is that they indicate patterns in the use of warm-water sites by manatees during the winter. This information then can be used to appropriately protect sites that are heavily frequented. Aerial survey data can be combined with photo-identification of known individuals to yield not only total counts but also information on the structure of the population at a given site. This combined approach has led researchers to conclude that two protected sites, Crystal River and Banana River, witnessed manatee population increases from the 1970s to the 1990s. Buddy Powell started detailed aerial surveys of Crystal River in the 1970s. Today, that long-standing tradition is carried on by Joyce Kleen of the Crystal River National Wildlife Refuge. Trends in results of those flights clearly show an increase in manatee use of the Crystal River over the last couple of decades. Jane Provancha of the Kennedy Space Center reports the same trends in Brevard County's Banana River, and ranger Wayne Hartley observes similar trends in Blue Spring on the St. Johns River based on his field observations. Wayne's steadfast determination, dedication, and eye for detail over the last 20 years at Blue Spring have made his observations of individuals in the population extremely valuable. Wayne has committed to memory the unique features of more than 300 manatees. He is one of the few old-school natural historians who can remember a stray encounter with a lone manatee from years before and make a present-day definitive match with just one casual glance. In 1978 there were 21 animals in Blue Spring. Today, nearly 200 manatees are known to visit the spring run in a single winter. Increase in the three subpopulations at Crystal River, Banana River, and Blue Spring is not simply due to an increase in the number of animals migrating to these protected sites, but reflects increased reproduction and a high adult survival rate for these areas.[14] Undoubtedly, the introduction of successfully rehabilitated captive manatees into these systems has benefited their populations, and habitat protection at the three sites is probably directly responsible for subpopulation increase. The less protected areas of the Atlantic and southwest Gulf coasts do not evince positive trends similar to those seen at Crystal River, Banana River, and Blue Spring. This discrepancy provides dramatic evidence that protected habitat is of great value to manatees in Florida.

At Crystal River, sanctuaries in place during the winter keep boats and swimmers from entering areas set aside for manatees to rest, feed, socialize, and thermoregulate without interference. In the late 1960s, Hartman reported an approximate high count of 38 animals at Crystal River.[15] In 1978 that number was reported at 72, and these days over 400 individuals are counted. The sanctuaries have worked commendably as the high number of manatees using them indicates.

Unfortunately, sanctuaries are not available to manatees in many parts of the state. Presently, several no-entry zones surrounding warm-water discharges protect manatees thermoregulating there during the winter, but they often fall short with regard to other necessities for their survival. What do manatees do when they leave these protected winter sites during the remainder of the year? Where do they find protection while they are feeding? Regrettably, there is precious little natural habitat left in Florida to set aside for manatee sanctuary status. Cam Shaw of the U.S. Fish and Wildlife Service (FWS), John Reynolds and David Laist of the Marine Mammal Commission, and Kipp Frohlich of the state's Imperiled Species Management Section are among those working to address some of these long-term concerns and needs.

Managers at the FWS have utilized long-term site fidelity data sets to calculate potential biological removal (PBR) levels. These calculations change as threats and habitats change, necessitating perpetual revision. Not including natural mortalities (from cold stress and red tide, for example), PBR level represents the maximum number of animals that may be removed from a marine mammal stock, while still allowing that stock to reach or maintain its optimum sustainable population. (To many Floridians, this number should be zero, as too many manatees are already needlessly killed every year through human carelessness.) The term "removal" includes, but is not limited to, deaths caused by boat strikes and other human activities. PBR is a theoretical but necessary tool for predictive model development. Such predictions are difficult to make, especially in light of the fact that manatees are endangered. There are obvious variations in mortality trends, and field counts of manatees can often be extremely variable, even within the same season. The ultimate goal established by the FWS for manatee recovery includes establishing a positive growth rate by stabilizing or decreasing numbers of manatee deaths.[16] This objective is best accomplished by allowing manatees appropriate habitat for healthy reproduction and by diminishing threats. Establishing sanctuaries and enforcing boat speed zones appear to be working; both are important strategies for meeting recovery criteria. Woodie Hartman, veteran observer of the Florida manatee scene, feels that greater enforcement of existing regulations on boat traffic is urgently needed. This sentiment is shared by many in the manatee research community as well as by boaters and other individuals who have carefully considered conservation issues and have witnessed the tremendous increase in Florida's human population over the years.

Population dynamics

In spite of the importance many people place on estimating the number of manatees in Florida, it has become clear that the future of the population is critically tied to factors such as the age structure of the population. This concept refers to relative proportions of calves, juveniles, and adults and is closely related to adult survival rates and reproductive parameters like the calving interval. Below, we discuss how such factors impact population models. But let us begin at the beginning.

Early studies on Florida manatee population biology were done by Joseph Curtis Moore in the 1950s and continued by Woodie Hartman in the late 1960s. With the help of Buddy Powell, Woodie logged and mapped much of what is known today about manatee natural history. With just 63 animals, Woodie made observations and generalizations about most of their life history parameters that have proven over time to be accurate.[17] His work laid the foundation for extensive studies that were to follow during the next few decades. Later studies in Crystal River were made by Galen Rathbun, Jim Reid, and Bob Bonde of the Sirenia Project.

Bob Bonde's first trip into the water with manatees occurred in 1978. "I remember the time like it was only yesterday. Two young, first-year manatee calves were as anxious to see me as I was to see them. With an enthusiasm not unlike that of an excited puppy dog, these twin calves of long time resident manatee, Piety, swam straight for me. One of the calves I first saw on that cold winter day in 1978 was later christened Narnia and is now a mother of several of her own calves. Often when I see Narnia and her calf, grandmother Piety is nearby." Piety was one of the original 63 distinctive animals cataloged and documented by Hartman in the 1967–68 field season.[18]

Today researchers travel to the Crystal and Homosassa rivers each winter to document manatees. Now there are more than 2,000 animals represented in a statewide photo-identification catalog maintained by Cathy Beck of the Sirenia Project.[19] Cathy has worked for more than 25 years with the project and has a keen eye for detail. In a cooperative effort involving Cathy and Amy Teague of Sirenia Project as well as colleagues from FWRI and Mote Marine Lab, a large amount of photographic data has been collected and validated. Significant contributions to the catalog and its usefulness have also been made by Wayne Hartley at Blue Spring State Park and by Kit Curtin, working in southeast Florida for over a decade. Each year thousands of photographs and notes submitted from researchers in the field are exhaustively sorted and analyzed by the team. These documents identify more than 400 individuals from the Crystal River population with the remainder distributed throughout Florida. Most manatees have a pattern of features such as propeller scars, tail notches, and other mutilations that can be used to identify them uniquely (fig. 5.2). Sadly, the most useful identifying features are scars inflicted by boats. With the aid of photographs researchers are able to gauge and monitor manatee survival and to study scar acquisition rates, other injuries, and reproductive parameters.

The Sirenia Project database has been used to determine the probability of survival for adult manatees. Cathy Langtimm and colleagues analyzed the pattern of photo-documented resightings of identified individuals in three regionally defined subpopulations: the Northwest, which includes Crystal

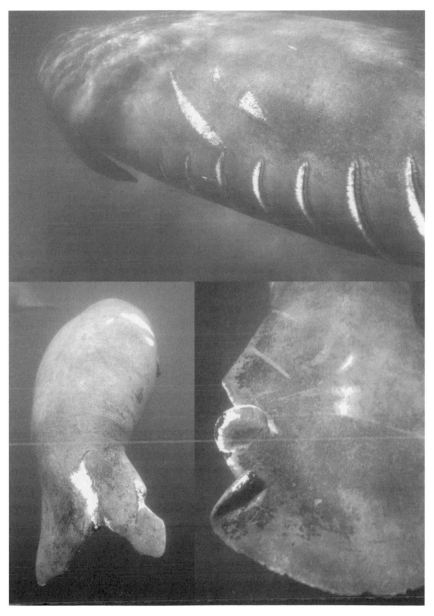

Figure 5.2. Scar patterns are used by researchers to recognize distinct individuals in the population. Here are examples on three different animals. (Photograph by U.S. Geological Survey.)

River; Blue Spring; and the Atlantic coast.[20] With so many manatee research-ers observing and photographing manatees every year at these sites, it ap-peared likely that a previously identified animal would be seen again if it were still alive. They found that at Blue Spring there was a 95 percent chance a sur-viving known adult previously seen at that site would show up again. At Crys-tal River the chances were also high at 74 percent, but on the Atlantic coast the probability was only 51 percent. They concluded that resighting probability, and thus adult survival, at Blue Spring and Crystal River is high enough to sustain growth in those populations, but that the situation on the Atlantic coast is cause for concern. More data are needed for southwestern Florida, from Tampa Bay south to the Everglades.

Population modeling is the science of using information about the indi-viduals of a given species in a given region to determine present trends in the status of that population.[21] Typically, these data include such information as the number of individuals of breeding age and the birth and death rates. Modeling of Florida manatee data suggests that as a group they are capable of maximal population increases of about 7 percent per year under ideal circum-stances.[22] This number is based primarily on the reproductively active period of female manatees, the interval between successive calvings, and adult sur-vival rates. Because of the extended period of reproductive activity and fertil-ity in these long-lived mammals, it turns out that adult survival is the primary factor influencing the potential for population growth. If one makes what appear to be reasonable assumptions about several population variables, a population viability analysis can be performed. This type of analysis takes a set of current conditions and projects into the future.

Miriam Marmontel and coworkers used statewide data on reproduction and survival derived from carcasses collected between 1976 and 1991 to per-form one such analysis.[23] The 1997 Marmontel study indicated a trend slightly toward negative growth (population loss). According to her model, however, only a 10 percent increase in annual manatee mortality would push the popu-lation toward extinction. On the bright side, a 10 percent decrease in mortality would result in slow positive population growth. This translates roughly to cutting boat-related mortality in half, since it constitutes about 25 percent of all annual mortality. This is one reason why so much energy has been focused on regulating boat traffic in Florida and preserving manatee habitat. Success is within our reach, but so is disaster. The human population of Florida, around 16 million as of this writing, continues to grow rapidly, and the number of registered watercraft mirrors this growth (440,000 in 1975, more than 830,000 in 2002). Based on these numbers, boat-related manatee mortality may continue to increase unless other factors change (fig. 5.3).

In addition to looking at the Florida manatee population as a whole, we may wish to analyze subpopulation trends in specific locations. The Manatee Population Status Working Group, headed by Dawn Jennings of the FWS and Elsa Haubold of FWRI, currently recognizes four subpopulations of manatees that correspond to state geographic regions and represent management units. These include the Northwest, the Southwest, the Atlantic (including the lower St. Johns River north of Palatka), and the upper St. Johns River (south of Palatka). In their 1995 analysis of three of these regions (Northwest, Atlantic, and upper St. Johns River), Eberhardt and O'Shea estimated that population growth rates were positive, between 1 and 7 percent per year (7 percent at Crystal River representing the Northwest region, 6 percent at Blue Spring representing the upper St. Johns River region, and 1 percent on the Atlantic

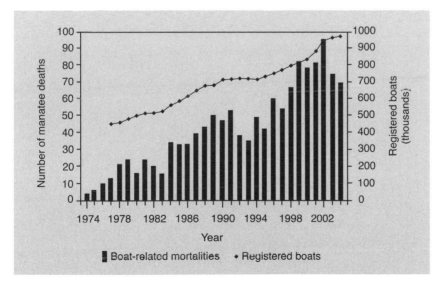

Figure 5.3. As the number of registered boats in Florida increases, so does the number of deaths due to watercraft-related injuries. (Graph by Fish and Wildlife Research Institute.)

coast).[24] A more recent detailed evaluation by Runge, Langtimm, and Kendall found that growth of the Northwest subpopulation is about 3.7 percent per year, while that of the upper St. Johns River subpopulation is about 6.2 percent per year.[25] The manatee subpopulation in the Southwest region, on the other hand, appears to have declined by about 1.1 percent per year over the past ten years. It is more difficult to assess the status of the Atlantic subpopulation because of uncertainty about adult survival rates. An optimistic analysis suggests positive growth of 1 percent per year, whereas a pessimistic analysis arrives at an estimated decline of about 3 percent per year.

The Florida Manatee Recovery Plan establishes specific quantitative criteria that must be met in order for the Florida manatee to be downlisted by the federal government from endangered to threatened status.[26] One criterion is that the average population growth rate must be greater than 1.0, a figure which appears to apply in at least two of the four management regions. Of the two remaining criteria, one requires that the average adult survival rate be greater than 90 percent and the other that the average fraction of adult females with a dependent calf be greater than 40 percent. Taken altogether, these criteria are indicators of a healthy population.

Reproduction

Births and deaths ultimately determine the makeup of a population of animals and how its composition changes. Other factors that influence population dynamics include available food resources, disease outbreaks, rate of predation, and weather conditions. On that note let's take a closer look at reproduction and early life among manatees. Unlike many marine mammals, Florida manatees are considered semisocial, meaning that they do not form long-term social bonds. Of course, they do interact with each other, but only a mother and her calf remain together for as long as two to three years during the nursing period and sometimes beyond.[27] Pregnancy lasts 12–14 months,[28] so females may have a calf as often as every 2.5–3 years (plates 7 and 8). The calf reaches sexual maturity between two and five years of age.[29]

Once a female becomes sexually mature and comes into estrus, manatees form a mating herd that consists of a transitory group of consorting males pursuing one receptive female (fig. 5.4). However, copulation has rarely been

Figure 5.4. Several males follow a female in estrus in an attempt to mate. These mating herds can last for several days. (Photograph by U.S. Geological Survey.)

observed in the wild, and it has not yet been verified that the female in any such herd is actually in a physiological state of estrus based on hormonal status. The mating herd is certainly the most visible potential breeding behavior manatees exhibit, but a more subtle behavior noted from field observations involves a single male diligently shadowing a female until she becomes receptive. The relative frequency of these contrasting behaviors is unknown. The individual male members of a mating herd try relentlessly to hold onto the female and roll over in attempts to gain access to her underside.[30] A major difficulty in consistently identifying the exact composition of these herds derives from the hazards of swimming among manatees to identify sex by viewing the undersides of otherwise indistinguishable individuals.

One winter morning, Bob Bonde was swimming among a group of mating manatees in Crystal River in very cloudy water. All of a sudden, an animal beneath him came lunging to the surface, hitting Bob squarely in the chest. Fortunately, the snorkel in his mouth kept him from biting off his tongue. "The impact reminded me of my days in high school when one was blindsided by an enthusiastic tackler in a less than friendly game of football. To this day, I am not sure what the manatee was thinking, but I feel he was just as startled as I was. Luckily, he didn't make me out for the receptive female or I'd have been in a great deal of trouble and would guess that I would have some very interesting stories to convey to you."

The female may be pursued by males for two to four weeks.[31] However, estrus may not necessarily be occurring during this entire period of pursuit, but instead may last for only a brief period during the whole mating herd scenario. The two to four weeks of male pursuit could represent actual receptiveness on the female's part, or it may reflect the establishment of dominance among males. It may also indicate a strategy of sperm competition, with males breeding as frequently as possible while the female is receptive.[32] In other mammalian species exhibiting sperm competition, the males possess markedly enlarged testes, but manatees do not. Two possible explanations of this apparent paradox have been suggested.[33] First, manatees *do* possess enlarged seminal vesicles, which may compensate for smaller testes through production of large volumes of seminal fluid. This tradeoff could be related to the low metabolic rate of manatees, if production of semen is less expensive metabolically than production of sperm. Another possibility is that the testes only appear small when scaled to the greatly enlarged overall body size. (A similar relationship applies to interpretation of relative brain size.)

Female manatees are thought to exhibit promiscuous breeding behavior, mating with several males in the herd. This mating system may more specifically be described as "scramble competition polygyny."[34] This reproductive strategy has also been described for Hawaiian monk seals (*Monachus schauinslandi*), humpback whales (*Megaptera novaeangliae*), and other species.[35] In manatees, a peak in this reproductive behavior appears to occur from April to May. Gestation length is estimated at 12–14 months, and manatees almost always give birth to one offspring at a time with twinning occurring in less than 2 percent of births.[36]

It has been suggested that Florida manatees may undergo suppression of reproductive activity during the colder months of the year. Changes in male and female reproductive anatomy, periods of increased calf mortality, and field observations of mating herds, pregnancy, and lactation also indicate that manatees engage in a "diffusely seasonal" reproductive pattern.[37] This kind of pattern enables species to breed throughout the year, with peaks and lulls in reproductive activity occurring during energy-rich and energy-poor periods. Manatees in Florida have abundant food resources year round, but may experience energy stresses due to cold water during the winter. Also, plant nutritional quality is lower in winter than in spring and summer. The fact that fewer mating herds are seen during the winter months, when individuals live in closer proximity to each other in warm-water refuges, further supports the hypothesis that reproductive behavior is suppressed during the winter.

The aquatic environment presents a thermal challenge to manatee reproductive tracts, but its exact character is opposite of what one might expect. Like many marine mammals, male manatees have their testes and associated structures located deep inside their bodies rather than in scrotal sacs. This makes manatees more streamlined during movement through the water, but presents a potential problem of heat buildup. Maturing sperm need a thermal environment that is not too warm, and this deep location beneath fat and muscle is subject to warming beyond the tolerable limit, even during the winter. To get around this, manatees possess an extensive blood vessel network between surface structures and the testes.[38] This network brings cooler surface blood to the testes, keeping them in the correct temperature range. Interestingly, female manatees have a corresponding arrangement which may protect their reproductive tracts from hypothermia. Similar arrangements are present in male and female cetaceans and some seals.

To ensure and maintain the reproductive viability of these endangered mammals, more knowledge of their reproductive physiology needs to be obtained. A better understanding of the manatee estrus cycle and the identification of seasonal hormonal fluctuations would help us to identify reproductively sensitive periods during the year. In addition, a clearer understanding of manatees' basic reproductive physiology would allow us to identify abnormal or unhealthy states.

So how can we measure hormone concentrations in wild and captive manatees while minimizing any stressful interactions with the animals? A noninvasive technique called a radioimmunoassay is used to measure concentrations of steroid hormones excreted in feces. In fact, this technique is commonly used in many zoos to monitor the reproductive status of numerous species. With this assay we can identify when animals become sexually mature, identify the gender of unknown individuals, and determine when a female is in estrus or pregnant. Utilizing this technique, Iske Larkin and her collaborators have begun to learn some interesting things about manatee reproduction. To begin with, not all manatees are alike. The hormone patterns measured in individual animals over the course of a year or more can vary quite a bit from one animal to another. Analysis of the data suggests that captive female manatees have an estrus cycle that lasts between 28 and 42 days, much longer than the observed duration for females among mating herds in the wild. This cycle is slightly longer than that of other herbivores such as cattle, with a mean estrus cycle length of 21 days, and horses, with an estrus cycle ranging between 19 and 22 days. Although Florida manatees do not appear to be strong seasonal breeders, slight seasonal increases in hormone concentrations occur during warmer months of the year. Coinciding with other studies that indicate suppression of manatee reproduction during the colder months, this finding would explain why fewer mating herds and birthing events are seen during the winter when individuals aggregate in warm-water refuges.

Most of the hormonal work done so far has focused on captive animals due to ease of access. The study of wild manatees would allow researchers to answer some intriguing questions. How often does a female come into estrus before she becomes pregnant? Does conception really happen at the same time the female is observed in a mating herd? After mating, how long does it take before we can determine hormonally that the female is pregnant? Further study of wild manatees would also enable researchers to better identify and resolve potential problems related to manatee pregnancy and birth.

Causes of manatee mortality

A significant share of manatee mortality in Florida is directly linked to several specific and extensively documented human causes.[39] In order to determine causes of manatee death, the Sirenia Project and Dan Odell of the University of Miami organized a statewide carcass salvage program in 1974. All carcasses were recovered and examined at necropsy in an effort to determine why each animal died. A detailed necropsy examination protocol was adopted.[40] In mid-1985 the program was transferred to the State of Florida, and over the next few years necropsies were done largely at the state diagnostic laboratory in Kissimmee and at SeaWorld in Orlando. In 1989 this responsibility fell to Scott Wright, a pathobiologist at FWRI who was interested in studying manatee diseases. Wright's research interest went hand in hand with the important salvage of carcasses to better understand Florida manatee population dynamics. Scott's job was challenging not only because of the physical labor involved, but also because of his primitive research facility: a simple pole barn out in the woods. He soon hired Mark Sweat and Donna Banowetz to assist him. Together, they made significant advances in the design of manatee salvage trailers, necropsy tables, and rescue boats. Largely through the efforts of John Reynolds, then a professor of marine science at Eckerd College, a modern facility for conducting necropsies and research was built in St. Petersburg in 1993 with funding from the federal government. Currently directed by Tom Pitchford and Butch Rommel, staff at the facility examines most of the carcasses recovered today. From 1974 to date, more than 4,000 dead manatees have been recovered and examined in detail.

Generally speaking, the causes of manatee death can be divided into three types: human-related, natural, and undetermined.[41] Human-related causes account for about 33 percent of total manatee deaths, a trend that has remained steady for many years. This category includes fatalities caused when a boat or other watercraft hits a manatee or when a canal lock or flood-control structure crushes or drowns a manatee. All the other human causes are grouped together to include manatee death from ingestion of fishing gear, entanglement in crab trap lines, gunshot wounds, poaching, and perhaps pollution.[42] Natural manatee deaths include those from cold stress, exposure to red tide, and from natural disease processes. Some calf mortalities may also fall into the natural causes category. The undetermined category most often applies to animals that are either very badly decomposed or exhibit no trauma or pathology.

In addition to elucidating cause of death, carcass recovery generates a wealth of other material: detailed anatomical studies of the reproductive, nervous, skeletal, and digestive systems (including digestive tract contents); genetic and age determinations for individuals; and data about animal health status and pathological conditions. Recovered carcasses also can be useful for determining population structure through assessment of carcass location, time of year, age, reproductive status, and genetic profile.

Determining the age of dead animals is essential for understanding mortality patterns by age class and how that may impact the future health of the manatee population. Miriam Marmontel, building on initial findings by Daryl Domning and Al Myrick, pioneered the measurement of annual growth layers in the periotic bone of the ear capsule as a way to determine ages of manatees found dead.[43] Many mammals can be aged through examination of the teeth, but manatees continually replace their teeth, making this technique unfeasible. Manatees undergo seasonal patterns of bone growth. Each year a period of rapid growth is followed by a period of slower growth. In a stained section of bone, for each year of life, a broad, light staining band represents the rapid growth phase, while a succeeding thin, dense staining band represents the slower growth phase (fig. 5.5). An individual therefore can be aged by our counting the number of these bands.

Bone is continually remodeled, meaning it is first deposited by one type of cell then sculpted to the proper shape by other cells that selectively erode it. In

Figure 5.5. Stained sections reveal growth layers that are deposited annually in the periotic bone, which forms a capsule around the manatee's inner ear. Each yearly deposit consists of a broad, light staining band, resulting from rapid growth, and a thin, dense staining band that corresponds to a period of slower growth. (From Marmontel et al. 1996: 74; image courtesy of the Society for Marine Mammalogy.)

many bones, remodeling results in a haphazard pattern of layers of new and old bone. But in the periotic bone of manatees the layers are usually preserved with fairly minimal rearrangement. Meghan Pitchford and Katie Brill of the FWRI Marine Mammal Pathobiology Lab are continuing the work pioneered by Miriam Marmontel by analyzing over 2,000 periotic bones collected over a 27-year span. Excluding deaths of newborns, the average age of Florida manatees at death is 7.6 years (12 years for those that are adults), and only 1 percent of animals recovered are greater than 30 years of age. This is rather disturbing for a species that can live as long as 60 years. Probably because of hormonal changes associated with puberty, the first year of sexual maturity is often associated with an abrupt change in the distance between growth bands. Sexual maturity occurs by age five in 86 percent of manatees. However, 73 percent of dead females were seven years old or younger. This means that they had only the opportunity to have one calf before they died and were not able to participate in the prolonged association that often occurs between mothers and calves even after weaning. It also means that a relatively small number of females was producing most of the calves—an issue of potential concern if this limits genetic diversity.

Boats and manatees

Boats hit manatees and sometimes inflict fatal wounds; watercraft collisions account for approximately 25 percent of the annual manatee mortality in Florida. Is it only larger boats that do lethal damage? A group of boaters in Brevard County claims that a local barge is responsible for most of the boat-related manatee deaths that occur there. How are we to know? Scott Wright and colleagues in 1995 examined scar patterns on 227 carcasses and found 79 percent of the scars located on the back, 19 percent on the tail, and only 2 percent on the head. Analysis of the scar patterns indicated that animals are struck at any orientation, both perpendicular and parallel to the long axis of the body. Animals killed by impact alone often showed no external signs of the boat strike. In most cases, it was not possible to determine the type, size, or speed of the vessel from the extent of the injuries.

More recently, Tom Pitchford and Butch Rommel at the FWRI Marine Mammal Pathobiology Lab have undertaken detailed analysis of wound patterns on manatees killed by boats in an attempt to determine the type of watercraft that inflicted the injuries. They are working in cooperation with members of the boating industry who provide knowledge about boat motors, propellers, skegs, and rudders. About half of the lethal boat wounds appear to be inflicted by impact with the hull rather than the propeller. However, for those wounds inflicted by propellers, the pattern of wounding is related to the propeller's diameter and pitch. Prop wounds usually look like a series of parallel lines (see fig. 5.2).[44] The length of the longest line is proportional to the diameter of the propeller, while the distance between the lines reveals the pitch of the propeller blades. Almost all outboard propellers turn in a clockwise direction, resulting in a rightward slant to the wound lines. Counterclockwise propeller rotation produces lines with a leftward slant, and their presence on a dead manatee indicates the likelihood of its encounter with a twin engine boat, even if there are no accompanying lines from the second propeller. The degree of slant to the lines is associated with the rake of the propeller, which is higher on outboard motors than on inboard motors (found on tugs and larger vessels).

In addition to parallel prop wounds, single wound lines oriented more or less perpendicular to the prop lines are often made by skegs or rudders. On an outboard lower unit, the skeg is located in front of the propeller; it is behind the prop on boats with inboard motors. On boats with rudders, the rudder is often offset from the propellers. The relationship of these single wound lines to the parallel lines produced by propellers provides a clue to the type of boat involved in fatal collisions. Tom's group hopes to refine this analysis and use it to evaluate the extensive catalog of photographs taken of dead manatees over the years in order to better understand what types of boats are involved in lethal strikes, how strikes may vary with location, and perhaps how they have changed over time.

Manatees that die from boat strikes often have broken bones. By analyzing broken bone patterns in dead manatees we can learn something about the forces involved. This information might also assist us in setting maximum speed limits in waterways used extensively by manatees. The Florida Manatee Sanctuary Act of 1978 and subsequent amendments give the FWC the authority to regulate boat speeds and to limit boating activities in areas essential to manatees. The 1989 "State's Recommendations to Improve Boating Safety and

Manatee Protection for Florida Waterways" identified 13 key counties and gave them the following options: to develop site-specific speed zones; to adopt 300-foot buffer slow speed zones within all inshore and coastal waters; or to maintain 30 mph within channels and 20 mph outside the channels. For the most part, the counties chose to develop their own county-specific zones, and most of these zones were adopted and approved by the State of Florida by the late 1990s.

To designate boat speed zones in high-use areas, the FWC primarily uses manatee aerial survey data, mortality records, documentation of areas used by tagged manatees, and boat-use data. Based on these datasets and the need to optimize boater traffic, speed zones are delimited by visual estimation of the areas used by manatees. Maximum speed limits are typically established based upon the density and use patterns of manatees frequenting the area; consideration of the nature and extent of watercraft use (for example, a nearby boat channel indicates frequent, high-speed activity); and concern for promoting ease of compliance by boaters. (Speed limits, however, are rarely based on information pertaining to the biological effects of boat strikes on manatees—the kind of information gathered by Tom Pitchford's group.) The proposed speed zones are then reviewed and modified in a series of public hearings and may be subject to legal challenge. The speed zones that are ultimately implemented by law are a compromise between the rules originally proposed by the FWC and FWS and the desires of the affected parties (commercial boating industries and recreational boaters).

Bone biomechanics

Kari Clifton is a graduate student working with engineers at the University of Florida to quantify the biomechanical effects of boat strikes on manatees. This involves integrating findings from postmortem specimens—including bone biomechanics, histological characteristics, and fracture healing—with data from impact tests. Manatee bone possesses unusual characteristics compared to that of other marine mammals. The general trend in marine mammals over time has been a reduction of bone mass and density.[45] In contrast, the sirenian skeleton is characterized by an increase in bone density and other structural differences.[46] The mechanical properties of bone have been well studied in humans and some domestic animals;[47] however, mechanical studies on the bones of marine mammals have been few. In addition, age and sex differences in bone structure and composition may directly influence mechanical properties.

The primary function of high density bones in manatees is to regulate buoyancy in shallow-water environments.[48] Manatees display an unusual response to skeletal fractures: bone deposited around and beyond the site of injury is not reabsorbed after the repair process is complete as it is in other mammals. This may affect the survival of an injured animal in several ways. Due to their high mineral content and density, manatee bones are relatively brittle.[49] The increased mass of the healed bones may increase their brittleness, diminishing the amount of energy needed to break them again. In addition, the damping effect of the soft tissues may not be enough to prevent refracture. An alternative possibility is that the unusual bone deposition is a mechanism for increasing the toughness (that is, resistance to fracture) of the repaired bone. Further studies will be instrumental in shifting the focus to a more objective basis for establishing boat speed zones adequate to help reduce collisions and lethal injuries.

Carcass recovery

In order to determine causes of death, make age determinations, and carry out studies of population structure, health status, and anatomy like those described earlier, carcasses are picked up throughout the state and transported by trailer back to the necropsy lab. On one such trip to deliver a carcass to the necropsy facility in Gainesville, Bob Bonde had to stop for gas. At the pump the smell of the decomposing carcass was so bad that the attendant asked Bob to pump his own gas and please leave the money on top of the pump. Heads turn when the occasional biologist, en route to the lab with a manatee carcass, takes the liberty to drive through the pick-up window at a local fast food establishment, and unsuspecting toll collectors almost always take a second look as the trailer rolls by.

Mark Sweat was on his first day of the job in July 1989. After spending a year putting up manatee speed zone signs, he had joined Scott Wright in the business of going around the state to collect manatee carcasses and perform necropsies. On a hot summer day, Mark went to the dock where the dead manatee was located and discovered that it was a large pregnant female. He loaded it onto the flatbed trailer they used in those days and headed for the necropsy facility. On the way, he stopped in Kissimmee at a strip mall to make a phone call and noticed some high school kids looking at the carcass (in those days they weren't even covered). He heard some shouting and looked again. The heat had caused gases to build up significant pressure inside the pregnant manatee and the dead fetus was expelled out the birth canal and into the parking lot!

All local color aside, this is a very sad business. To see these magnificent creatures hacked by deep propeller wounds and lying prostrate on a flatbed trailer is to receive a sober reminder of what happens when humans carelessly trespass the manatee's habitat. To this day, even the hardened researcher still feels pangs at the sight of a manatee killed by a speeding boat or crushed in a flood control structure.

An upward trend in the number of manatees recovered dead in Florida has been apparent since the mid-1970s. This trend correlates directly with the upward trend in human population growth, the number of boats registered, and possible increases in manatee numbers. In 2004, nearly 300 manatees died in Florida's waterways, with 69 of these attributed to boat collisions. If we are to coexist with these creatures we will need to make sacrifices to help protect the species and its habitat. Conservation measures can be as simple as slowing down our boats in areas where manatees aggregate and establishing no-entry sanctuaries. These apparently sensible and relatively simple procedures have already been implemented in specific locations with good results. Even so, the active lobbies against additional manatee protections in Florida reveal the extent to which these helpless, gentle creatures are victims of our burgeoning, thrill-seeking population and its supporting technologies.

6 Where Do They Go?

Chessie

On a warm, late summer day in 1994, a lone manatee was observed far from what is considered typical manatee habitat. It had been spotted for a number of weeks in Chesapeake Bay off Maryland's shore. Initially, manatee experts in Florida assumed it was probably a subadult male that had gotten lost wandering outside its usual range. Managers and researchers were notified, and with winter approaching, a full-scale rescue effort was initiated.[1] On October 1, 1994, a large (600 kg) adult male manatee was rescued, and arrangements were made to transport him back to Florida. After a short rehabilitation at SeaWorld Orlando, the animal, dubbed Chessie, was released off the Kennedy Space Center in Central Florida with a satellite-monitored radio tag.

Chessie surprised managers and biologists alike when he traveled another 200 miles south to the Ft. Lauderdale area where he overwintered with a large aggregation of manatees in the warm waters of the Port Everglades power plant. As temperatures rose in spring of 1995, Chessie moved north and continued all the way up along the Atlantic seaboard, reaching Rhode Island by late summer. By mid-fall Chessie had returned south again and spent the following winter in Florida's warmer climate. This extraordinary journey totaled more than 4,000 miles round trip, and in subsequent years, including 2001, Chessie was still observed making this trek into the new frontier, forging a path that one day others might follow.

Surprisingly, the nearshore habitat doesn't change much from North Florida to Long Island. All along the way are salt marshes containing cord grass (*Spartina*), a favorite manatee food.[2] The new growth of spring cord grass is especially nutritious, so it is not surprising that manatees spending the winter in Brevard County on Florida's east coast move north to Jacksonville and southern Georgia during the spring, feed on *Spartina,* then head back south in the fall. Food sources like cord grass may drive these movements. In the Carolinas and farther north, we start to encounter sea grasses like eelgrass (*Zostera*) that are also eaten by manatees.

Historical records of manatees in the Chesapeake Bay date back 300 years, although such sightings have been few. These were probably animals that were traveling widely during the warmer months. So Chessie was not behaving strangely but rather using normal manatee habitat in a way typical for those few individuals that make long-distance travels. Incidentally, early reports of "Chessie the sea monster" in Chesapeake Bay may very well have resulted from manatee sightings, hence Chessie's name. Sightings of seals occur in the vicinity of Long Island, so some reported sightings of manatees that far north may have actually been seals. Every year since Chessie's remarkable voyage there have been around 10 manatee sighting reports in the region of Chesapeake Bay, further indication that Chessie does not represent a lone "crazy manatee" but rather a fairly typical though comparatively rare phenomenon.

Chessie exemplifies one among myriad surprises that lie ahead for researchers. After more than 25 years of intensive research on this species, scientists continue to learn a great deal. These intriguing animals guide us along a path to better understanding our fragile planet and its complex ecosystems. This alone makes studying the manatee a great pleasure.

Tracking

Our ability to move around in our environment is second nature to us. So much so that only when that ability is restricted by mishap, injury, or disaster do we fully appreciate the significance of movement to our sense of independence. Most wild animals are dependent upon movement for their survival, because that is how they obtain food and shelter. By tracking the movements of individual manatees, we learn about the location of critical habitat—those sites where large numbers of manatees spend lots of time feeding, obtaining freshwater, mating, calving, or keeping warm. We can also begin to appreciate the complexity of seasonal migration paths and gain insight into learned patterns of movement as well as foraging habits. This information is important to conservation managers, who make decisions about sanctuary locations and boat speed zones with the aim of helping to preserve the manatee population at a sustainable level.

Where manatees go is largely determined by food distribution, mating opportunities, freshwater, and, during winter cold spells, warm water. Movement patterns change as individuals get older and vary between males and females. The most detailed information on manatee movements has been obtained through the use of telemetry, which involves attaching a transmitter assembly to a belt around the manatee's peduncle (that's the narrow "waist" region between the body and tail). As the animal travels, the transmitted signals can be received by a hand-held antenna or, more commonly these days, a satellite. Recorded locations can be converted to dots on a map. Connecting the dots reveals the path taken by the animal.

Radio tracking equipment

The first manatees tracked in Florida in the late 1970s were tagged by Blair Irvine, Michael Scott, and colleagues at the Sirenia Project.[3] Since that time, more than 300 manatees have been tagged in Florida. Most were wild, free-ranging animals caught and restrained in nets (plate 9). Some were tagged as part of a post-release monitoring project to gauge the success of releasing rehabilitated and captive-born individuals into the wild. Presently, the most common method of capture involves nets deployed from boats. Once netted, the animal is pulled up onto the boat's deck for examination, fitted with a transmitter, and then released.

Designing a manatee radio tag proved challenging. It had to work in salt water and have a suitably strong signal. It couldn't hinder the animal's natural movement and had to be retrievable before the batteries expired. The earliest version looked like a rubber belt with a bulky protuberance in the middle, from which a 50-cm-long antenna sprouted.[4] The protuberance was actually the transmitter and battery pack sheathed in a protective layer of epoxy wrapping. The whole apparatus weighed about 1.5 kg. First of course, it had to be put around the manatee. Large numbers of people were recruited to capture a wild manatee in a net and then pull it onshore where the radio tag belt could be attached. It was fixed around the animal using nuts and bolts made from two different types of metal, which would corrode slowly so that eventually the bolts would break and the belt fall off. This "breaking belt" design prevented the apparatus from constricting the body of a growing manatee. The belt also contained a homing device so that it could be recovered, fitted with fresh batteries, and redeployed. In order to find and track the manatee, its signal had to be picked up using a hand-held antenna located on land, in a boat, or in an airplane. In any case the whole creative engineering process was a time-consuming endeavor.

Today the tagging assembly consists of an improved belt first engineered in 1984 by Galen Rathbun, Buddy Powell, and Jim Reid of the Sirenia Project.[5] It is placed around the peduncle, just in front of the wide tail fluke (fig. 6.1). A floating transmitter is attached to the belt by way of a short, stiff, nylon tether. This produces a stronger signal than the one on the initial belt design because the antenna is usually not submerged. (In salt water, signals are attenuated and cannot be heard with tracking equipment when the antenna is underwater.) However, use of a tether does increase the likelihood of entanglement, so both tether and belt are designed to break free should they get snagged on an object in the water. Similarly, the belt is designed to fall off after a couple of

Figure 6.1. Different transmitters are used to track manatees. The units are attached by a flexible tether to a belt that is wrapped around the manatee's tailstock. These devices allow researchers to monitor the animal's movements. (Photographs by U.S. Geological Survey.)

years due to corrodible pins used in the buckle. On many occasions, transmitters have been recovered after detaching from a manatee. In some cases, concerned citizens have grabbed the floating tag and pulled it free, thinking the manatee entangled in fishing gear or a crab trap float. In one case it appeared that an alligator tracked the floating tag, approached it from the rear, and grabbed it with its sharp teeth. The tag broke free from the manatee and was later recovered by trackers on land, cradled under the front legs of a protective adult gator. The tag was still working and was deployed on another manatee later the same day! One individual manatee named Moon carried more than 26 different tags (involving 34 tagging bouts) over more than 1,700 days of tracking over an eight-year period.[6]

In 1985 the first satellite-linked transmitters were deployed, making it possible to track manatees from a desktop computer rather than by traipsing around the countryside holding an antenna and trying to pick up a signal from a manatee that might or might not be in the vicinity. Again, a tether design was used to float the battery pack and antenna about 2 m behind the animal (plates 10, 11). Throughout the 1980s most of the radio tracking was carried out by researchers at the Sirenia Project. They began with 14 animals at Crystal River in 1984, advanced to 18 per year at Fort Myers in 1985 and 1986, and after that to about 20 per year along the Atlantic seaboard. During the 1990s the state's Fish and Wildlife Research Institute (FWRI) also became involved. The most extensive state effort has centered on Tampa Bay and other west coast sites. In addition, state researchers and members of the Manatee Rehabilitation Partnership have primary responsibility for tracking captive-release animals. While most of these animals have been in short-term rehabilitation for injury or sickness, some have spent longer periods in captivity in public display settings. The federal and state manatee biologists often work cooperatively to capture, tag, and track manatees.

Different types of transmitters are used to track manatees.[7] Ultrasonic pingers are used for underwater detection; very-high-frequency (VHF) units are used to locate animals in the environment; and ultra-high-frequency (UHF) tags (also called PTTs or platform terminal transmitters) are used for remote monitoring by polar-orbiting satellites as part of the Argos system, a network of satellites and computers that transforms received signals into locations. The sonic tag is used with a hydrophone to precisely locate the animal underwater at close range and sometimes as much as a half mile away. Under ideal conditions, the VHF tags can be heard from a vehicle or boat up to seven miles away and from an airplane more than 50 miles away. The direction of the signal allows the tracker to locate the animal. The PTT tags can be taken anywhere on the face of the earth, since locations are relayed from satellites in space back to ground-based stations. Scientists can access the information by computer and relay the locations to teams in the field. Accuracy for these locations varies, but generally they are precise to a few hundred meters.

Tracking manatees is an art, but on the horizon new technologies show promise for more efficient and accurate tagging and monitoring of manatees. Integration of GPS (global positioning system) tags into current configurations is being done today. The high spatial resolution of GPS, coupled with the downloading capabilities of satellite uplinks, allows biologists to supply managers with very detailed information on manatee habitat-use patterns. Also, cellular technology incorporating a "call home" system that would allow transmitters on manatees to periodically call in their locations might soon be possible. Smart tags with acoustic recording and other special features will eventually measure environmental parameters like temperature, salinity, currents, turbidity, travel speed, heading, and depth, allowing researchers to better interpret manatee behavior.

So where do they go?

In addition to movements related to obtaining food, water, and mating opportunities, manatees actively seek warmer water during the winter when temperatures drop below 20°C.[8] Some even travel hundreds of miles (Chessie traveled thousands) on this quest. Such long-distance, seemingly directed travels are usually to sites used habitually by an individual. Many of the sites used for thermoregulation are artificial; that is, they have been significantly altered by power plants, industrial effluents, or other human activities. In 1974 Hartman recognized 25 primary warm-water sites available to manatees in Florida, a significant number of them artificial.[9] By the year 2000, 16 were classified as artificial, and some of them were utilized by several hundred manatees.[10] As plants age and close, the number of artificial warm-water sites will diminish, literally leaving manatees in the cold.

The historical winter range for the Florida manatee may once have extended from the southern tip of the state north to Sebastian Inlet on the east coast and to Charlotte Harbor on the west coast, sometimes including natural springs northward.[11] As Florida was developed at the beginning of the twentieth century to accommodate a rapidly growing human population, much suitable manatee habitat in the south was lost. Low wetlands were filled with soil, and standing water was channeled out into the sea. In the 1950s and even earlier, several power plants were built along the coasts to supply energy to the growing human population. Dotting the coasts like stepping-stones, power plants provided warm-water sanctuaries for manatees, enticing them to overwinter further north than they had before (plate 12). A great deal of fine winter habitat previously unavailable to this semitropical species opened up to the local manatee population in the north. Ultimately, manatee dependence on these artificial warm-water sites may not be beneficial to long-term prospects for manatee survival in the southeast United States.

With radio tags, manatee travel in excess of 50 miles per day has been documented. Movements are often direct, with little time taken to stop and feed or rest. One of Bob Bonde's experiences is illustrative here. "One day several years ago fellow trackers Jim Reid, Beth Wright and I . . . followed a manatee traveling north off the coast of Jacksonville. The animal came out of the sheltered Intracoastal Waterway and went out into the sea, possibly to take advantage of a current that would make the trip easier. When she reached the mouth of the St. Johns River she stopped. We suspected that she was resting, and as we tracked her we crossed a bridge over the neighboring Ft. George River, and noticed that the fishermen on the bridge were all on the same side that was facing the sea. We picked up the manatee's signal once again and noticed that she was active and moving. As she approached us, we crossed the same bridge. However, this time all the fishermen were on the other side of the bridge facing upstream as the tidal current had recently turned. Just as the current helped keep the fishing lines from fouling up under the bridge suspension pilings, our manatee swam under us, apparently using the current to help make her journey even more effortless. I have learned over the years that manatees seldom leave anything to chance. Even movements in their natural habitat are premeditated and deliberate."

East coast

A large radio tracking study of 78 east coast manatees was conducted by the Sirenia Project from 1986 to 1998. In a detailed analysis, Chip Deutsch and colleagues discovered a range of seasonal movement patterns and identified seven different classes of manatee migration.[12] These classes are very different with respect to home range, which is defined as the area typically covered during an animal's routine patterns of movement. Some manatees range within a few miles over the course of a year, whereas others use a large portion of the Florida Atlantic coastline. Once a manatee adopts a specific migratory pattern, it is unlikely to change that behavior over time (figs. 6.2, 6.3). Shifts in power plant use patterns, however, have forced some manatees either to change their behavior or die from cold stress. Manatees also make travels of

Warm-season Range

Winter Range

Figure 6.2. Betty, a well-known manatee tracked for several years by the Sirenia Project, displayed regular patterns of habitat use. In the summer she frequented feeding sites in the Banana River, Brevard County. During the winter she was found most often at Port Everglades Power Plant in Broward County and the Coral Gables Waterway in Dade County. (Diagrams by U.S. Geological Survey.)

hundreds of miles, possibly in an effort to find certain types of vegetation.[13] They certainly have dietary preferences that are probably nutritionally driven.

In one common pattern, manatees winter in South Florida, migrate north to Brevard County in the spring, move farther north to the Jacksonville area in summer, then turn around and head south, spending the fall around Brevard County and returning to South Florida for the winter. Manatees utilize the Intracoastal Waterway like a manatee highway because it provides a means of rapid migration. In Brevard County, Haulover Canal provides a connection

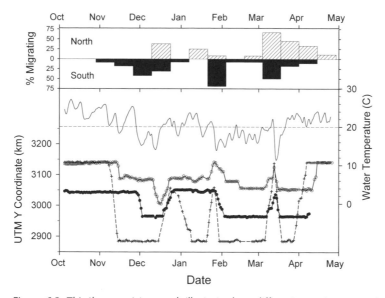

Figure 6.3. This three-register graph illustrates how different manatees move in response to changes in temperature. The top register shows travel directions of tagged migrants throughout the year. In spring most manatees travel north, and in the fall most travel southward. Spanning an eight-month period, the middle register shows that as temperatures decrease in winter (right Y axis), manatees travel south (left Y axis). As depicted here, most manatees decided to travel south when water temperatures dropped below 20°C around late November/early December. Some manatees travel the entire coast, while others utilize only half the coastline of Florida. In the bottom register, UTM coordinates correspond to latitudes. Here, the uppermost line indicates Duval County, the middle line Brevard County, and the bottom line Dade County. As temperatures started to climb back up, the manatees returned to typical warm weather summer feeding sites. (From Deutsch et al. 2003: 25; graph courtesy of The Wildlife Society.)

between the Indian River and Mosquito Lagoon, so manatees don't have to travel out into the ocean to continue their travels north or south.

Placing a transmitter on a manatee yields a great deal of information about the behavioral biology of both that individual and the species as a whole.[14] Through tracking, we have learned that manatees use the same waterways that boats use to navigate from area to area. This habit of sharing canals and channels with boats puts manatees directly in harm's way. Manatees also use industrial areas to thermoregulate in warm water and as places to obtain freshwater. Tracking manatees in Florida often places the biologist at power plant discharges and sewage treatment facilities. In effect, these areas have become very important to the long-term survival of manatees, especially in Central and North Florida. Warm water is necessary to help manatees cope with cold winter temperatures, while industrial effluent and treated sewage discharge help satisfy their freshwater intake needs. Long-term effects on manatees of drinking treated discharge have not been investigated to date.

The dynamics of herd organization and social activity around these locations is very interesting. Industrial sites quite literally become watering holes where aggregations of manatees pass the time feeding, drinking, sleeping, and cavorting. Manatees travel great distances to reach them. One late fall day Bob Bonde was tracking a manatee from the Georgia border down the east coast of Florida and into Brevard County. The animal, Diane, had spent the last four days traveling south at a rate of about 50 miles per day. She swam through the Haulover Canal into the Indian River and continued south into Titusville, stopping at the local sewage plant discharge for a drink of freshwater. Unfortunately, the plant was having repairs that day, but this did not stop the experienced manatee. After examining the off-shore discharge pipe and realizing that the water was off, she continued on to a small marina to the south, negotiating through a brief maze of canals to a dead end. There, to Bob's surprise, a small storm drain discharged a trickle of fresh running water. Diane lifted her head out of the water and drank. Amazingly, Diane had traveled several hundred miles through apparently familiar territory and headed straight to an established manatee watering site. Realizing that water was unavailable there, she immediately switched to plan B and obtained freshwater from a second remembered site to quench her thirst.

Water quality can be an important issue with respect to manatee health.

One manatee was recovered dead in south Florida with a case of toxoplasmosis (a parasitic disease that is spread by ingestion of parasitic cysts excreted in cat feces).[15] The animal had been recovered near a trailer park where untreated sewage was being discharged into the adjacent river system used by manatees. It is suspected that someone at the trailer park had recently cleaned a contaminated kitty litter box and the infected material came into direct contact with the water and thus the manatee. Unfortunately that exposure proved fatal.

Calves stick close by their mothers during the two years or so they are nursing. In the process they learn where to go for food, rest, freshwater, and warmth. Researchers tracked C-Cow and her aptly named calf, D-Cow, for several years. Born in 1987, D-Cow spent two years with his mother prior to being weaned. Their summer range followed the Banana River in Brevard County—a favorite manatee hangout along the northeast coast of the state—and every winter, they both traveled south to power plants in the Ft. Lauderdale area. Prior to weaning, D-Cow was captured and tagged. After weaning, both manatees (under the watchful eye of Sharon Tyson) stayed in Brevard County during the summer but moved independently of each other. With the first hint of colder weather in early September, C-Cow departed and moved south for the winter, arriving at the inland Ft. Lauderdale power plant. Two weeks later, D-Cow, still in Brevard County, departed during the next cold front and was sighted by manatee tracker Kit Curtin within 20 meters, but still independent, of his mom. In subsequent years, they have both been resighted many times as they pursue the same migratory strategy. During the warmer months, adult male manatees generally travel farther per day than adult females.[16] This is because males seek mating opportunities at these times, while many females are caring for calves. Such range patterns among related manatees have been demonstrated by John Bengtson for manatees using the St. Johns River,[17] as well as by Jessica Koelsch of Mote Marine Laboratory for manatees using Sarasota Bay.[18]

Radio tags have not hampered reproduction in tagged manatees. Many of the tagged adult females have mated, given birth, and successfully reared their calves to weaning.[19] In fact, births have been documented in the wild by field personnel. During the weaning process, the mother may travel several miles to a new location with the presumed intention of "losing" the calf. Sometimes mating activity can facilitate the weaning process. Mating herds often move animals sizeable distances and sometimes last up to 19 days with travels of more than 30 miles. Herding activity may be beneficial to the health of the population by giving manatees genetic exposure to individuals from different geographic regions.

Studies utilizing manatee radio tracking data have illuminated many interesting aspects of manatee behavior. John Bengtson studied manatees in the St. Johns River in the late 1970s.[20] His work led to the theory that adult male manatees establish travel circuits along the river that increase their chances of intercepting estrus females. Behavior that apparently increases mating opportunities is evident in other areas as well. Jim Reid tells us that male manatees often linger off major inlets and narrow passages, apparently in hope to increase exposure to receptive females. As an example, he describes the case of Ross, a male manatee, who usually ranged around Jupiter Inlet, near the intersection of the Intracoastal Waterway and the Loxahatchee River. Periodically, Ross took off and was tracked 30–40 miles away, most typically to a mating herd. He may have used his intersection as a kind of "pickup" zone. Ross's movement pattern consisted of long periods of close-range activity interspersed with longer distance movements followed by a return to home base.

Studies by Chip Deutsch and Sirenia Project colleagues emphasize the diurnal activity patterns of satellite-monitored manatees using the east coast of Florida.[21] In winter, manatees generally keep to canals during the daylight hours and go out to forage at night along the Atlantic coast. This pattern may have developed as a response to lower boat activity during the night hours. Research suggests that if they are given enough time to acclimate, manatees flourish in areas where boats are not allowed to enter. Of course, such areas must constitute suitable manatee habitat, having ample vegetation and a nearby source of freshwater. These criteria are used today when managers look for suitable manatee sanctuary sites. Richard Flamm and scientists at the Florida FWRI have developed models to predict manatee habitat use and travel corridors based on manatee tracking data.[22] Additional detailed models incorporating new information on manatee biology are being developed under the direction of researcher Brad Stith with the USGS Sirenia Project.

Manatees are often observed in groups. It is common to see a small group of manatees from a summer site reappear in the same group months later at a fall or winter site. But aside from mating herds and large winter aggregations at warm-water sites, these groups probably represent rather loose social assemblies. Manatees travel together if their habits converge, and some appear to recognize specific individuals, but they apparently maintain only loose social organization.[23] There is much we have to learn about manatee social structure.

Tampa Bay

Tampa Bay is the largest open-water estuary in Florida—more than 400 square miles in area and home to many manatees. It provides everything a manatee needs in the way of food, freshwater sources, secluded areas for reproduction and nursing, and warmth during winter cold snaps. Aerial surveys done in Tampa Bay between 1987 and 1996 showed that about 50 manatees were found there at any given time during the warmer months of the year.[24] Over this same period, there was a steady increase in the number of animals seen during winter: from 50 to over 300. It is likely that the warm-water sites in Tampa Bay attract temporary winter visitors.

The Tampa Bay manatees were the subject of a six-year radio tracking study by Brad Weigle, Beth Wright, Monica Ross, and Richard Flamm at the FWRI.[25] The team tracked a total of 44 manatees and followed individuals for periods ranging from one week to six years, using as many as 14 separate tags per animal. With lots of hard work, the researchers discovered some interesting patterns. In the winter (December–February), the manatees stay in the bay and aggregate around four warm-water sites, including three power plants and one natural spring. During the warmer months (March–November), more than half the animals travel to sites outside the bay; longer excursions are made and individual patterns of movement become more pronounced (plate 20). Most of the larger males of breeding age move 100 km or more away from Tampa Bay along the west coast. This wanderlust increases their chances of encountering new females, which would help maintain genetic diversity in the population should breeding occur. Younger males that are not yet reproductively mature often stay in the bay throughout the year, but as they mature they gradually expand their ranges.

Mature females without calves travel outside the bay like adult males, but young females and older females with calves tend to stay within close range of the warm-water sites and freshwater, like the young males. In fact, for all manatees, the location of freshwater sites influences their movements during the warmer months. These sources include rivers like the Hillsborough and Manatee, streams, springs, and storm-water discharges. A female with a nursing calf gradually expands her range of movement. During this time, her calf learns where to go for food, freshwater, and warmth. Once weaned, calves often visit the same sites as their mothers. Imprinting of learned travel routes may explain why some young animals travel longer distances than others.

As it does throughout much of Florida, the human population around Tampa Bay continues to grow. In addition to the direct effect of more boats in the bay, the increase in human numbers can also impact manatees indirectly by leading to decreased water quality and degraded underwater grass beds, though the latter may recover fairly quickly.[26] One way to help mitigate these potentially negative effects is to establish protected manatee sanctuary areas that keep people and watercraft out. Once these areas are protected, the benefits of improved water quality and grass beds will follow. Undoubtedly, information gathered from radio tracking and aerial surveys will prove very useful in sanctuary-establishment efforts.

Ten Thousand Islands

Another recent Florida manatee tracking effort led by Jim Reid, with the help of Susan Butler, both of the USGS Sirenia project, centers around animals in the Ten Thousand Islands area of southwestern Florida. Reid's study is designed to assess the impact of the Everglades restoration project on manatees. In order to gather highly specific information, data from GPS tags deployed on these manatees reveals their location every 15 minutes rather than every few hours (plate 13). Manatees in this region typically forage the near-coastal area containing numerous small islands and periodically travel up a nearby river to get freshwater. When an individual goes back and forth it tends to utilize the same pathway through the maze of islands. Other manatees duplicate similar routes of their own. Observations like these suggest that manatees know their way around quite well and can navigate precisely even in a rather murky, intricate environment like Ten Thousand Islands. To put the navigational skills of manatees in perspective, we might consider how frequently boaters in this area strand on shallow oyster beds.

Captive-release animals

Captive manatees released into the wild with radio tags comprise part of the larger radio tracking efforts undertaken in Florida.[27] The first captive fitted with a radio tag, an adult named Beauregard, was released in 1985. Since that time, more than 77 formerly captive manatees have been monitored in our effort to learn about successful readaptation to the wild. A manatee named Mo provides a useful illustration of the complexities involved in the readaptation process.

Originally rescued as an orphan calf in August 1994 in the Withlacoochee River, Mo was released in 1998 in the Crystal River area, near his rescue site. After a couple of weeks in and around the river, he ventured out into the Gulf of Mexico. Monitoring his locations by satellite, biologists noted that as he moved south along the west coast of Florida his positions began to shift out to sea. Wary that this manatee was not acting like other wild manatees, researchers initiated a rescue operation. Through the efforts of a team led by Jim Reid with assistance from SeaWorld, Mo was tracked, intercepted, and rescued many miles offshore of the Dry Tortugas (more than 300 miles from Crystal River). Had it not been for the information provided by his tag, Mo most certainly would have been carried by currents out into the Gulf of Mexico and lost forever. Mo was a very naïve animal and had little experience in the wild. Handlers are now faced with the charge of conditioning him for his third trip out into the wild. He will be taught to forage on natural vegetation and released during the winter when other manatees are present. Mo has helped to educate manatee researchers and managers about the difficulties and decisions involved in releasing young or naïve animals back into the wild.

Movement patterns and genetics

We know that manatees overwinter with very high site fidelity to particular locations. In the early days of manatee research, biologists thought that manatees comprised discrete subpopulations that did not intermingle. It wasn't until manatees were finally matched to specific sites—through radio tracking and photo-identification—that we were able to develop a clearer picture of breeding scenarios. The presence year after year of tight groups of the same individuals in the same close quarters (for many months at a time in some cases) had researchers worried that inbreeding might be taking place.

In most cases, we still don't know where actual breeding does occur, but due to the extent and potential for manatee movements between adjacent regions, it appears that there is at least the potential for good mixing and therefore some regional genetic hybrid vigor within the population. On the other hand, a low level of heterozygosity (genetic diversity) within the entire population does suggest that Florida manatees may have experienced a founder effect or population bottleneck that is still reflected in their genetic makeup today.[28] This occurs when a limited number of individuals establishes a population, which may have been the situation when manatees became established in Florida. It can take a long time for genetic diversity to increase when starting from a relatively homogeneous stock.

Males tend to travel more than females, but there are homebody males and wide-ranging females. Young females in Brevard County have been observed to stay in that vicinity until coming into estrus, when they wander north to become the focus of mating herds near Daytona Beach. This type of wandering behavior, seen in both males and females as they mature, probably promotes genetic mixing. Research conducted by Angela Garcia-Rodriguez at the University of Florida and the Sirenia Project used samples of mitochondrial DNA to investigate genetic relatedness among populations of manatees ranging from Florida to South America.[29] All manatees examined in Florida to date share the same mitochondrial DNA profile (mothers bequeath their genetic heritage to offspring through mitochondrial DNA, thereby indicating family lineages). The data suggest that Florida manatees originated from Caribbean stock that migrated northward after the last glaciation about 12,000 years ago. However, there seems to be little genetic mixing between west and east coast manatees, a finding borne out by radio tracking data that shows scant evidence of manatees moving between the east and west coasts of Florida. The northern end of Florida Bay is shallow with no freshwater, and this inhospitable environment may represent a geographical barrier to widespread mixing between west coast and east coast animals.

Current studies coordinated by Pete McGuire of the University of Florida are focusing on nuclear DNA markers where maternal and paternal contributions can be assessed. Eventually these markers may reveal more genetic diversity among Florida manatees than we can determine with mitochondrial DNA, but the 14 nuclear genetic markers examined thus far indicate low diversity.[30] These genetic studies are a crucial adjunct to assessment of population dynamics through carcass salvage data, radio tracking, aerial surveys, and photo-identification.

Moving on

We have learned a great deal from the radio tagging of manatees in Florida. This useful technology becomes more sophisticated each year. Methodologies established to better understand manatee migratory behavior are also helping researchers in several other countries. Fellow scientists in Mexico, Belize, Costa Rica, Jamaica, Colombia, Brazil, Indonesia, and Australia have benefited from migration monitoring projects in the United States. Cooperative efforts like these should be nurtured so that sirenians can be better protected globally.

As we have seen, calves appear to learn movement patterns from their mothers. In addition to learning the location of prime feeding habitat and freshwater, young calves learn the location of warm-water sites. Increasingly, however, these warm-water sites are located at power plants that can shut down temporarily for a variety of reasons including equipment malfunction. Some plants may also face permanent closure due to age, obsolete technology, or energy sector deregulation. Plant shutdowns pose a significant problem for manatees that have learned to visit adjoining sites for feeding and habitat utilization. Nobody knows how strong the manatee's habitual tendencies may be, but we don't want a catastrophe to find out.

Manatees that have been taught to use natural springs as overwintering sites also may be vulnerable to extended periods of cold. From historic levels, most springs in Florida have suffered flow reductions due in large part to increased water demands and drought conditions. As long as manatees depend on these warm-water havens, they must be maintained through strict monitoring and management to ensure adequate winter habitat.

7 Brains

Life underwater

Try to imagine 45 million years of evolution that leads you from life on land to a life spent entirely in water. The water is often murky, and you spend much of your time finding and eating submerged vegetation. For a couple of years as a youngster you tag along with your mother to suckle and learn where to find food and warm water. When separated from her, you communicate using simple squeaks. Luckily, you don't have to worry about natural danger in the form of predators. In the colder months you seek warm water. If male, upon reaching sexual maturity you look for receptive mates whenever possible and then go on your way. If female, you will be approached—often in a very aggressive, persistent manner—by several determined males.

We are so accustomed to experiencing the world through our own perceptual abilities that it is easy to forget just how profoundly these fundamental facts of life, coupled with millions of years of evolution, have shaped reality for manatees. The single fact of being in the water all the time has consequences for a variety of organisms. Water affects the way sounds and vibrations are conducted, how light is refracted, how chemical and electric signals are sent and received, and what kinds of food resources are available. Living in water also places much greater thermal demands on the body than does living on land. We have seen in the case of manatees that the combination of herbivorous diet with aquatic environment has resulted in a low metabolic rate and the large body size that reduces threats of predation. A trait that exists due to one kind of selection pressure can become useful in an entirely different context.

Throughout the animal kingdom, what one eats is directly related to specific behavioral adaptations. Bats that eat insects utilize skilled flying and echolocation to find and capture their prey. Nine-banded armadillos rely on their sense of smell and long, sensitive snouts as they forage for prey among the leaves of the forest floor. Certain fish find the organisms they eat by detecting the weak electric fields emitted by their moving bodies. Some frogs use their visual system to track the movements of flies and to determine where to aim their long, sticky tongues. Humpback whales work in cooperative groups to create cylindrical "bubble nets" that trap fish by confusing them and then feed by lunging through the concentrated schools with open jaws.

Some philosophers claim that imagining the perceptual world of another species is frivolous because we can never really know the experience of another creature. Even if this is true, we can still approach a kind of sympathy with other animals by allying imagination with observation and scientific reasoning. Besides using observation, we can seek insight into the perceptual world of a species by examining the organization of its nervous system, the machinery that defines the capacities and boundaries of its perceptual world.

Brain size

Lots of attention has been paid to relative brain size, largely because attempts to link brain size to intelligence have a long tradition across many disciplines. But not all brain regions are associated with intelligence, and there are many purely biological reasons why brain size is large or small in a given species. Variations in brain size among individuals of a single species are more difficult to explain but probably occupy the realm of naturally occurring variations, such as height, and have little or nothing to do with intelligence. During the nineteenth and twentieth centuries various and bold claims were made about comparative brain size and intelligence among the different races. Such theories had more to do with political expediency and outright prejudice than with scientific data. Fortunately, that era seems to be behind us.

There is also the whole question of what we mean by "intelligence." Well-intentioned people disagree about this concept all the time, and any test or indicator of intelligence can be criticized because it ignores so many of the attributes we find meaningful as human beings. How many kinds of intelligence are there anyway? What about artistic creativity, social acumen, and emotional depth? How about decision making in a crisis? In addition to considerations such as these, there is the very daunting challenge of specifying what is meant by intelligence in other species. We know that among humans it takes a different set of skills to be a concert pianist than to be a nuclear physicist. How different must be the intelligence required of a successful polar bear than of a successful zebra. And that's just within the domain of mammals. What about birds, fish, insects? We can make long lists of the various sensory abilities and motor skills we imagine would be useful, but these do not really capture the essence of what we mean by intelligence, which is a more integrative, evaluative capacity utilized in contexts like problem solving. Regardless of how we define intelligence, we can consider brain size purely as an observable biological variable that is related in some poorly understood way to perceptual, cognitive, and behavioral capabilities.

Relative brain size refers to the size of a given brain in relation to body size. It is certainly reasonable to expect individuals of smaller stature to have correspondingly smaller organs, including brains. The same goes for species. We would not expect a tiger to have a brain as large as that of an elephant, because tigers are smaller overall (fig. 7.1). So one way we can compare brain size across species of different sizes is to measure the average brain/body weight ratio for adults of each species. In the simplest possible case, the brain would always represent some fixed amount of overall body weight, say 10 percent, and the brain/body weight ratio would be the same for all species. But such is not the case.

If the data are plotted for lots of mammalian species, brain size *does* increase with increasing body size across species, but at a slower rate (fig. 7.2). In other words, an adult elephant brain is larger than an adult tiger brain, but not by the same proportion that their body sizes differ. In scientific lingo, the scaling exponent for all mammalian species together is less than 1.0, something like 0.74. If it were 1.0, this would mean that the brain scaled in exact proportion to body weight. We can take this "average mammalian curve," then, and ask which species lie well above or well below the average line. Those well above the line have very large brains, while those well below it have very small brains. The degree of deviation is turned into a number called the encephalization quotient (EQ), which is the ratio between the observed brain weight and the weight expected for that body weight according to the average mammalian line. Thus, a species with EQ = 1.0 has a brain weight that exactly

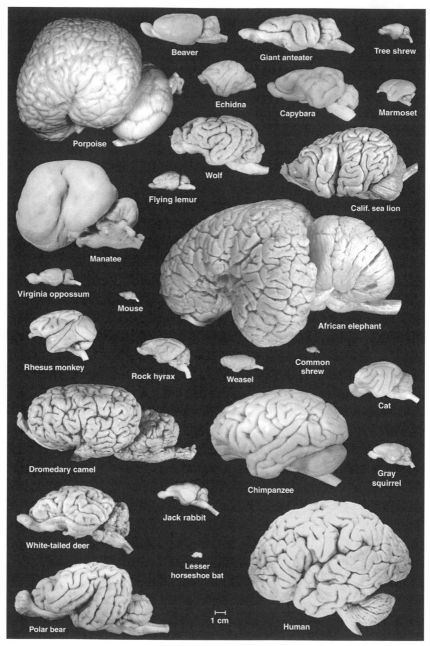

Figure 7.1. Mammalian brains exhibit great variation in size and degree of folding of the cortical surface. Manatee brains are very smooth for their size. (Illustration by Carol Dizack, courtesy of Academic Press.)

matches the expected value. EQs greater than 1.0 represent brains that are larger than expected, whereas EQs smaller than 1.0 represent smaller-than-expected brain sizes. Humans have a very large EQ in the 7.5 range. Bottlenose dolphins are up around 3.2. Chimps and some other primates range from 2.0 to 3.7. Carnivores, ungulates, elephants, and rodents tend to be right near the average line. At the other end of the spectrum, the hippopotamus, some marsupials, insectivores, and bats lie in the 0.3 to 0.8 range.

It turns out that the Florida manatee, with an EQ of 0.27, has perhaps the smallest relative brain size of any mammal.[1] Dugongs aren't far off, with a value of 0.38. So what does all this mean? Are manatees dumb? Perhaps a low EQ is simply one consequence of living an aquatic existence. Most of the brain/body weight data for mammals is based on terrestrial species. Living in the water removes some of the constraints of gravity, and over evolutionary time body size might be free to increase well beyond the limits found on land. Indeed, the largest mammals are whales. When compared to cetaceans (whales and dolphins), manatees have an EQ of 0.25, an even lower value than that derived from comparison with all other mammals. When matched with pinnipeds (seals, sea lions, and walruses), the manatee EQ goes up to 0.5. In

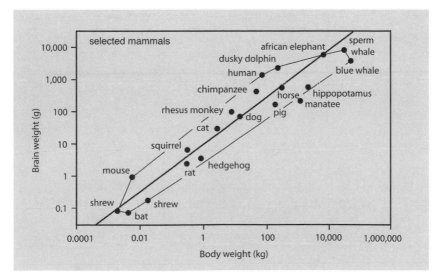

Figure 7.2. Brain size scales with body size across mammals. Manatees have small brains for their body size. (Modified from van Dongen 1998: 2,100, courtesy of Springer.)

other words, sirenians have low brain/body weight ratios no matter how you cut it, and this does not appear to be merely a consequence of life in water. In fact, low EQ appears to have been a sirenian trait for a very long time. The recently extinct Steller's sea cow had a low EQ, and the earliest sirenians from the Eocene exhibit small brain cases in relation to overall skull size.[2]

As it became clear that interpreting relative brain size in terms of intelligence was fraught with problems, scientists began looking at biological variables to see if they were correlated with EQ. A step forward occurred in the 1970s when researchers discovered that among bats, brain size correlates with feeding strategy, and this association cuts across taxonomic categories.[3] Bat species specialized to feed on fruit, nectar, blood, or other animals all have larger relative brain sizes than do aerial insectivores (bats specialized for catching and eating insects on the wing). In the early 1980s renowned mammalogist John Eisenberg and others explored the possibility that a variety of life history traits in addition to feeding strategy might be associated with relative brain size.

John's analysis suggested that passive strategies against predators (for instance, rolling up into a ball) indicate low relative brain size, whereas active strategies (flight, running, counterattack) indicate large brain size. In other words, having a highly three-dimensional arboreal existence gets you a larger brain than dwelling on the largely two-dimensional ground. The situation for the aquatic environment was less clear. Pinnipeds and dolphins have large EQs, but baleen whales have very low EQs. As we have seen, manatees and dugongs also have exceedingly low EQs. So there appears to be no overall effect on brain size that comes from living in water. However, the popular name "sea cow" may be more relevant than it first appears, because mammalian herbivores generally have lower EQs than carnivores, regardless of whether they are terrestrial or aquatic.[4] This suggests that feeding habits may be closely related to relative brain size in mammals generally, not just in bats.

In the 1980s it began to appear that other life history variables—single or multiple birth patterns, longevity, length of parental care, social structure, and behavioral characteristics—might also play a role in relative brain size. Tom O'Shea and Roger Reep considered the life history traits of manatees: large bodied, long-lived, exclusively herbivorous, exclusively aquatic, with single birth patterns, strong mother-calf bonds for at least two years, little vocal communicative behavior, and no cohesive social structure.[5] Large body size in manatees makes sense for three reasons: it enables the animal to keep warm, to process large amounts of food, and to reduce predation. When the body is small, body surface is large relative to body volume. Heat is lost rather rapidly, especially in water which has far greater thermal conductivity than air. As body size increases, the body's volume increases faster than its surface, and heat is lost more slowly. Because sirenians are fully aquatic herbivores that eat large quantities of relatively low-energy food, they require a large digestive tract. Low metabolic rate is also typical of manatees, and this probably reflects the constraints of eating plants and needing to conserve heat. Even so, Florida manatees and other sirenians are limited to fairly warm tropical and subtropical waters. So these two factors—the constraints imposed by eating plants and the need to conserve heat—appear to have driven the evolution of large body size.

O'Shea and Reep hypothesized that in the case of sirenians, natural selection for large body size may have been so strong that the typical mammalian relationship between brain and body growth gradually decoupled.[6] The basic idea behind this relationship is that if a body continues to grow after the brain is fully developed, then the brain/body weight ratio will get smaller and smaller. In fact, though manatees do have an unusually prolonged period of body growth, we still don't know how long their brains continue to grow. Therefore, for now, the O'Shea and Reep hypothesis must remain a provocative theory. Clues can be had by looking at other species. Lori Marino, a biologist at Emory University, has investigated the issue of relative brain size, focusing on cetaceans and primates.[7] In species like orangutans and gorillas where males are much larger than females, it is the females that have relatively larger brains. This is probably due to the fact that males have more prolonged body growth in order to attain their larger size. Because this body growth occurs without similarly prolonged brain growth, the males end up with smaller relative brain size. So, it may be that within some general developmental constraints the growth of brain and body are rather independent.

In the end, differences in relative brain size may reflect two factors. The first factor is variation in body composition due to phenomena such as seasonal fat deposition or production of very dense bone (as in Sirenia). Consider the large whales. They have very low EQ values, but most researchers feel that this is due to the large amount of seasonal blubber they carry on their bodies, which increases body weight and thereby lowers relative brain size. Therefore, an adaptation of this kind—which has nothing at all to do with the brain itself or with intelligence—results in a lower EQ. The second factor that appears to play a key role in explaining variations in relative brain size has to do with growth patterns and takes two forms. (1) Prolongation of a preexisting growth pattern (like that in the primates described above), simply extends the duration of the normal process by which the brain grows at a slower rate than the body after the embryonic phase. This magnifies the divergence of growth rates of brain versus body. (2) Alteration or extension of body growth rate results in a body that continues to grow independent of further brain growth.

In the case of manatees, we simply do not have enough information to say whether low EQ results from a prolongation of the normal brain and body growth curves or whether body growth continues for an extended time period in the absence of further brain growth. O'Shea and Reep concluded that the manatee brain is not small in relation to the body; rather the manatee body has become large in relation to the brain. This way of viewing the issue emphasizes the need to look at all the life history traits of a species when interpreting brain-body relationships and suggests that great caution be taken when thinking about relative brain size in terms of intelligence.

The full story of sirenian brain evolution awaits the quantitative examination of fossil sirenian skulls and a fuller appreciation of the range of variation among mammalian brains in general. Although we will never know what the interior structure of these ancient brains was like, it is apparent that present-day sirenian brains exhibit unusual and in some cases unique traits compared to the brains of other mammals.

Brain folding

Manatee brains are about the size of a grapefruit and are lissencephalic or smooth-surfaced. This is unusual because all other mammalian brains of comparable size or larger are gyrated (having folded surfaces), including the brains of cows, large cats, horses, elephants, sea lions, and humans (fig. 7.1). Gyrated brains start out lissencephalic but begin to develop convolutions well before birth. This folded surface characterizes the cerebral cortex, one of the major regions of the brain in mammals. In fact, this region is so large that during development it overgrows much of the rest of the brain to become the dominant feature visible upon examination. Is the degree of folding in the cerebral cortex related simply to size? Perhaps larger brains are convoluted whereas smaller brains aren't. It turns out that each mammalian order has its own characteristic pattern of folding. Within an order (Carnivora, Artiodactyla, Primates) it is indeed the case that the brains of larger species have more folds, but the pattern of folding is different for each order. The brain of the least weasel, the smallest carnivore, is more convoluted than the brain of the manatee, which is about 100 times greater in size. So degree of brain folding appears to be influenced first by brain size and second by the evolutionary lineage to which a species belongs.

All four living species of sirenians have brains with smooth surfaces. In order to quantify the degree of folding, scientists compute a gyration index (GI) or the ratio of total to exposed brain surface. In other words, the more convoluted the brain, the more hidden cortex there is, and the higher the GI value. The GI is near 1.0 for smooth brains like those found in many rodents. For carnivores and ungulates the GI is around 2.5, and for some whales and dolphins it is up around 4.0. Manatees have a GI of 1.06, very near the low end of the spectrum.[8] Convolutions in the cerebrum can leave their impression on the interior of the brain case during fossilization. Consequently, it is possible to determine whether brains of extinct mammals were convoluted. From the fossil record, we know that sirenian brains have been almost totally lissencephalic throughout their entire evolutionary history.[9]

Traditionally, cerebral convolutions have been considered indicators of intelligence. This is partly due to the fact that we humans possess highly convoluted brain surfaces. But this conclusion may turn out to be just another case of hubris. As far as we know, the degree of folding appears to be related to the development of neural connections. A greater density of connections results in an outgrowth of cortex (a gyrus) surrounded by fissures where such outgrowth did not occur.[10] Take the case of the raccoon, which possesses astonishing dexterity and sensitivity in its fingers. Each finger has its own representation in the region of cerebral cortex devoted to forepaw sensation, and these digit maps are separated by fissures. From other similar examples we know that fissures often demarcate functional boundaries.

So what does this mean in the case of manatee brains, which lack fissures? Nobody knows for sure, but it may be that the unusual thickness of the manatee cerebrum constrains its ability to fold. Cetaceans represent the other end of the spectrum. Dolphins and whales have very thin cerebrums, and their brains exhibit some of the highest degrees of folding among all mammals. Understanding the dynamics of gyration represents one of the enduring challenges in neuroscience. A recent theory suggests that gyral development may be related to the tension produced by bundles of nerve fibers as they develop and collectively innervate the cortex. It may be that in larger brains there are so many nerve fibers projecting to functional zones like the digit representations (in comparison to the relatively sparse fibers located between them), that mechanical forces come into play and the gyri grow outward like mushrooms.

In 1902 the respected British anatomist Grafton Elliott Smith recorded his impressions of sirenian brains.[11]

> Amongst the whole series of placental mammals there is no other animal in which the brain presents features so extraordinary and so bizarre as in the Sirenia. The only parallel which can be found for the peculiar cases presented by the manatee and the dugong is that presented by the brains of idiots, in which the process of elaboration has ceased in the earlier months of intrauterine life, and the organ has simply grown in size without becoming perfected in structure.

Among the bizarre features observed by Elliott Smith were lissencephaly and enlarged ventricles. Even in 1902 he knew that some kinds of human mental retardation are associated with lissencephaly—smooth hemispheres lacking the convolutions found in normal individuals—and with enlarged lateral ventricles. A brief anatomy lesson will be useful here. The brain starts out embryologically as a tube; it is even called the neural tube in early stages of development. The space inside the tube is called the ventricular system, and this is where cerebrospinal fluid is made and flows in adults. As the brain grows and changes shape, this ventricular space undergoes local enlargements and deformations, but it remains one continuous channel, like a pipe that twists and turns. The two lateral ventricles are the portions of the ventricular system that lie inside the cerebral hemispheres. In humans, enlarged ventricles are most often associated with hydrocephaly in which a greater-than-normal pressure of the cerebrospinal fluid causes the ventricles to expand. Increased pressure can result from a blockage or overproduction of cerebrospinal fluid. As one might imagine, increased pressure can deform the neural tissue that comprises the walls of the tube, and this can lead to compromised brain function. We can get some idea, then, of why Elliott Smith thought as he did.

Inside the brain

Brain size and surface folding are external features that are easily compared among species. But what if we look at the internal structure of the brain? How do manatees rate in complexity based on the sizes of various brain regions and the arrangement of nerve cells? Data on regional size exist for relatively few mammals, about 160 species altogether. Rather amazingly, the size of any particular brain region is determined mostly by total brain size, belying our intuitive expectation that a species dominant for a given sensory modality will exhibit extra large brain regions devoted to processing that kind of information. Such expansions appear to be constrained by the developmental linkages involved in brain growth.[12]

For any given brain size, the size of a particular region varies by about 3x across all species. So, for example, owl monkeys may appear to have very large visual areas, but their size is still within this 3x range when compared to other brains of comparable overall size. We can also go in the other direction and ask what happens when a sensory system is reduced or lost. Marine mammals collectively exhibit reduced olfactory systems due to their adaptation to the aquatic environment where the sense of smell is seldom used. Interestingly, this loss cascades through much of the rest of the brain that receives olfactory connections. Thus, pinnipeds and manatees have brains with relatively large cerebral cortices but relatively small olfactory-associated regions.

Cerebral cortex is responsible for much of the higher order information processing that goes on in the brain. The geometric arrangement of nerve cells into layers and columns is one of the hallmarks of mammalian cerebral cortex, and this orderly arrangement probably reflects maximization of information processing in each cubic millimeter of cortex. The neuronal inputs and outputs of the cortex are arranged topographically, also largely in terms of layers and columns. Primates like us exhibit exquisitely detailed layering patterns with over 100 cortical areas distinguishable on this basis. In contrast, bats and insectivores have much simpler geometry and thus far fewer areas. Hoofed mammals and carnivores are intermediate between these extremes. Cetaceans have very thin cortices with a very simple layering scheme, but they have a lot of cortex. The manatee cerebral cortex is abnormally thick and exhibits lots of interesting layering patterns, comparable to those of carnivores and some primates.[13] As with gyration, size probably plays an important role here. It is known that the wiring pattern of the cortex is arranged to maximize the efficiency of its pattern of connections. As brains get larger they can probably accommodate more functional specializations.

Rindenkerne

In the next chapter we discuss the uniqueness of manatee hair, which is structurally the same as the whiskers (vibrissae) in other mammals. In mice, rats, and some marsupials, these vibrissae are so important that the nerves from each vibrissa connect with a group of cortical neurons called a barrel, which is devoted to processing information from that vibrissa alone. The so-called barrels have an apparent analogue in sirenians, suggesting that sirenian hair is doing something very significant.

In 1961 a scientist visiting the University of Wisconsin from British Guiana gave a talk about manatees and emphasized their potential use in clearing canals of excess vegetation. Upon hearing this, our colleagues Wally Welker and Jack Johnson consulted Elliott Smith's compendium on vertebrate brains, which documents the brain collection of the Museum of the Royal College of Physicians and Surgeons where he was curator in the early 1900s. Through this they discovered the anatomical work of James Murie, done in the 1800s, which included beautiful engraved illustrations of the body and organs (including the brain) of manatees from Guiana (fig. 7.3). A few other papers from the late 1800s and early 1900s reported on the external morphology and vascular supply of the manatee brain. Only one, by the German scientist Dexler, presented microscopic findings on the cellular structure of the brain in a dugong.[14] Perhaps the most striking feature noted by Dexler was the presence of large clusters of neurons in the deepest layer of some areas of the cerebral cortex. Dexler called these Rindenkerne (German for "cortical nuclei"). This cluster arrangement is highly unusual, considering that in all other mammals the cells of the six cortical layers are usually arranged in uniform sheets (I is the surface layer, VI is the deepest layer), uninterrupted by clumps such as these.

A notable exception was discovered in the 1970s in the cerebral cortex of the mouse. It was found that the part of the cortex in which the facial whiskers are represented contains spheroidal clusters of nerve cells in layer IV—the main processing layer for neural inputs of a sensory nature. More importantly, researchers found that each of these clusters is preferentially related to one of the whiskers. The whiskers are arranged in orderly rows on the face, and the clusters in layer IV reflect that same topography, so that the geometry

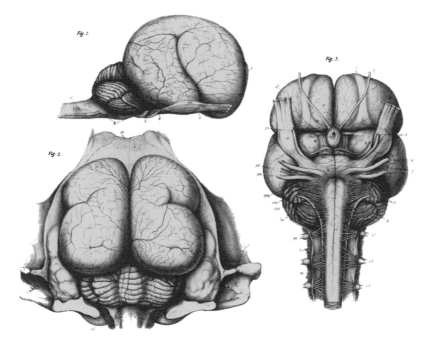

Figure 7.3. Manatee brains viewed from the right side (fig. 1), in the skull from above (fig. 2), and from ventral perspective with blood vessels and cranial nerves visible (fig. 3). (From Murie 1880.)

of the periphery is reflected in the geometry of the cortex. This is the general principle underlying the localization of function in the cerebral cortex. For example, in all mammals the face is represented on the lateral margin of the sensory cortex, whereas the legs are represented nearer the midline. This simply reflects the fact that, in general, the spatial arrangement of nerves coming from the periphery (face, arms, legs) is maintained as those nerves enter the brain and contact various information processing centers, which in turn project to other centers, all the way up to the cerebral cortex.

We rediscovered Dexler's Rindenkerne during more recent detailed studies of manatee cerebral cortex aimed at understanding how the manatee brain is organized (fig. 7.4).[15] To explore brain organization in a monkey, cat, or rat,

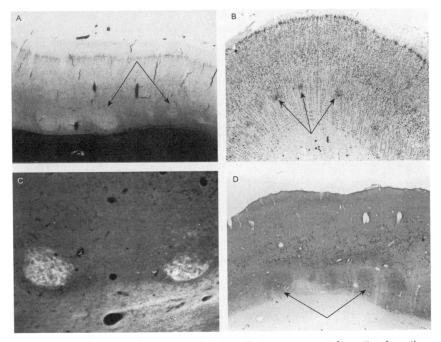

Figure 7.4. Rindenkerne, the neuron cell clusters that may process information from the tactile hairs found on the face and body of sirenians. A. Myelin stain makes large and small Rindenkerne visible in the cerebral cortex. B. Small Rindenkerne demarcated with a Nissl stain. C. Rindenkerne stained for acetylcholinesterase. D. Rindenkerne stained for cytochrome oxidase. Arrows indicate examples of Rindenkerne. (Modified by Joe Cheatwood from Reep et al. 1989: 381, 383; reproduced courtesy of Karger Press.)

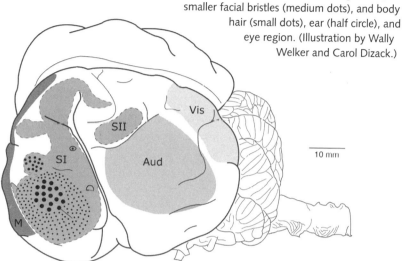

Figure 7.5. Manatee brain schematic viewed from the side. Probable locations of the cortical areas involved in sensory and motor functions are shown. Aud = auditory cortex; M = motor cortex; SI and SII = somatic sensory cortex; Vis = visual cortex. Depicted within SI are the hypothesized representations for the large facial bristles (large dots), smaller facial bristles (medium dots), and body hair (small dots), ear (half circle), and eye region. (Illustration by Wally Welker and Carol Dizack.)

the usual approach would be to perform combined anatomical and electrophysiological experiments. A typical experiment of this kind would involve (1) recording electrical activity from a group of cortical cells; (2) finding out that they preferentially respond to the touching of the hand; and (3) injecting a neuronal tracer like a fluorescent dye to follow the connections of those cells. By repeating this kind of experiment over and over again, scientists have gradually been able to develop detailed maps of the way the body surface is represented in the brain.

Such experiments are hard enough to conduct in a controlled environment using animals that are small and for which anesthesia is well worked out. But because of the endangered status of manatees, not to mention their very large size, we had to use a different strategy known as the comparative approach. Basically, this involves doing the descriptive anatomy as completely as possible and then comparing the findings with more detailed experimental work known for other species. We found that Dexler's Rindenkerne come in two sizes, large and small. The large ones are located primarily in the region of the cortex that we suspect is devoted to the face, based on its position on the lateral side of the brain where the face is represented in other mammals (fig. 7.5). What we don't know, however, is whether each of the large Rindenkerne processes information from a single manatee facial whisker, as it does in mice and other species that have been studied experimentally.

This is certainly our suspicion, but it is hard to prove. There are many more cell clusters than there are facial whiskers, so one possibility is that every hair on the body is represented by a cell cluster in the brain. This would make sense if the hairs on the nonfacial portions of the body convey significant sensory information as we expect. Because the brain is an exceedingly expensive organ to maintain, nature does not allot neural space without a good reason. In other words, these clusters of nerve cells, the Rindenkerne, must represent something of functional significance. That's as close to faith as science gets. The rest is actual work.

8 Perception and Behavior

Specialized hair

Hair is one of the defining features of being a mammal. But few of us regularly pause to consider its functional significance in other species. Manatees have a lot of facial hair but scant body hair. As we shall see, less is sometimes more.

Many mammals depend upon hair in the form of fur in order to keep warm. This is called pelage hair, and it is the kind found on our bodies. We are familiar with the cycle of shedding that occurs in many animals in anticipation of warmer weather. In these cases, the hair follicles remain beneath the skin surface but the hair shaft is shed. Each hair has its own follicle, a small organ that lies in the dermis, the deep layer of skin that is not visible from the outside. The follicle is a cylinder that includes a sheath for attachment of the hair shaft, a few nerves that provide sensory innervation to the follicle, and associated glands that secrete sweat and sebum into the follicle so it can reach the skin surface.

Consider for a moment the extreme forms that hair takes and why. Porcupine quills are modified hairs quite effective in defense against intruders or predators. They are positioned in the erect state by means of muscles attached to every hair follicle (the same state as when our hair "stands on end"). Similarly, one species of tenrec, small insectivorous mammals of Madagascar, has a small patch of quills on its back. It uses these quills to stridulate—that is, to make sound by rubbing them together at high speed as do some insects by rubbing their wings and legs. These sounds are used to communicate alarm signals and to enable pups to find their mothers. So, in both cases, modified hair serves a specific purpose beyond insulation.

Whiskers are present on many commonly encountered mammals including cats, dogs, mice, hamsters, and manatees. Whiskers are a special type of sensory hair called a vibrissa. Vibrissae send signals to the brain indicating that contact has been made with something in the environment and helping to localize it for further investigation. Other than sirenians, almost all mammals that have been studied possess lots of pelage hair but many fewer vibrissae. Many mammals have vibrissae on the face, the largest group of these being the whiskers of the upper lip region known as the mystacial (mustache-like) whiskers. A few other vibrissae may be found above the eyes or on the sides of the face and chin (take a look at your pet cat or dog). Some mammals, notably some squirrels, also have vibrissae near the paw, the elbow or knee, or on the underside of the body.

Among the aquatic mammals there is great variety in the degree and pattern of hair distribution. Baleen whales have vibrissae on the head, but in most odontocetes (toothed whales) the only hair present is found prenatally. Prenatal vibrissae atrophy before birth, leading to a completely hairless condition postnatally.[1] Freshwater river dolphins are an important exception to this condition, with reduced visual systems and well-developed, bristle-like vibrissae along their upper and lower jaws. River dolphins are fond of eating fish and crustaceans, and the vibrissae are reportedly used to detect these prey along river bottoms.[2] Elaborate vibrissae are found on the faces of pinnipeds (seals, sea lions, and walruses), in addition to the dense pelage hair covering their bodies.

Vibrissae are used in several functional contexts. Mice are nocturnal rodents and they use the vibrissae on their faces to find their way in the dark. In order to perform this specialized tactile function, mice often engage in "whisking" behavior, rhythmic movements of the vibrissae in active exploration of the environment very similar to our waving our hands around to navigate in the dark.[3] Pinnipeds have very long, elaborate vibrissae. When they are hauled out of the water onto land, they may often be seen waving their vibrissae around in dramatic displays that are used for social communication, often in conjunction with loud vocalizations.[4] When underwater, they use the vibrissae in order to locate prey and other objects in the environment.[5]

Along with their specialized function, vibrissae likewise have a specialized structure that is different from that of pelage hairs.[6] Instead of a simple sheath as in pelage hair, the vibrissal follicle wall consists of an elaborate blood sinus surrounded on the outside by a dense capsule and lined on the inside by a thin wall. If the hair shaft on the inside of the follicle cylinder moves around, it bangs into the thin wall where many sensory receptors are located. These receptors undergo mechanical deformation when the hair contacts the thin sinus wall and, in turn, convert that mechanical deformation into electrical energy. The receptors are associated with 100–200 nerve fibers per follicle that convey these electrical signals into the brain.[7] The sensitivity of the system is tuned by the blood pressure inside the sinus; the higher the pressure the greater the tension on the wall and the more likely that the receptors will respond to hair movements. As mentioned in the previous chapter, information concerning the direction, magnitude, and timing of vibrissae movement is conveyed to the cerebral cortex and processed by specialized sets of cells called barrels, with one barrel dedicated to each vibrissa. This organization differs quite markedly from the more continuous brain representations found in the visual and auditory systems. Barrels are known to exist in about 21 species of rodents and marsupials, but most other mammalian species have not been examined in this regard.[8]

Hair-like appendages are not just the province of mammals. For example, when insects fly, their wings rub back and forth across the tegula—a plate of hair-like protrusions innervated by about 30 neurons—thus signaling the nervous system about the position of the wings.[9] In addition, insects have a variety of hair-like appendages on their bodies and legs. Hairs such as these are one member of a class of sensory receptors known as mechanoreceptors because they transform mechanical deformations (like the bending of a hair) into electrical signals that then travel into the central nervous system. In general, mechanical energy is transmitted by the movement of hairs or joints, by the deformation of touch receptors on the body surface, and by vibrations. Specialized cells of the auditory and vestibular (balance) systems of many animals possess cilia, which are hair-like appendages. These cilia respond to the movement of fluid in the inner ear. Those in the cochlea are involved in hearing, and those in the semicircular canals in balance.

The oral disk and tactile scanning

So what about manatees? The face of a manatee is not necessarily a thing of beauty, and it is difficult to imagine how sailors reportedly mistook it for a mesmerizing siren (until we recall the transforming effect of weeks on end at sea together with the fermented grape). Manatees have very fleshy, hairy faces, and the region between the mouth and nose, called the oral disk, is greatly expanded compared to most mammals. The oral disk contains about 600 stout bristle-like hairs that are brought into contact with novel objects in the environment (figs. 2.4, 2.5; plate 14).[10] As mentioned in chapter 2, manatees prepare to "scan" or feel an object by first broadening and flattening the oral disk. This causes the bristle-like hairs to protrude and prepare for contact. (Normally these hairs are hidden between the fleshy folds of the oral disk when it is loose and relaxed rather than flattened.) Then, the manatee moves the oral disk back and forth, scraping the hairs against the object. Interestingly, prior to contact, manatees often close their eyes, perhaps to improve tactile discrimination. Recently, we found that all of these bristle-like hairs are vibrissae whose follicles are innervated by numerous (50–75) nerve fibers (plate 15).[11] These vibrissae correspond to the mystacial vibrissae of other mammals and represent a dramatic increase in number from about 50 in mice, cats, and dogs to 600 in manatees. Moreover, manatees possess clusters of nerve cells (the Rindenkerne) in what we believe to be the face region of the cerebral cortex, like the barrels in mice.[12] We suspect that some of these Rindenkerne are associated with the vibrissae of the oral disk, perhaps in a one-to-one fashion like the mystacial vibrissae in mice.

Sirenians are not the only mammals with an extraordinary number of mystacial vibrissae. The Pacific walrus (*Odobenus rosmarus*) has around 450, many more than the typical pinniped, and these are long and stiff. Like manatees, walruses sweep the head and vibrissae across objects that are under tactile investigation. The vibrissae located in the center of this array appear to be the most sensitive and are used most often.[13] Bearded seals also have a profusion of long mystacial vibrissae. The proliferation and elaboration of vibrissae in walruses and bearded seals may be related to the fact that both appear to use their vibrissae to locate and identify the marine invertebrates on which they feed.[14]

Is the oral disk of manatees used simply in casual investigation, or does it play a significant role in their behavior? Chris Marshall observed manatees searching for food by making quivering movements of the oral disk in a side to side motion, while sweeping the entire head vertically and horizontally, most often with the eyes closed.[15] Once food was located, the larger bristles of the upper and lower lips were used to grasp the plants. Daniel Bachteler, a member of Guido Dehnhardt's research group in Germany, tested the ability of a captive manatee to discriminate between objects using the oral disk.[16] He trained the manatee to approach an underwater wall on which two panels were fastened. The surface of each of these panels had grooves. Using food rewards, the manatee could be trained to indicate which panel was the standard one with grooves 2 mm wide. This task proved easy for obvious comparisons of 2-mm to 10-mm groove widths (or even of 2-mm to 5-mm widths), but as the grooves of the nonstandard panel approached 2 mm, the manatee's performance became random. In the beginning of training, the manatee would scrape the bristle-like hairs of the oral disk along the grooved panel and would then try to grasp the panel using its large facial bristles and lip movements as in feeding. After a few training sessions—perhaps having discovered that the panel was not something good to eat and that real food was the reward for correct performance—the manatee used only the oral disk to make contact with the panels.

This type of behavioral testing, whether done on humans or other animals, is called psychophysics because a learned behavioral response is used to indicate the sensitivity of a sensory ability involving many components of the nervous system. These components include the sensory receptors (in the manatee's case, located in the hair follicles), sensory nerves that project into the brain, various regions inside the brain, and motor output pathways that result in the observed behavior. In order to compare the performance of different individuals or different species, psychophysics investigators utilize the concept of a "just noticeable difference"—in the Bachteler and Dehnhardt experiment, the smallest difference between two groove widths that can be reliably distinguished. But what does reliable mean? Well, if the best performance is 100 percent correct and the poorest (in a two-choice situation) is 50 percent correct, then 75 percent correct represents the halfway point. The manatee could tell the difference between 2.00-mm and 2.28-mm grooves with 75 percent accuracy, so the just noticeable difference (JND) was 0.28 mm or 14 percent of the standard (2 mm).

How does the manatee's tactile discrimination ability compare with that of other animals? This is where the JND becomes useful because, expressed as a percentage, it is a relative measure and thus applicable across species, assuming of course that similar testing has been done with other animals. Bachteler's manatee performed better than sea lions using their facial vibrissae (JND=24 percent),[17] the same as elephants using their trunks (JND=14 percent),[18] but not as well as harbor seals (JND=9 percent),[19] and much poorer than humans using the tips of their fingers (JND=4 percent).[20] Two manatees currently being studied by Gordon Bauer's group at Mote Marine Laboratory in Sarasota, Florida, exhibit even better acuity: JND=2.5 percent for one and JND=7.5 percent for the other.

An elaborate sensory-muscular complex such as the oral disk was likely to find some use even if its evolution was the by-product of selection for other traits. In the next section, we explore the possibility that one such trait was the development of a widespread distribution of vibrissae over the entire body.

The body hairs and life underwater

In 1915 a German anatomist named Dosch reported that all the hair on the bodies of manatees and dugongs is of the vibrissal type.[21] The manatee face alone contains around 2,000 hairs.[22] If each of these were a vibrissa, a very extensive array of sensors would be represented. Given the detailed tactile information conveyed by the oral disk, we might not be surprised to find that all of its 600 hairs are vibrissae. But what about the rest of the body? In a recent investigation we found that the manatee body actually contains another 3,000 sparsely distributed hairs. Furthermore, each of these indeed has the characteristics of a vibrissa, complete with an encapsulated blood sinus and innervation by 20–50 nerve fibers (plate 15).[23] Why would manatees have vibrissae all over their bodies when vibrissae in other mammals have such a restricted distribution?

Consider that manatees are large-bodied, slow-moving aquatic herbivores that usually reside in turbid habitats, have greatly reduced visual systems and poor visual acuity, do not appear to utilize echolocation, and do not possess thick pelage. Let's look at these traits one at a time. As discussed in the previous chapter, large body size in sirenians probably evolved in order to accommodate the thermal stresses of an aquatic lifestyle (as in other marine mammals) together with an herbivorous mode of life where these animals consume

5–10 percent of their body weight per day in vegetation.[24] This amounts to at least 23 kg of food a day for a 450-kg adult! That's a lot to put in your gut, and manatees possess enormous digestive tracts. Although manatees evolved in tropical locales, they do encounter colder water, particularly in more temperate regions like northern Florida. So it also pays to have a large body in order to reduce heat loss.

Slow movement is characteristic of manatees, although they exhibit short powerful bursts of speed on occasion. One reason their generally relaxed pace may be possible is that manatees have no predators trying to catch them. If they did, they would probably need to be capable of sustained escape behavior. Likewise, being herbivores, they are not trying to catch fast-moving prey. Thus, there has likely been no selection pressure for the capability of sustained rapid movement. By comparison, many terrestrial herbivores (like certain animals on the plains of Africa) are constantly in danger of being caught by predators. So although, as plant eaters, they do not require the capacity for fast movement in order to catch prey, they do need this capability to escape predation themselves.

Even though manatees in Florida are most easily observed in clear-water springs, the water is turbid in most of their coastal and near-coastal habitat. This murkiness lessens the usefulness of vision and probably explains why manatees have such reduced visual systems. Having a well-developed visual system means having lots of brain tissue devoted to processing visual information. So reduction potentially frees up that tissue for other functions, though we are not sure exactly how this works during brain development much less during evolution. Some whales and dolphins generate high-frequency sounds that are used as sonar to echolocate objects, but manatees apparently have not evolved this ability. In their lack of fur, manatees resemble the cetaceans but not most pinnipeds. Cetaceans have a thick blubber layer that performs an insulating function. Manatees inhabit warmer waters and do not have thick blubber, but they do have a remarkably thick and dense dermis that may be more protective than insulating.

Bringing all these behavioral and anatomical characteristics together, it would appear to be adaptive to utilize tactile hairs distributed over the body as a three-dimensional tactile array, even though we are unsure how this wide distribution of vibrissae came about or why manatees were apparently the only mammals to evolve such an array. It may be that the combination of large size, slow movements in shallow-water habitats, and lack of echolocation were conducive factors in sirenians. But the developmental quirk that enabled vibrissae to establish themselves over the entire manatee body was also required, and how this came about is totally unknown.

Based on the known functional properties of vibrissae in other animals, the manatee tactile array is probably capable of encoding the intensity and direction of underwater pressure gradients and low-frequency vibrations impinging on the body surface (in other words, various forms of water movement). Pressure waves, including compression (or sound) waves, travel about 4.5 times faster in water than air (depending on water temperature, depth, and salinity) and undergo less rapid energy dispersal than in the air. Therefore, pressure waves are potentially useful stimuli in the denser aquatic environment. In the absence of vision, wave information would be very important in detecting and localizing significant environmental stimuli such as approaching animals, water currents, and tidal flows.

Woodie Hartman and John Reynolds were the first researchers to suggest that the body hairs of manatees might be used in this way.[25] In his pioneering field study of Florida manatees during the late 1960s and early 1970s, Hartman observed groups of manatees resting together on the bottom of Crystal River. Every 10 to 15 minutes, one animal slowly floated to the surface to breathe and then sank back down again to rest. The other animals followed this cue so that the whole group appeared to rise and fall together. But they did this with their eyes closed! That ruled out visual cues, and Hartman heard no obvious sounds associated with the behavior. He conjectured that the body hairs were used to sense movements in the water and that this sensitivity might be the means by which a group of animals, resting with eyes closed, could rise in unison to breathe. He also suggested that this system of body hairs might enable manatees to detect other manatees moving in the vicinity. Ed and Laura Gerstein, who made a detailed study of manatee hearing abilities, think it possible that manatee body hairs also detect low-frequency sounds.[26] One of their manatee subjects consistently rotated his body and bent his head down when acoustic stimuli less than 400 Hz frequency were played. This body posturing was consistent with maximizing the exposure of body hairs to the low-frequency stimuli. The Gersteins refer to this response as vibrotactile in order to distinguish it from typical responses involving the auditory system, which did not include posturing.

The manatee system of body vibrissae, which appears to represent a tactile array capable of detecting and localizing water displacements associated with significant environmental stimuli, is analogous to the lateral line system in fish and some amphibians. The lateral line system is located beneath the black stripe running down each side of a fish, and it is the reason why we can sneak up behind a fish but cannot grab it. This system consists of specialized cells that are stimulated when water flows over them. Nerves associated with these cells convey motion information to the brain, often triggering rapid escape behavior. The function of the lateral line system has been likened to "touch at a distance," a function markedly different from that of facial vibrissae involved in direct contact tactile scanning.[27]

In fish, the lateral line system has been shown to mediate behavioral orientation to water currents such as those generated by moving animals, but it can also be used to detect underwater objects.[28] Stationary underwater objects create distortions in the flow fields generated by animals moving through water, and fish obtain information about object size and distance through the lateral line system's analysis of the velocity distribution of the flow field over the entire body.[29] If the distributed system of body vibrissae in Florida manatees is used in a similar way, the large body size of manatees may enhance this analytical ability by providing a larger detector array. Thus, manatee body vibrissae may be used to detect and localize fixed objects of various sizes in the underwater environment, including outcroppings such as limestone formations and boundaries such as river banks. Such a capability would be of obvious use in navigation.

Manatee field biologists have long wondered how manatees find their way back to previously visited sites in murky water. Manatee biologist Tom O'Shea once observed several animals cruising along one side of the St. Johns River, which is quite dark because of its tannin content. Suddenly, they turned and headed for the opposite side where they entered a spring. This spring was probably too far away to have been detected by changes in water temperature, chemistry, or visibility. It is plausible, however, that the manatees oriented to some landmark in the underwater environment or to a change in current flow and, based on this information, zipped across to the other side.

Nice stories, but is there any real evidence that vibrissae are sensitive enough to be used in the same way as the lateral line system? Well, consider seals. Their specialty is finding and eating fish on the run. How they manage to get close enough to capture them has long remained a bit of a mystery. It turns out that when a fish swims it leaves a wake, and now it has been demonstrated that seals use their facial vibrissae to detect and track this wake or hydrodynamic trail. Dehnhardt's group in Germany tested two captive harbor seals and found that, in the absence of acoustic cues and even when blindfolded, they could reliably track the hydrodynamic trails left by a miniature submarine.[30] These trails were similar in magnitude to those produced by fish. During the tracking behavior, the seals held their vibrissae extended outward from the face. When fitted with a stocking mask that held the vibrissae against the face, they could no longer track and locate the submarine. It is still anyone's guess how sensitive the body vibrissae of manatees might be, but these findings on seals certainly raise the possibility that other marine mammals use their vibrissae to detect underwater movements.

If body vibrissae function anything like facial vibrissae, manatees may be the only mammals to have developed a mammalian version of the lateral line. And let's not forget dugongs. Dosch, the German anatomist who first claimed that all manatee hairs were vibrissae, actually made this claim for all sirenians, dugongs as well as manatees, because he had studied specimens from both species. More recent anatomical observations have been consistent with Dosch's hypothesis, but no systematic study of dugong vibrissae has yet been made.[31]

Vision

The eyes of manatees are small and covered by a circular eyelid. The optic nerves, which convey visual signals to the brain, are also reduced in size. The external eye muscles and the nerves that control movement of the eyeball are all small, as are the brain regions that process visual information. All of this suggests that manatee vision is rather poor, which makes sense for a species adapted to turbid-water environments. But some observers have suggested that manatees utilize vision as a major means of exploring their environment, at least in clear water.[32] So what is the evidence regarding manatee vision?

Eyes exhibit significant variation in structure across mammals, including differences in lens shape, cornea thickness, and photoreceptor types. The geometry of the eye influences its optic characteristics, but the resolving capability and the ability to detect dim light and color are primarily determined by the photoreceptors and nerve cells in the retina. Mammalian photoreceptors are of two types, rods and cones. Rods are more numerous and are more sensitive detectors of light, but cones have specialized pigments that allow them to discriminate color. The retina also contains a variety of nerve cells that process the light signals gathered by the photoreceptors and turn them into information that is sent to the brain for interpretation and integration with other neural traffic. The most important of the retinal nerve cells are the ganglion cells; more ganglion cells mean better resolution of spatial detail. Their long axon processes comprise the optic nerves, which act as cables connecting the eyes to the brain (actually, the retina is an outgrowth of the brain that moves farther and farther from the brain center during development).

Ganglion cells are distributed nonuniformly in most mammals, with regions of high density organized in a central region in vertical or horizontal stripes or other patterns. These patterns have perceptual significance and are related to particular adaptations. Species with frontally placed eyes (humans, cats, pinnipeds) have a high density of ganglion cells—and thus maximum spatial resolution—in the portion of the retina devoted to the binocular region of the visual field (the area perceived by both eyes). Species with laterally positioned eyes (rabbits, squirrels, ungulates) often have a horizontal streak of high density, probably related to scanning for movement of predators on the horizon. Elephants have both a horizontal and vertical streak, and the latter is associated with the binocular region of the visual field in which the trunk moves back and forth. Most cetaceans exhibit two regions of high density, one related to underwater vision and the other for vision above water. By comparison, manatees exhibit a rather rudimentary condition where there is no localized grouping of ganglion cells and the overall concentration is low.[33] Interestingly, this same combination of traits is also found in river dolphins and may be associated with adaptation to short-distance vision in turbid water. Behavioral observations also suggest that manatees are nearsighted. Based on estimates derived from ganglion cell density and eye geometry, manatees appear to have significantly poorer spatial resolution than cetaceans and pinnipeds and only marginally better resolution than river dolphins.[34]

Because vision ultimately is the result of multiple processes involving optics and nerve cells, visual performance must be measured behaviorally rather than simply inferred from anatomy.[35] Visual acuity is the official term for spatial resolution ability—the ability tested when the optometrist asks us to read ever-smaller letters on an eye chart. One common way to test animal acuity is to present the subject with two panels having evenly spaced vertical lines and to give a food reward if the subject correctly picks the panel with the wider spaced lines. The subject may not be able to see the difference between the two panels as the line spacings become similar at test distance, even though the difference may become apparent on closer inspection. Visual acuity is basically the smallest difference in spacing that can be detected at a fixed distance, and it is expressed in degrees and minutes of visual arc. The smaller this value, the better the acuity.

Hugh and Buffett are two manatees at Mote Marine Laboratory in Sarasota, Florida, that have been studied by Gordon Bauer's research group.[36] They have been trained to station themselves about 3 m from a pair of panels and then to swim toward them. A divider positioned 1 m from the panels forces the manatee to decide which panel to swim toward, and this choice determines whether or not he will be rewarded. By running many trials of this kind, the researchers can reliably define the line-spacing difference that corresponds to 75 percent correct performance, as in the tactile testing described above. By this criterion, Buffett's visual acuity is 23' (23 minutes of arc)—close to the value of 20' predicted by calculations involving ganglion cell density and eye geometry.[37] In contrast, Hugh's acuity is greater than 1° (or 60'), suggesting that he may be visually impaired. To put these values in perspective, the acuity of cows at about 22' is similar to that of Buffett. River dolphins have poorer acuity at 41'. Humans, dogs, pinnipeds, and bottlenose dolphins all have significantly better acuity with values less than 10' (fig. 8.1).

One finding that may influence our understanding of manatee vision is that the corneas of 26 manatee eyes examined to date are vascularized.[38] In other mammals this represents an abnormal, pathological condition that affects visual acuity. Because this condition was present even in a manatee fetus, it is likely to be the normal condition for manatees rather than the result of an environmental influence like water contamination. The small size of the blood vessels observed in the manatee corneas suggests that they may not affect vision, but this is not known for sure.

The internal structure of the manatee eye reveals the existence of two types of cones as well as rods, suggesting that manatees have color vision.[39] This was tested behaviorally by giving manatees a choice of two targets to touch with their snout.[40] One target was a particular color, the other was gray. The subject was given a food reward if it correctly chose the colored target. Through repeated presentations in which the target positions were randomly switched and a variety of colors and gray shades used, the investigators could distinguish between the use of brightness cues and true discrimination based on color. Manatees were able to distinguish green from gray and blue from gray, but could not distinguish red. This indicates the existence of dichromatic vision, similar to that seen in pinnipeds, and supports the anatomical evidence for two cone types, one tuned to blue wavelengths, the other to green. Bob Bonde reports peak curiosity about his leaf-green bathing suit from inquisitive wild manatees, most of whom ignore his yellow and blue swim trunks.

Compared to air, the coastal aquatic environment of the Florida manatee is characterized by relative darkness, reduced contrast, and reduced visibility. Under these conditions, color vision may enhance contrast and thus facilitate the object detection useful in finding specific kinds of plants to eat.[41] Manatees' ability to discriminate different degrees of brightness independent of

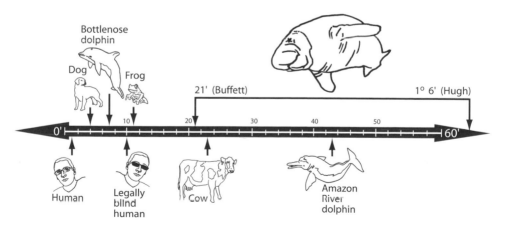

Figure 8.1. Visual acuity among selected animals. Manatees have rather poor eyesight by this measure. (Adapted by Rachel Henriques from diagram by Wendi Fellner, © 1999–2003.)

color is comparable to that of fur seals. Human brightness discrimination is about three times better than that.[42] Consider two panels distinguished only by degree of brightness. For a human to detect a difference between them, the panels' brightness must differ by about 1 percent in low light conditions. For a manatee or fur seal to distinguish the panels, their brightness would have to differ by about 3 percent.

Manatees can use visual cues to solve problems. In tests carried out independently by Dale Woodyard and Ed Gerstein, captive manatees were able to use size, shape, pattern, brightness, and color to discriminate targets presented in settings in which reward was given for success. During his study of manatee feeding behavior, Chris Marshall found that manatees came quickly when they saw carrots, apparently recognizing the characteristic color, size, or shape of one of their favorite foods. One captive animal at Homosassa Springs Wildlife State Park even stashed his carrots under a ledge down in the main spring! At close range (less than 1 m), visual investigation by manatees involves repeated shifting of the head so that first one eye then the other is focused on the object of interest.[43] This suggests that binocular cues are no longer available in the near field. Similarly, it is commonly observed that manatees often bump into objects. It appears likely that under many circumstances, including feeding and interaction with other manatees, manatees switch from using visual to tactile cues at close range.

Hearing

Field observations of wild manatees indicate that, given adequate time, they can accurately determine the location of an approaching boat and move rapidly in the opposite direction. So why do so many manatees have scars indicating multiple collisions with boats or their propellers? Perhaps they don't always hear boats coming or don't have sufficient time or ability to localize their direction of travel. Perhaps they don't have enough time to escape to a safer area. Or maybe they simply ignore the sounds. The issue of manatee hearing ability is one of the reasons why slow speed zones have been established in areas where manatees congregate. But as we shall see, the sounds generated by slow-moving boats may actually be more difficult for manatees to hear than those of fast-moving boats. Understanding the hearing abilities of manatees and learning about the acoustic environment in which they live therefore bears a direct relationship to their survival in Florida.

Unlike the visual system, auditory components of the central nervous system are well developed in manatees. This includes the peripherally located auditory nerves, which convey signals from the inner ear, and the brain regions that process this information. The hearing abilities of manatees have been investigated in detail by Ed and Laura Gerstein and their colleagues.[44] For months at a time over several years, Ed and Laura lived in a small trailer behind Lowry Park Zoo in Tampa, Florida, so they could run tests on manatee hearing at night after the crowds had gone and it was sufficiently quiet. Similar to the visual experiments described above, these were behavioral psychophysical tests, which many consider the most direct way to assess the perceptual capacities of an organism. Their subjects were Stormy and Dundee, two captive-born manatees. This was the first time manatees had been trained to perform a specific hearing task, and it took over a year's time and lots of food rewards to get them to understand the task and to keep them motivated enough to perform. As illustrated in figure 8.2, each manatee was first trained to station himself underwater at a hoop. When a light came on, it alerted the manatee to listen for a tone. If the animal heard a tone, he was trained to press a striped pole, and if he heard nothing he was to press a plain pole.

Through the use of thousands of such trials covering a wide range of tone frequencies and intensities, audiograms were constructed for Stormy and Dundee (fig. 8.3). The audiogram is a curve that defines the total frequency range of hearing and also reveals the specific range in which hearing is most sensitive. In the case of the two manatees housed in a quiet pool, the range of detected sound was 500–38,000 Hz or cycles per second (1 kHz=1000 Hz), with greatest sensitivity at 16–18 kHz and rapid declines in sensitivity below 2 kHz and above 25 kHz. In comparison, humans underwater have less sensitivity overall, and their greatest sensitivity is around 1 kHz (fig. 8.3). Compared to cetaceans, the manatee audiogram is rather flat in the range of 5–20 kHz. This is similar to most pinnipeds and is consistent with the anatomical structure of the cochlea of the inner ear.[45] In addition, the anatomy of the cochlea shows none of the specializations associated with the ultrasonic (very high frequency) or infrasonic (very low frequency) hearing found in cetaceans.[46] In two other experiments, the audiogram was derived not from behavioral re-

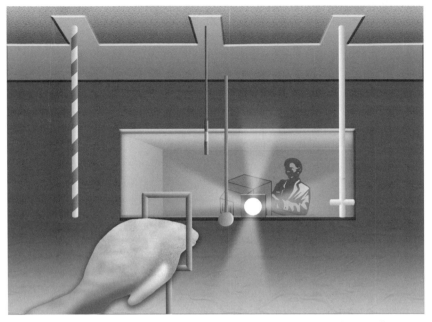

Figure 8.2. Auditory testing setup for the Gersteins' study at Lowry Park Zoo. (Illustration by Rachel Henriques.)

sponses but from the recorded electrical activity of the brain with reference to tones of various frequencies and intensities. The first study was done on an Amazonian manatee. Similar to the psychophysical results in Florida manatees, maximum sensitivity was found in the region of 10–20 kHz.[47] Apparently, it makes a big difference if hearing occurs underwater. A similar study done on four Florida manatees, but with sound stimuli delivered in air, found peak sensitivity at 1–1.5 kHz.[48]

These findings have significant implications for the question of how well manatees can detect boat noise, most of which is below 1 kHz, radiates in all directions, and occurs in a significantly noisier environment than the quiet pool Stormy and Dundee occupied. In order to test the ability of manatees to localize sounds, an underwater speaker array was used to play a variety of sounds.[49] Although the manatees were able to localize recorded manatee vocalizations and sounds over 10 kHz 90 percent of the time, their ability to localize low-frequency sounds of idling boats was less reliable. They localized higher frequency sounds of a cavitating boat propeller with moderate success. This implies that slow-moving boats may generate low-frequency sounds that are less detectable by manatees than those of faster moving boats. Further investigation of the underwater sounds generated by moving boats revealed that this is in fact the case. A typical outboard boat traveling at fast speed (38.6 km/h) produced sound that should be detectable by a manatee at a distance of about 200 m, or 16 seconds before impact, whereas the same boat traveling at slow speed (4.8 km/h) produced sounds that a manatee would probably not hear until the boat was 4 m away, or about 2 seconds before impact.

A recent study evaluated the response behavior of manatees in the wild to an approaching boat similar to many outboard pleasure craft found throughout Florida.[50] A team of researchers used a remotely operated aerial video camera to record manatee responses to boat approaches made at various speeds and distances from specific individuals. The most significant finding was a tendency for manatees in shallow water to respond to approaches within 10 m by moving quickly to the nearest deep water. Although this did not always take them out of the path of the boat, it may have removed them from

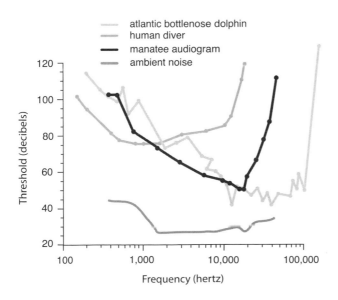

Figure 8.3. Audiograms for manatees, humans, and Atlantic bottlenose dolphins. (From Gerstein 2002: 156; graph reproduced courtesy of *American Scientist.*)

harm by positioning them deep enough to avoid contact with the boat or its motor. Once again, this finding emphasizes the apparent difficulty manatees have in localizing sounds associated with boats, especially in shallow water. Such findings have generated an interest in the development of warning signals to keep boats and manatees apart. These are discussed further in chapter 10.

Vocalizations are the naturally occurring flip side of hearing. The main frequency of vocalization coincides with that of the maximum sensitivity of hearing across a wide variety of vertebrates. In his early field studies, Woodie Hartman noted that manatees were relatively quiet and tended to vocalize most during play, sexual activity, and when alarmed.[51] He found that the most frequent communications occurred between a mother and her calf, and more recent studies have confirmed this. Manatee vocalizations consist of short (about 300 msec) chirps or squeals, with several frequency bands in the range of 3–20 kHz (fig. 8.4).[52] A recent study of Amazonian manatees showed that adult females produce sounds of shorter duration and higher frequency than those of adult males.[53] Juveniles produce even shorter sounds of higher frequency, and calves produce the shortest, highest sounds. Manatees may therefore be able to discern both the age class and sex of individuals that vocalize.

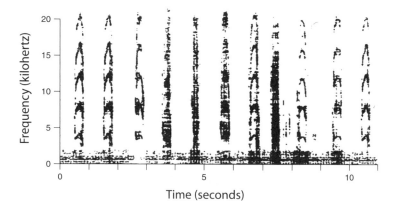

Figure 8.4. Manatee vocalization spectrum. Each vertical array represents a single squeak or chirp sound and consists of a fundamental low frequency plus several higher harmonics (overtones). (From Gerstein 2002: 159; graph reproduced courtesy of *American Scientist*.)

More significantly, individuals appear to produce "signature" calls that uniquely identify them to others.[54] This is particularly important for mother-calf pairs that become visually separated in turbid water. Incidentally, it is not yet clear how manatees produce sound. They apparently do not have vocal cords, so it is possible that they vocalize by expelling air out of the nasal cavity or within its membranes, although this possibility needs to be tested.[55]

Olfaction and taste

The usefulness of olfaction is probably directly related to how much time is spent breathing. For the cetaceans and sirenians who spend all their time in the water, this isn't much. But the semiaquatic pinnipeds that haul out onto land represent an altogether different situation. Not surprisingly, manatees have undergone significant reductions in all components of the olfactory system. They lack altogether the vomeronasal organ, an accessory olfactory structure that is prominent in terrestrial herbivores and is involved in driving mating behavior initiated by pheromonal cues.[56] This reduction of the olfactory system in manatees is similar to the condition in baleen whales. The toothed whales, which spend even less time near the surface, lack olfactory structures altogether.[57]

Taste is potentially another matter. In some species the aquatic environment has encouraged the evolution of elaborate taste reception. Catfish are known for their barbels, the fleshy appendages that hang from their chins. In fact, these are elaborate chemosensory devices covered with taste receptors. Some fish even have taste receptors on other parts of the external body surface. But manatee tongues contain precious few taste buds, and there is no evidence for taste buds in more exotic locations.[58] Field observations have shown that manatees seek out fresh water to drink, and some of their food preferences may be based on taste, perhaps driven by nutritional urges. In addition, manatees may have a keen ability to sense temperature changes and to taste salt or other chemicals in the water, abilities which may act as cues in navigation. Much remains to be learned about the taste capacities of manatees.

The unusual constellation of sensory abilities, behavior, and brain traits exhibited by living manatees (and dugongs) reinforce the view obtained from the fossil record that sirenians represent a significant departure from other mammalian lineages. We have discussed the intimate associations that exist among brain traits, sensory capabilities, feeding behavior, body size, metabolism, and other anatomical and physiological features. The interdependence of these factors suggests that this departure may have occurred very early in sirenian evolution.

9 Rehabilitation and Release

Manatees in captivity

During the 1800s and early 1900s manatees were occasionally plucked from their environment and transported on ships to museums for scientific research or public display.[1] Often the animals died a short time after capture. One of several bungled manatee captures made in the Everglades in the early 1900s *did* succeed in acquiring a specimen for the New York Aquarium.[2] That manatee was wrestled and finally restrained by a determined team of hunters who kept it tied to trees for a couple of days before placing it in a tank for transport by ship to New York. Unsurprisingly, it only lived a short time. The captive rearing of manatees is a science that requires adequate facilities and a great deal of specialized knowledge. At great expense to the individuals culled from the population early on, only a little information was gained about their husbandry. But as conservation efforts improved, more manatees graced Florida's waterways. This growing manatee population, coupled with the advent of a recreational watercraft industry and ever-more-powerful outboard motors, increased the incidence of injured, orphaned, and distressed manatees.[3]

The longest-lived captive manatee to date is Baby Snooty, housed at the South Florida Museum and Planetarium in Bradenton. In 1948 an adult female manatee, aptly named Lady, was rescued and taken to the Miami Seaquarium. A couple of months later, Lady gave birth to a healthy male calf. That manatee was named Snooty. He was moved to a pier pavilion run by the City of Bradenton in the early 1950s and later moved to the museum, where he resides today. Every year the community holds a special birthday celebration for its pride and joy.

Several manatees have been housed in captivity for a long time.[4] Like Baby Snooty, others kept more than 20 years in captivity include Romeo (1957), Juliet (1958), Rosie (1967), Amanda (1973), Ariel (1973), Lorelei (1975), Gene (1977), and Rita (1982). A few manatees have been born in captivity and remain there, including Snooty (1948), Ariel (1973), Lorelei (1975), Hurricane (1983), Hugh (1984), Dundee (1986), Buffett (1987), Betsy (1990), Slip (1991), Webster (1991), and Stoneman (1994). In recent years managers have restricted rather than encouraged birth of Florida manatees in captivity. Captive breeding has not been deemed necessary as it is thought that wild manatees are reproducing adequately in the natural environment and limited resources are better spent on rehabilitating orphaned or injured manatees or on protecting critical habitat. Therefore, captive male and female manatees are kept at different facilities.

A group was convened in 1991 to address issues related to manatee capture, rehabilitation, and release. The Interagency/Oceanaria Captive Manatee Working Group assisted the U.S. Fish and Wildlife Service (FWS) in supplying guidance for releases of captive manatees into the wild. Jim Kraus of FWS assembled the working group along with Bob Turner and Jim Valade. Today that group is coordinated under the expert direction of Nicole Adimey. It is a daunting task to plan for the eventual release of captive manatees. Participants in the working group include veterinarians and other representatives of the oceanaria; researchers from the U.S. Geological Survey (USGS) Sirenia Project, the Florida Fish and Wildlife Conservation Commission, and various

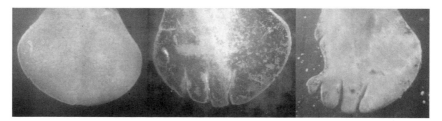

Figure 9.1. Scar patterns can change over time, as on the tail of this Crystal River female who has been observed in the field since 1991 and is known to have given birth to two calves. Shown from left to right is the appearance of her tail in 1991, 1996, and 1999. Note that new lesions obliterate or mask previous scars used to ID the animal. Therefore, it is important to maintain consistent sighting records over time. (Photographs by U.S. Geological Survey.)

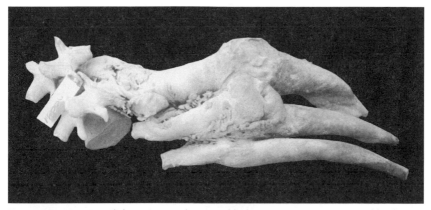

Figure 9.2. Manatee rib bone is very dense and lacks a marrow cavity. Wound healing often leads to grotesque bone overgrowth like that shown in the midportion of these ribs. Vertebrae are visible on the left. (Photography by Kari Clifton.)

academic institutions; representatives from Save the Manatee Club; and wildlife managers. All have the same goal: to facilitate the transition of manatees from captivity to the natural environment. Since the first rescue of an injured manatee in 1973, through 2002, 608 injured or orphaned manatees have been assisted on site or taken into captivity. Seventy-seven previously captive individuals have been monitored with radio tags after release, and an additional 390 were returned to the wild without electronic monitoring.

Rescue

Rescue and subsequent medical procedures are most often performed when manatees are injured, cold stressed, or orphaned as calves. Most injuries are the result of blunt trauma or propeller wounds from encounters with boats (fig. 9.1), and these are often serious (fig. 9.2). Individuals have been found with broken bits of boat propeller in their heads, others with their lungs ballooning out of their backs and floating beside them from open wounds caused by a boat. The telltale sign of a previous encounter with a spinning propeller is a series of parallel lesions, usually seen on the dorsal body surface.[5] Ironically, such wounds, if not life threatening, generally form permanent scar tissue that helps researchers identify individuals in the wild.[6] Analysis of scars has also helped researchers identify certain types of watercraft associated with manatee mortality.[7] However, when manatees are struck and the wounds are life threatening, the individual may be captured by an experienced rescue team and transported to a critical-care facility for medical treatment and subsequent rehabilitation. Unfortunately these injuries are common, and rescue facilities have been overtaxed during the last several years. Nonetheless, no manatee is ever turned away.

Manatees are also rescued for other reasons. Entanglement by crab trap lines or monofilament fishing line is a significant problem and can lead to infection and sometimes amputation of affected limbs. When an orphaned calf is recovered, rescuers seldom know exactly why it has become separated from its mother. Occasionally, the mother has been killed by a boat strike or some other cause. Recovered orphans often exhibit emaciation, metabolic exhaustion, or constipation. Cold stress often produces acute problems associated with hypothermia as well as longer-lasting problems, including immune system compromise and severe bacterial dermatitis.[8]

Once a manatee is identified as needing assistance, experienced biologists or animal care specialists are dispatched to the scene to evaluate the animal's condition (fig. 9.3).[9] In consultation with veterinarians and animal husbandry experts, a decision is made either to continue observation or to rescue the animal. If rescue is necessary, a team is assembled and sent out with a net to catch the manatee. These nets are often deployed from a large rescue boat. Once netted and pulled into the boat, the animal is taken to a waiting vehicle and transported as quickly as possible to a suitable facility. Currently, there are three primary critical care facilities in Florida: SeaWorld Orlando, Lowry Park Zoo in Tampa, and Miami Seaquarium in Key Biscayne. Once the animal is stabilized, it is placed in a holding tank until ready for release back into the wild. Federal law requires that manatees be held only as long as necessary to make them medically and developmentally fit for return to the wild.[10]

There are several other facilities in Florida that house manatees, including manatees that have undergone critical care and face prolonged rehabilitation. These include Homosassa Springs Wildlife State Park, Mote Marine Laboratory in Sarasota, Living Seas at Epcot in Orlando, and South Florida Museum and Planetarium in Bradenton. Additionally, manatees are currently being held at the Columbus and Cincinnati zoos in Ohio, SeaWorld San Diego in

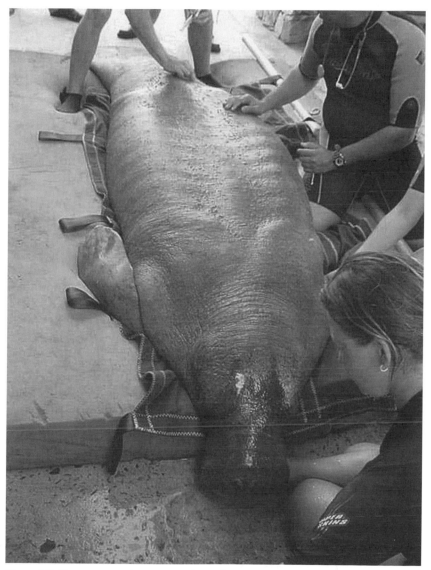

Figure 9.3. Here, a very sick manatee is brought into captivity for rehabilitation. Note the emaciated state evidenced by the visibility of the underlying ribs through the skin. (Photograph courtesy of Caribbean Stranding Network, Puerto Rico.)

California, and the Dallas Aquarium in Texas. Altogether, about 50 Florida manatees are being housed at facilities throughout the country. Puerto Rico, Brazil, Mexico, Belize, Japan, and several European countries also currently have Antillean manatees in captivity.

Rehabilitation of injured and sick manatees requires the expertise of many dedicated people. Veterinarians, animal care specialists, behaviorists, dieticians, water quality experts, and researchers all contribute to the care and treatment of captive manatees. Dedicated veterinarians that have long-term expertise in medical care of manatees include the late Jesse White of Miami Seaquarium, Deke Beusse and Mike Walsh of SeaWorld Orlando, Greg Bossart of Harbor Branch Oceanographic Institute, Maya Daugherty and Mike Renner of Miami Seaquarium, Dave Murphy of Lowry Park Zoo, Charlie Manire at Mote Marine Laboratory, and Mark Lowe of Homosassa Springs Wildlife State Park. All these medical experts worked to open the path to our present-day understanding of manatee medicine. Animal handlers with combined decades of experience include Bob Jenkins of Florida Marineland, Bob Wagoner, Randy Runnels, and Steve Lehr of SeaWorld Orlando, Betsy Dearth of Homosassa Springs Wildlife State Park, and many others. Much of the expertise gathered by these individuals is currently assembled into a Manatee Husbandry Manual that helps guide others in the field of manatee care and handling.

A career in manatee rescue and rehab is full of surprise, grief, delight, and, not infrequently, encounters with the bizarre. The final rescue mission of Deke Beusse is a case in point. A few years ago Deke was retiring after 31 years as a veterinarian with SeaWorld Orlando. Thursday was to be his last day, and he was looking forward to spending Wednesday night saying goodbye to all the friends he had made over the years. Then came a call that a manatee needed to be rescued from a canal near Titusville on Florida's east coast. By the time Deke and his crew got their boat in the water, it was around midnight and the moon was up. As they traveled up the canal, the churning water glowed phosphorescent with myriad bioluminescent microorganisms. The rescue team received word that the manatee had died, but that another animal was hovering about. The whole scenario sounded awfully familiar: death of a mother manatee, survival of a now-orphaned calf. Now the mission was potentially two-pronged: rescue the calf and retrieve the mother's carcass for necropsy. When they arrived at the site they found a large dead female but no calf. So, they tied the animal behind the boat and started back, chugging along very slowly because of what seemed the unusual size and weight of the carcass. On docking back at the boat ramp, Deke tried to winch the animal up on the trailer, but it wouldn't budge. In the darkness, they discovered that a large male manatee was so fully locked in amorous embrace with the immobile female that he would not let go. With strenuous effort they dislodged the male and pulled the female out of the water. At last, both phases of the mission were accomplished—though clearly the attachment of the second animal to the female was something other than a calf's.

Treatment

Modern medical methods and technology are used to treat a variety of marine mammals including manatees.[11] Manatees are usually treated on land because of their capacity to make sudden, powerful movements in water (fig. 9.4; plate 16). A manatee can be safely restrained for treatment by draining its pool or by putting the animal on a stretcher in shallow water and then pulling it onto dry land. Once out of the water, the typical manatee becomes docile. If necessary, intramuscular injections of sedative can provide 60–90 minutes of calming. Other agents can be administered to provide adequate sedation for performing procedures such as wound cleaning, removal of bone fragments, or intubation. More extensive procedures like surgery require inhalation anesthesia using isoflurane.[12] Afterward, reversal agents may be administered to speed recovery to full consciousness. Blood samples are obtained by venipuncture of the region of the flipper corresponding to the radius and ulnar bones in a human forearm. Urine samples are difficult to obtain through catheterization, but sometimes urine flow can be stimulated by pressing the abdomen. A Frisbee placed under the manatee during examination helps to catch urine. Oral administration of medication is done by feeding tube or by mixing medicine in prepared food. The gastric tube is also used to administer water, nutritional support, and mineral oil in cases of constipation. Some animals require prolonged tube feeding: up to six months.

Physical examination of the patient, clinical chemistry (analysis of the blood serum), and hematology (analysis of blood cells) compose the cornerstone of medical diagnosis of disease in any species. Manatees are known for producing robust bubbles associated with large amounts of intestinal gas. In fact, flatulence is considered a positive clinical sign as it indicates normal digestive function.[13] More sophisticated diagnostic tests are especially important in aquatic and marine species such as manatees, which frequently show minimal overt signs of malaise, even when seriously ill. Therefore, aquatic animal veterinarians need accurate and useful hematologic and biochemical analyses to successfully diagnose and treat their patients.

Normal blood values are known for a sample of healthy manatees and consist of 40 value ranges for various blood cell types, enzyme levels, glucose levels, and other variables.[14] These values are used as a baseline by which to evaluate the values obtained from sick or injured animals and to determine if the patient has some type of organ dysfunction such as liver disease or kidney failure. Some individuals regularly have concentrations at the low end of the normal population's range, while some individuals regularly have concentrations at the high end. Additionally, it is important not to misconstrue normal seasonal and reproductive physiologic flux in values as pathologic change. To obtain the best diagnostic information, both population and individual reference intervals should be generated using one methodology.

In many species, leukocyte (white blood cell) counts and fever are moderately sensitive indicators of internal inflammation and infection. In a few species, such as the cow, leukocyte counts do not become elevated unless disease is severe, and they may proceed to drop precipitously because consumption of leukocytes quickly exceeds their production by the bone marrow. For this reason, white blood cell counts in bovine species are an insensitive indicator of inflammation. Clinical reports from veterinarians indicate that manatees' leukocyte response seems to be similar to that of cows. Additionally, adequately assessing the core temperature of a 500-kg aquatic animal can be inaccurate at best, so fever is not a good indicator of inflammatory disease in manatees.

The University of Florida veterinary clinical pathology laboratory is investigating alternate ways to assess inflammatory disease states. One important diagnostic approach involves the assessment of proteins associated with the inflammatory response. The acute phase reaction (APR) is a nonspecific response to inflammation associated with infection or autoimmune disease or to tissue damage due to trauma, surgery, or tumors. Positive APR proteins are

Figure 9.4. Biomedical samples and data are collected from every manatee handled. Here Bob Bonde is measuring back fat thickness with a portable ultrasound scanner. (Photograph by U.S. Geological Survey.)

produced by the liver in response to molecules released at the site of injury to either protect the body or to combat a potential pathogen. In humans, APR proteins are nonspecific indicators of disease similar to fever or leukocyte counts. Additionally, APR proteins are used to assess other disease conditions. For example, in humans, C reactive protein is used to assess risk for potential heart attack. Blood levels of the individual proteins change at different rates after the initial insult or injury, thereby providing useful information not only about inflammation but also about the duration of disease. Sequential measurement can also aid in assessment of response to treatment. In Europe, appropriate APR proteins are used as mandatory screening tests for inflammatory disease in livestock. APR proteins could be a valuable screening diagnostic for inflammation in manatees, as they are in cows and other large domestic animals.

Manatees that are thin, near comatose, or suffering neurologic signs of red tide toxicity may require buoyancy support in the form of a flotation jacket. These are most often required, however, for manatees that have developed a pneumothorax (air released from punctured lungs into the thoracic cavity) as a result of trauma from a boat strike. Manatees with a pneumothorax have difficulty righting themselves, so they need buoyancy aids. Some pneumothoraxes heal themselves over time.

In 1990 a 10-year-old adult female manatee suffering cold stress and weight loss was brought into SeaWorld Orlando for treatment. She was fed with a nasogastric feeding tube and quickly gained weight. But then she bit off the end of the tube and apparently swallowed it. In the days succeeding this incident, she lost weight and did not pass the piece of tube. SeaWorld Orlando veterinarians Deke Beusse and Mike Walsh were concerned that the swallowed tubing was causing her to avoid eating and might lead to further complications. They decided to attempt to retrieve the broken piece. To do this, they would need to anesthetize the animal and thread an endoscope down the digestive tract until they could locate the tube section and bring it back up. Because nobody had ever anesthetized a manatee before, they called in Dr. Alistair Webb, a veterinary anesthesiologist at the University of Florida. Conventional wisdom held that marine mammals should not be anesthetized, primarily based on experiences with sedated dolphins drowning. The fear was that an anesthetized manatee might stop breathing altogether.

After serious discussion, the doctors decided to go ahead with their plan and removed the manatee from the water. They constructed a mask that would fit tightly around the animal's snout, then pumped in the anesthetic gas, isoflurane, until the animal reached a stable plane and was still able to breathe on its own. Next Mike threaded a small endoscope into one nostril to guide Alistair's endotracheal tube, which was sent down the other nostril. The endotracheal tube was passed by the larynx and into the trachea, allowing anesthetic to continue to be delivered to the lungs in a controlled fashion after the mask had been removed. Next, they threaded a larger endoscope into the digestive tract but were unable to find the broken piece. The manatee came out of the anesthesia just fine and made a full and healthy recovery. The location of the missing tube remains a mystery to this day. Since this initial episode, many manatees have been successfully anesthetized for abdominal or thoracic surgery, treatment of traumatic wounds, and difficulties during calfbirth.[15] These days, instead of using an inhalation mask, veterinarians usually sedate the animal with intramuscular injections of Demerol followed by intubation for deeper anesthesia.

In another incident from around 1990, a female manatee started showing signs of having trouble giving birth. She was going through the characteristic body contortions associated with labor, but no calf appeared. Suspecting that the calf was turned around inside her, and fearing for the mother's life, the SeaWorld Orlando veterinarians performed a Caesarean section and delivered a fetus that lived for two days. After full recovery, the mother was released back into the wild and later bred and calved successfully. This experience demonstrated conclusively that interventions of this kind can be performed with no harm to the manatee.

Many Florida fishermen get their fishing lines tangled in grass beds. A common solution is to cut the line, but this leaves hook and line behind in the grass. When manatees feed on the grass bed, the hook can get caught in their lips, mouth, or throat, and the fishing line can get swallowed or tangled around their flippers. Deke Beusse discovered he could diagnose the presence of hooks in the throat by a characteristic rattling noise the animal makes when it comes to the surface to breathe. If fishing line ensnares a flipper, it can dig so deeply into the skin that the limb becomes infected and either self-amputates or, in some cases, has to be surgically removed. Manatees may also become entangled in crab trap lines. Some individuals have been observed dragging a crab trap behind them for several days before finally being rescued. Entanglement usually does not interfere with swimming, diving, or feeding, but it poses a significant threat to the health of pectoral flippers. Most documented entanglements (69 percent) involve crab trap lines, while most of those remaining (23 percent) involve monofilament line.[16] Interestingly, female manatees are more likely to become entangled than males. This may be due to their proclivity for rubbing their teats, either to relieve irritation or for pleasure. Injuries to pectoral flippers from crab trap lines or fishing lines are treated with disinfectant and waterproof ointment to lessen the chance of infections and amputation.

Made up of members of several organizations, a Manatee Entanglement Working Group has made considerable headway in helping to clean the environment of discarded monofilament line and other trash that presents a hazard to manatees. Strategic placement and use of recycling bins at boat ramps, fish camps, and piers has been very encouraging. The team has a long way to go, however, and needs the support of fishermen and Florida citizens to help prevent this problem from becoming more widespread.

Cold stress is a major problem for manatees in Florida, where they are at the northern end of their tolerable winter range. If they are unable to find warm water by migrating southward or by taking refuge in springs or warm-water power plant sites, they may experience prolonged exposure to cold water (less than 20°C or 68°F). This can initiate a series of behavioral and physical changes that constitute the manatee cold stress syndrome.[17] In the short term, cold stressed manatees exhibit lethargy and hypothermia due to inability to metabolically regulate their core temperature.[18] This renders them less likely to eat and more susceptible to potentially life-threatening dehydration, constipation, and metabolic breakdown. In addition, their immune system becomes compromised, so they are more susceptible to opportunistic pathogens and fungal infections of the skin. If rescued, these animals are first given water through a tube to reverse their dehydration, then fed a calorie-rich gruel that is gradually increased in amount and solidity.

An inadvertent experiment illustrates the relationship between cold stress and immune suppression.[19] Homosassa Springs Wildlife State Park is located near the Gulf coast of Florida and is centered around a natural freshwater spring that discharges two million gallons per hour. This spring is about two acres in area, and the immediate vicinity ranges from 1–12 m in depth. The water temperature varies between 22.5 and 23.5°C year-round. The park has held captive manatees since the early 1980s. These days, they typically house nine females. Like other captive manatees, these were either born in captivity or are undergoing rehabilitation before release. A bridge and underwater gate keep the animals confined to the spring area.

In 1996, this group of manatees experienced an outbreak of papilloma virus, which shows up as lesions on the skin (fig. 9.5). Immunologic testing revealed that the white blood cells from these animals were not as robust physiologically as those from healthy manatees. Based on what is known about this virus in other species, it appears that manatee papilloma virus is a latent infection that becomes activated to produce the observed lesions only after immune suppression. Baseline studies on manatee immune system response have been conducted by Cathy Walsh of Mote Marine Laboratory and Mark Sweat of the University of Florida. One hypothesis for the observed immune suppression in the captive Homosassa animals is prolonged exposure to the cool spring water. So, even though the water is not cold enough to induce full-blown cold stress, it may have stressful effects over the long term. Other factors, though, may also be involved. In any case, the wisdom of keeping manatees confined to a spring for long periods of time should be seriously questioned.

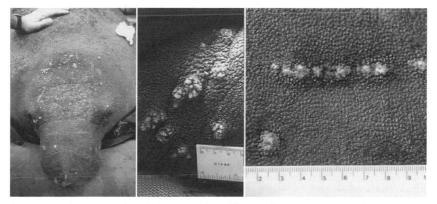

Figure 9.5. Three examples of lesions produced by papilloma virus. Research is underway to determine the etiology of this disease. (Photographs by U.S. Geological Survey.)

Red tide

From March through April of 1996, more than 150 Florida manatees died along an 80-mile stretch of the southwest coast of Florida in the region between Venice and Naples.[20] This event mobilized a large number of manatee biologists, critical care staff, and resources which hadn't existed decades earlier. Sick manatees were taken to various locations, including Lowry Park Zoo and SeaWorld, where they were held for observation and treatment. Many exhibited neurological signs including strained breathing and inability to maintain position in the water. These individuals were fitted with flotation devices and held in shallow water to prevent their drowning. Dead animals were taken to the Marine Mammal Pathobiology Laboratory in St. Petersburg and to various field sites where Scott Wright and his staff and colleagues performed necropsies to determine the cause of this mysterious mass die-off. Numerous tissue samples were collected and forwarded to various investigative laboratories. Some of the sick manatees recovered, and some did not. As we shall see, the cause of death was discovered mainly because resources were in place that allowed much valuable scientific and clinical information to be obtained. This information will continue to be useful in the future.

Around the same time as the 1996 die-off in southwest Florida, there was a large red tide bloom in this same region, suggesting a possible connection. This was not the first time red tide had been suspected in a manatee die-off. Over a 10-week period in 1982, a large red tide bloom coincided with the deaths of 39 manatees found in the same vicinity. Both the red tide bloom and manatee deaths were accompanied by an excess of sick or dead birds and fish. Another red tide event that affected 98 manatees in southwest Florida occurred in the spring of 2003. Events of this kind, where a sudden disease outbreak selectively affects one or a few species, are called epizootics. Several other epizootics involving dolphins, whales, manatees, and sea otters that occurred from the 1940s through the 1980s and continue today have been suspected to involve red tide poisoning.[21]

Red tides in southwest Florida are periodic explosions ("blooms") of dinoflagellate organisms, usually a species named *Karenia brevis* (after Karen Steidinger, a red tide researcher at the Florida Marine Research Institute in St. Petersburg). This single-celled organism is often referred to as an alga or phytoplankton (fig. 9.6). Like other dinoflagellates, it is photosynthetic—able to manufacture its own food from sunlight, carbon dioxide, and dissolved nutrients, most notably nitrogen. Along the Gulf coast of Florida, *K. brevis* is always present at low concentrations several miles offshore.[22] Under certain environmental conditions the population reproduces in such great numbers that the water appears changed in color, producing a "red tide." At such times a single liter of seawater containing over 100,000 *K. brevis* organisms is sufficient to kill fish.[23] In recent years, counts have been reported in excess of a million organisms per liter.[24]

The organism stays near the surface in the daytime, then disperses to varying depths at night. If a large surface mat of *K. brevis* is blown closer to shore by the wind, marine life and birds suffer because these dinoflagellates produce toxins. About 20 out of 1,000 species of marine dinoflagellates produce toxins, and up to nine different toxins are contained within each cell of *K. brevis*.[25] When wind action or wave turbulence breaks the cells apart, toxic particles are liberated in sea spray and may be carried ashore by the wind, producing respiratory irritation or distress in humans present on beaches. Although red tide blooms represent an intermittent, naturally occurring process that has been observed since the 1500s, some scientists suspect that in recent years nutrients supplied by coastal pollution have promoted the formation of certain red tide blooms, possibly increasing their frequency and duration.[26]

In Florida, red tide blooms are most frequent along the Gulf coast from Clearwater to Sanibel. They are thought to develop in a process that begins with the Yucatan Current. This current travels northward between Mexico's Yucatan Peninsula and Cuba and then enters the Gulf of Mexico where it becomes the Loop Current when it circulates clockwise off the west coast of

Figure 9.6. Responsible for causing red tide in Florida, this single cell organism (*Karenia brevis*) is a type of phytoplankton called a dinoflagellate. (Drawing by Joe Cheatwood courtesy of Fish and Wildlife Research Institute.)

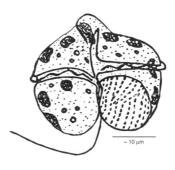

~ 10 μm

Florida (fig. 9.7). As the Loop Current encounters the coastal shelf many miles offshore, it induces a front of upwelling water. Such fronts represent dynamic regions of nutrient flow and light conditions that can favor blooms.[27] Most red tide blooms occur 20–75 km offshore in late summer or early fall.

Researchers now suspect that one critical factor driving a bloom may be iron-rich dust from Saharan Africa that arrives in the summer months on seasonal winds.[28] If this is coupled with adequate rainfall, the iron becomes available to a nitrogen-fixing phytoplankton called *Trichodesmium erythraeum*, which then excretes nitrogen in a form available to *K. brevis*. After two to eight weeks, the concentration of *K. brevis* can increase from 100 to 1,000 times normal levels. Wind and wave action can then bring the organisms to the nearshore environment, causing fish kills, sick and dying manatees, and neurotoxic shellfish poisoning in people that ingest exposed mollusks.[29] Because of the nitrogen connection, it has often been suspected that pollution caused by humans plays a role in red tide outbreaks. However, red tides have been observed since 1542; and because the frequency of red tide blooms has not varied since the 1950s, it may be that human nitrogen sources are not presently a major factor driving offshore blooms.[30] Incidentally, the same Saharan dust that appears to promote red tide blooms also contains chemical contaminants and microorganisms that are suspected to adversely affect the health of coral reefs and can ultimately affect the health of the environment overall.[31]

Was the episodic death of 150 manatees in 1996 caused by red tide, or could it have been merely coincidental? In order to address this question, an important study of the manatees affected in the 1996 epizootic was made by veterinary pathologist Greg Bossart of the Harbor Branch Oceanographic Institute along with his colleagues.[32] They examined postmortem tissues from some of the manatees that died during that episode and compared them with tissues from postmortem Atlantic coast manatees not exposed to red tide. The animals exposed to red tide consistently exhibited hemorrhagic lesions and congestion throughout the respiratory tract, liver, kidney, and brain, along with iron deposition in many organ systems. Using an antibody to one of the red tide toxins—developed by Dan Baden, then at the Rosenstiel School of Marine and Atmospheric Science at the University of Miami—they found that the toxin was present in lymphocyte cells of the immune system, which were present in great numbers in the affected tissues. Red tide toxin was not present in tissues from Atlantic coast animals or in a Gulf coast animal that died from boat-related injuries and was not exposed to red tide. These findings demonstrated that a significant amount of red tide toxin was present in the tissues of the exposed animals and suggested that it was the cause of the lesions observed on and the subsequent deaths of these animals.

The means by which dinoflagellate toxins produce illness or death are incompletely understood. Two neurotoxins produced by *K. brevis* probably produce many of the symptoms commonly reported. One acts on the sodium channels of neurons, and the other is a hemolytic toxin that destroys blood cells.[33] Neurological dysfunction was observed in four manatees that were exposed to red tide in 1996 but were rescued, given supportive care, and released after eventual recovery. These animals exhibited muscle fasciculations, lack of coordination, and an inability to maintain body orientation. They had to be fitted with floats to maintain their normal body position in the water or held in tanks containing very little water to prevent their drowning. The iron depo-

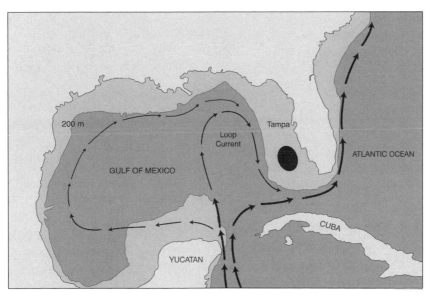

Figure 9.7. Currents in the Gulf of Mexico facilitate development of widespread red tide blooms, often off the west coast of Florida in the area indicated by dark shading. (From Tester and Steidinger 1997: 1040; map courtesy of American Society of Limnology and Oceanography.)

sition observed in affected manatees probably resulted from destruction of red blood cells. The magnitude of deposition observed suggested that this had been going on for some time, which implied that red tide exposure did not cause death immediately. Bossart and his colleagues hypothesized that toxin entered the system through inhalation and then was taken up by macrophage cells whose job involves clearing foreign substances from the body. But through its action on specific enzymes, the toxin may trigger the death of the macrophages, resulting in a cascade of toxin release followed by uptake by other cells and their subsequent death. In addition, the toxin may trigger a chain of inflammatory events that result in toxic shock and death.

Red tide toxicity may occur by ingestion of toxin as well as by inhalation. Typically, this occurs in people who eat contaminated shellfish that have acquired the toxin through filter feeding.[34] Toxicity by ingestion may have been the cause of the manatee epizootic of 1982.[35] In that case, 39 dead manatees were found in and around the mouth of the Caloosahatchee River near Fort Myers over a 10-week period from February to April. Both sexes and all sizes of animals were affected. During the same period, manatees in this region were observed to be disoriented (as evidenced by swimming in circles) or exhibited listlessness, labored breathing, or inability to maintain a horizontal position in the water. Two were rescued and brought to SeaWorld Orlando where they recovered. Two deaths were attributed to boat strikes, but the animals may have been affected by red tide intoxication. High numbers of dead or sick cormorants and fish were also noted in this area during the same period. The same general region experienced a red tide bloom of *K. brevis* from January to March. The dead manatees exhibited no consistent lesions of the respiratory tract or other systems, but one third of the brains examined did show hemorrhagic lesions associated with cerebral blood vessels. In most of the dead manatees the digestive tract contained a large number (thousands) of ascidians or filter-feeding tunicates. The manatees had ingested them incidentally while feeding on underwater plants. Among other factors, the temperature had been warm, so the cause of the deaths was unlikely to have been cold stress. Salinity at the mouth of the Caloosahatchee River had been higher than normal due to a prolonged drought and subsequent lack of freshwater discharge from an upstream dam connected to Lake Okeechobee.

After ruling out other potential causes of death including cold stress, heavy metal poisoning, and inhalation of red tide toxins, O'Shea and colleagues proposed that the manatees may have died by ingesting red tide toxin. But if so, how did this occur? Like other dinoflagellates, *K. brevis* changes its position in the water column, so that it is more likely to be found on the surface during the day and underwater at night.[36] Thus, manatees feeding on underwater grasses and breathing at the surface could have incidentally ingested some quantity of *K. brevis* as well. In addition, ascidians, which concentrate red tide toxins, could have been a more potent means by which manatees were exposed after ingesting these tunicates along with vegetation. Increased salinity may have also played a role as *K. brevis* cannot survive in freshwater. This would have promoted the organism's intrusion into the Caloosahatchee River, where most of the feeding by manatees on grass beds occurred. Currently, the health of aquatic plants is being used to establish the tolerable range of freshwater inflow to the Caloosahatchee estuary.[37] The salt-tolerant, freshwater species *Vallisneria americana*, which occurs at the head of the estuary, is an indicator of the minimum flow required, while the estuarine species *Halodule wrightii*, present at the estuary mouth, is an indicator of the maximum flow tolerated.

The consequences of red tide outbreaks for manatees are potentially severe. A catastrophic loss of up to 150 individuals out of a total population of 3,000–4,000 is far from trivial, particularly when it represents a significant proportion of a local subpopulation. Although isolated losses of this magnitude probably do not have a long-term effect on the population as a whole, several such catastrophes occurring in near succession could. Large winter aggregations would make Florida manatees especially susceptible to such events. To the extent that red tides are promoted by nutrients associated with human-related pollution, it is reasonable to conclude that in the near term we may witness an even greater increase in manatee mortality due to red tide.

Abrupt losses of large numbers of individuals from an already endangered population represent not only a diminution of total numbers, but a potential loss of genetic diversity as well. Thus, in considering what number of Florida manatees represents a robust population, it is important to consider a safety factor so that losses due to episodic events like red tide are not devastating to the population. Fortunately, some steps can be taken by humans to lessen the impact of red tide on manatees. These include reducing water-borne pollution, ensuring adequate freshwater discharges to promote salinity reduction when red tide is present, and rescuing and treating manatees exhibiting signs of red tide toxicity.

The responses of manatee biologists, sanctuary managers, veterinarians, and others to the red tide epizootics of 1982 and 1996 exemplify the best in people. Not only because of their desire to protect the health and welfare of Florida manatees, but also because of their determination to gain a deeper understanding of the dynamics that drive red tides. This in turn bears directly on the welfare of humans affected by respiratory distress or shellfish poisoning due to red tide outbreaks as well as on economic impacts on the tourism industry. The fates of manatees and people in Florida are distinctly intertwined.

Release

Before a manatee is selected for return to the wild it must first be deemed medically fit by a facility veterinarian. It is then classified by factors that rank the amount of potential risk the individual manatee faces for success. These factors include age, sex, age at rescue, length of time in captivity, and general circumstances related to the original rescue. Generally, animals held in captivity for longer periods of time or with little or no prior wild experience are considered more "at risk" than animals held for short periods with much free-ranging wild experience. Manatees unfamiliar with a natural environment may not know where to go to feed and may not move to warm-water sites during colder weather. These are matters of real concern for manatee rehabilitators.

Once the candidate has been cleared by veterinarians for release, the facility submits the animal's name and history to the FWS management team and a release plan is established. The plan is designed around the needs and circumstances of that individual manatee. An appropriate location and time for release is identified, and a decision is made about whether or not to radio tag the animal. If radio tagging is appropriate, the manatee is fitted with a transmitter that will allow researchers to monitor its movements and activities.[38] Tagging also allows the team to locate the animal periodically in order to catch it and perform medical assessments. Tagging and postrelease monitoring of a manatee is an extremely time-consuming commitment and requires numerous resources. It is nonetheless crucial to adequately assess the manatee's acclimation to the wild. James Powell and Monica Ross of Wildlife Trust lead the field effort to monitor the manatees selected for postrelease studies. The Manatee Rehabilitation Partnership (MRP) was established in 2002 as a consortium of all interested parties (governmental, nongovernmental, scientific, and oceanographic). This group is charged with monitoring released captives and maintains committees dedicated to research, education, and fund-raising.

Three years after the first captive manatee was tagged and released by the USGS Sirenia Project in 1985, a large-scale study was begun to examine the success of rehabilitated manatees after their return to the wild. In that study a manatee named Magoo was selected and fitted with a radio tag. Magoo had been rescued in 1983 from the Banana River near the Kennedy Space Center in Brevard County. He had suffered caustic chemical burns to the face and had scar tissue around his eyes that resembled glasses (hence his namesake, the myopic cartoon character, Mr. Magoo). Manatees are curious creatures and often seek freshwater sources from culverts and hoses. It was believed that Magoo had investigated a discharge pipe that must have been releasing a caustic agent into the water. Unfortunately his face was burned, but otherwise he was in good physical condition. In preparation for release, Magoo was freeze-branded to help facilitate identification later. Today, manatees lacking scar patterns for individual identification are still freeze-branded and are fitted with PIT (passive integrated transponder) tags.[39] Used in the pet industry for identification of animals, PIT tags, about the size of a rice grain, are implanted under the skin. They allow for the positive identification of an animal or carcass, even if it is badly decomposed, when other identifying marks such as scars and freeze-brands are not discernable. An electronic PIT tag reader is routinely used to scan all carcasses that are recovered through the state's manatee salvage and necropsy program. If a PIT-tagged manatee is detected at recapture or during a necropsy examination, researchers can check the records and positively identify the individual.

After five years in captivity, Magoo was fitted with a radio tag and released in June of 1988 near his original recovery location. At first, Magoo's movements were undirected and very slow. He seemed to travel backward one tail stroke for every two forward as he explored his surroundings. At one point field trackers were not even convinced that he could see. Was it possible that Magoo had been blinded by the chemical discharge and spent five years in captivity without anyone recognizing his visual limitations? Most manatees live in turbid, dark waters and have an extraordinary ability to investigate their habitat without the aid of vision. Field trackers were convinced that Magoo was either blind or visually impaired. Despite his false starts and researchers' worries, within a few days, Magoo had begun to investigate his environment more systematically and confidently, and within a few weeks he had established a range over which we tracked and assessed him for follow-up medical care.

Years ago, captive manatees were sometimes conditioned to come to station when they heard a clicking sound generated by an underwater dive communicator. Trackers would use these devices in the field to call a manatee over for an in-water physical examination. Bonde describes Magoo's response to one such clicker. "One winter day in the Sebastian River we were tracking Magoo, who was swimming mid-channel several hundred meters from shore. I went to the end of the dock and placed the 'clicker' in the water. I snapped it a few times and Magoo immediately changed direction and swam in a bee-line directly to the shore where I rewarded him. He looked great, was healthy, and in no time at all left station and continued on his way up the river. These sound generating devices do not produce very intense amplitude in the water and their frequency is low (700–1500 Hz). To this day I am amazed by the manatee's uncanny ability to detect even the slightest of sounds in the water."

As winter approached, trackers were very concerned about whether or not Magoo would find appropriate warm water to survive the approaching cold. He was often in the vicinity of other manatees, selected appropriate habitat, and seemed keen on emulating the activities and behavior of his cohorts. But as winter approached, he was slow to depart to one of the traditional wintering sites. He did finally leave the Banana River and went to the Sebastian River where he was afforded warmer water during the rather mild winter of 1988–89. Fortunately, the strategy that he adopted was also used by several other manatees in the herd, so we were convinced that Magoo would make it in the wild. Because he has not turned up among recovered carcasses, we are confident that Magoo has made a successful adaptation.

Another successful release was a female manatee named Georgia. Rescued as an orphaned calf in 1991, she spent six years in captivity. She was considered a high-risk case because she had been rescued at such a young age and had spent nearly her entire life in captivity. A release site was selected in the St. Johns River at Blue Spring State Park. Blue Spring has a resident winter population of manatees, ample vegetation, and good habitat adjacent to the spring run. The transition there should have been easy for Georgia. She was released in April 1997 and quickly adopted the behaviors of other manatees with one exception: she liked people. As a captive she had been exposed to humans and this affected her behavior in the wild. When people visited the state park in the summer to go swimming, Georgia rushed to them in anticipation of being petted or fed. This became quite a problem, because the park rangers were required to make swimmers exit the water when a manatee swam into the run. At the first sight of human swimmers, Georgia raced into the swimming area, and all the people were asked to exit the water. By herself, Georgia would inevitably get bored and leave the area. The swimmers then jumped back into the water, only to be herded out again when Georgia shortly returned. This game of cat and mouse continued all day long to the consternation of the park visitors. Since then, husbandry experts have limited contact between humans and captive manatees in order to minimize the occurrence of such behavior in the wild.

Georgia was distracted from this behavior in May of 1998 when she gave birth to a healthy male calf, Peaches. Presented with the responsibilities of parenting, her interest in park swimmers waned, and she devoted her time to instructing her calf. One measure of a successful release program is the released animal's reproductive contribution to the wild population. Clearly, Georgia was a great success, and she continues to be productive as part of the upper St. Johns River manatee subpopulation.

Another noteworthy success on the opposite coast of Florida is a manatee named Rachel. Rachel was rescued as a baby in 1990 from the Chassahowitzka River, just south of the Crystal and Homosassa rivers. The Chassahowitzka River is not frequented by wild, experienced manatees because it is very shallow. Field observations suggest that manatees instinctually feel vulnerable in shallow water. Rachel must not have known better, for when she was released in the Homosassa River after seven years in captivity, she abruptly swam several miles south to the Chassahowitzka River. Researchers felt concerned that she would be too vulnerable in this area, so she was caught and rereleased in Crystal River. But, in only a short time, she once again returned to the Chassahowitzka River. Finally, managers gave in to her persistence and allowed her to stay where her instinctive nature had driven her. In fact, like Georgia, she has also had multiple calves in the wild since her release and continues to do well in the Chassahowitzka system.

Not all releases have been successful. The myriad threats that haunt wild manatee populations can of course victimize released manatees. Some have been hit and killed by boats, while others have been unable to locate appropriate habitat. Moose was an emaciated orphan calf weighing a mere 14 kg when he was rescued and taken to SeaWorld Orlando in 1991. There, he underwent a prolonged rehabilitation. He became a close member of the SeaWorld family and often used his flippers to pull himself out of the water at the edge of the pool in order to interact with the staff. He grew to a healthy 545 kg and was released in 1994. The staff were elated to return a healthy manatee to the wild. Unhappily, Moose was hit by a boat and killed just 18 months after release. In honor of his memory, SeaWorld named their rescue boat "Moose."

The manatee rehabilitation and release program in Florida, and those elsewhere in the world, have implemented various strategies to help facilitate the return of manatees to the wild. We have learned a great deal from their cases. An active program is designed to return manatees to the natural environment as quickly as possible in order to keep them from developing dependency on captive life. Currently, animals judged to be at high risk are deconditioned of captive behaviors prior to release.[40] Special efforts are taken to ensure that manatees are also prepared behaviorally for release. This entails offering them natural vegetation, exposing them to the salinity of the selected release site, and minimizing their interactions with humans. It is hoped that by investing this effort prior to release, we will enable the manatee to weather most of the challenges that will confront it in the wild.

On the other hand, we must be cautious in our attempts to return manatees to the wild. As documented in other species, some released manatees may threaten the integrity of the wild population by introducing diseases or threatening the group's genetic health and fitness. Moreover, considering cases like that of the released killer whale, Keiko, sometimes an animal does not have the temperament necessary to survive in the wild. This may be especially true for older, long-term captives, and we must question the humanity of subjecting vulnerable individuals to the rigors and challenges of life in the wild. In an ideal case, we would not be able to distinguish a released manatee from a wild one. When that actually occurs, the release is a success!

10 The Future

People who work closely with manatees and study manatee biology have a passion for their work: manatees are such fascinating creatures, we often find ourselves captivated by their mystique. When we started studying manatees more than a quarter century ago, we were overwhelmed by the chore of compiling information on the species. Because very little information existed then, our jobs were extremely demanding and sometimes daunting. Today there is still much to learn about the animals, and we meet each challenge with fresh enthusiasm. During the last few years some exciting new science has been accomplished that fuels the inner fires that keep us all going.

In Belize, under the watchful direction of James "Buddy" Powell and Nicole Auil, biologists have been using radio tags to study manatees since 1997. Their work has given us the chance to share technology and knowledge with managers and researchers in this progressive Central American country (plates 16, 17). As we walk along the sandy beaches of San Pedro or Caye Caulker, "See the Manatees" signs remind us of ones Woodie Hartman used to see hanging in the windows of Crystal River dive shops back in the early days. They make us grateful to be at a point in time where conservation efforts in Belize can be supported by tried-and-true research on manatees in Florida. The models are there, and hopefully implementation will be easy.

New technologies tested in Belize hold great promise. During a recent trip there, our research group was joined by colleagues Kyler Abernathy and Greg Marshall of National Geographic and Nicole Adimey of the U.S. Fish and Wildlife Service. Their team has modified a device called the CritterCam (plate 18). This special camera fits snugly on the back of a manatee (and other marine wildlife) and, when successfully deployed, takes digital video of what a manatee actually sees as it moves about over a six-hour period in the water. By outfitting one manatee with CritterCam, Bob Bonde got the thrill of watching manatees interact naturally with each other: "For the first time we were in the water with the manatee, but miles away and not affecting the animal's behavior!" This type of remote monitoring offers lots of possibilities for observing manatee behavior and foraging strategies. Scientists hope to one day couple CritterCam with GPS tags for more detailed information about location. We also hope to gain better information on dive parameters from innovative data collection devices called TDRs or D-tags.

A few years ago, we were fortunate to welcome four pioneering scientists to our research team: Randy Wells and Doug and Stephanie Nowacek of Mote Marine Laboratory and Mark Johnson of Woods Hole Oceanographic Institute. They brought with them a new tag called the D-tag. The D-tag records movement information—including travel direction, speed, and depth—while making audio recordings. Successfully deployed, this unit literally put us in the water with the outfitted manatee. As soon as we recovered the tag, we eagerly downloaded its information and, via computer, heard and saw things that would have been difficult, if not impossible, to observe live. We listened to recordings of the manatee's breathing intervals during midnight sleep, watched changes in its orientation and depth as it surfaced to breathe, and witnessed changes in its behavioral rhythms apparently caused by another animal's approach. Data of this kind will help us monitor the reactions of manatees to oncoming boats. We hope one day to better understand their avoidance behaviors and the different strategies they use to cope in a world rife with boats and threats of deadly collision. Such detailed information will assist managers in implementing boat operation regulations and guidelines around areas where manatee/watercraft interactions are greatest.

Sophisticated technologies are also being developed to better understand manatee physiology. Graham Worthy, a colleague at the University of Central Florida, employs stable isotopes to gain insights into manatee predilections. Through Worthy's work, we can interpret general patterns in individual manatees' habitat use and feeding preferences by examining only small pieces of sloughed skin. In the next couple of decades, we will reap benefits from genetic and immunologic studies, which will expand and enrich our understanding of manatee diseases and their impacts. We will learn a great deal more about manatee reproduction and other life history parameters, which will give population modelers better data to discern trends in the Florida manatee population. These are only glimpses into the future of our research.

Through new technologies and data, we will travel further than ever before into the precariously balanced and beautiful world of manatees.

Back in Florida

Manatees in Florida face two major challenges in the future: ever-increasing boat traffic and reduction of winter habitat due to projected power plant losses.[1] The latter is a serious concern, and because of it the long-term survival of manatees in much of Florida is uncertain. In order to survive, manatees will have to develop new strategies for coping with a rapidly changing environment. While manatees will be required to utilize natural warm-water sites to a greater extent, we will have to guarantee that those habitats are available and that springs maintain adequate flow rates. We must therefore be proactive about preserving and enhancing natural areas before they fall to development. The continuation of healthy manatee populations depends upon our doing just that.

To get a sense of what it's like to endure as a sea cow in Florida waters, follow a year in the life of a typical manatee in James Powell's recent book *Manatees: Natural History and Conservation.*[2] In a habitat fraught with dangers, manatees are rather unreasonably forced to accommodate human interests. If we want manatees to live alongside us, we must accommodate their interests, too: mainly by complying with laws that promote manatee-friendly waters. It may take a bit longer to reach a favorite fishing spot, but how big a sacrifice, really, is a brief delay? We may be kept out of manatee sanctuaries or required to offset the impacts of a dock and the boats that use them. But what represent minor inconveniences and costs to us may be major boons to the manatee. People who need to place a price on natural heritage might consider manatees' significant contribution to Florida's economy. Once prized as food, manatees today are prized as subjects for the camera. Through them, Florida reaps the substantial benefits of ecotourism. Perhaps a mutually advantageous relationship between humans and manatees is possible after all.

As John Reynolds of Mote Marine Laboratory has stated so eloquently, successful long-term conservation efforts must recognize and incorporate a diversity of perspectives and values in order to arrive at balanced public policy via compromise.[3] Good conservation should enhance the lives of humans as well as other species and should provide the greatest good for the greatest number of people in a sustainable fashion. A cooperative approach is fundamental both to establishing links between policy makers and people and to driving management and recovery efforts for any species. Couple this with sound biological science, and an educated decision-making process has a chance to endure. This approach will almost certainly become important in other countries where manatee conservation may become the cornerstone of wildlife protection.[4]

In many respects, the challenges we face with regard to manatees in Florida are intimately linked to global issues of overpopulation, poverty, urban development, climate change, and environmental degradation. As Joel Cohen points out in *How Many People Can the Earth Support?*, the quality of our environment very much depends on our wisdom and the quality of the lives we choose to live now.[5] Similar considerations apply to manatees in Florida, where our decisions will largely determine their future as well as our own. Under natural conditions, devoid of human noise and machines, the availability of warm-water wintering sites is probably the main limiting factor for manatees because they have abundant food resources,[6] some of which have been restored.[7] Nobody knows how many manatees could be accommodated in Florida in the absence of boats, but it is certainly greater than the present number. Where watercraft are concerned, the fact that manatees are endangered is less relevant than the issue of how we treat a unique mammalian life-form that shares its aquatic world with us. As reasoning creatures, perhaps we should bear the burden of generosity.

At the time of this writing, turmoil surrounds Floridians' divergent opinions about their relationship to manatees. Some favor a total ban on recreational boating in manatee-frequented areas. Others defend their right to recreate whenever and however they please. This conflict is symptomatic of other struggles that arise from overpopulation and overdevelopment in Florida and has to do with such fundamental issues as water quality and land use. In counties with significant manatee populations, county commission meetings often include heated discussion about boats and manatees. Marinas cannot be built in certain areas until a manatee protection plan has been implemented. In order to ease restrictions that inconvenience them, some people want to remove the manatee's federally sanctioned endangered status. (Of course, protection under the Marine Mammal Protection Act would still apply.) Claims that manatees have "recovered" are often heard together with claims that slow speed zones "don't prevent manatee deaths anyway."[8]

Not long ago in Brevard County, boaters congregated on the Merritt Island Barge Canal to protest slow speed zones that they viewed as overly restrictive. They complained that speed limits lower the value of waterfront homes, inhibit water sports, and hurt the economies of communities that depend on boating. Steven Webster of Citizens for Florida's Waterways, the boater-advocacy group that organized the event, warned "We feel it's possible to protect manatees without destroying dreams. Until we do, there won't be peace on the water."[9] The gulf that separates people is perhaps best embodied by Brevard County commissioner Ron Pritchard when he claims, "These radical environmentalist groups are simply in it for themselves, not the species and not for the people."[10]

Public opinion polls regularly indicate that a majority of Florida citizens support the protection of manatees through the establishment of slow speed zones. A recent survey of 77 University of Florida students randomly chosen from a wide range of disciplines revealed that 74 percent had seen a manatee. When asked to estimate the number of annual manatee fatalities in Florida, most replied correctly that it was over 100. The students estimated annual fatalities caused by boats at 50 to 75. That answer was correct for 2003 during which 73 manatees were slain by boats, but in recent years this number has been closer to 100. When asked their opinion about the single most important action that should be taken to protect Florida manatees, many students recommended better enforcement of boating laws and fines for speeding boaters; others advocated enhanced educational efforts and creation of protected sanctuaries.

As the survey responses of the students suggest, efforts to keep boats and manatees from colliding have historically centered on the establishment of slow speed zones. As these zones have multiplied, boaters have understandably become confused. On one 20-mile stretch of the Caloosahatchee River near Fort Myers, over 130 federal signs join a host of state and county signs related to manatees. Boaters call the river's navigation an "exhausting exercise."[11] Many signs are difficult to read, and signs in close proximity sometimes post contradictory information. Under such conditions, it isn't difficult to see why many boaters throw up their hands in frustration and just do their own thing. Fortunately, the situation is improving. Law enforcement efforts have expanded in the area, signage is clearer, and consequently, there is greater compliance.

Are further compromises to be had in this standoff? One solution may be the development of technologies to reduce the likelihood of boat-on-manatee collisions. Such technologies might be substituted for the blanket slow speed zones that impinge upon boaters whether manatees are present or not. Deke Beusse and Chris Niezrecki of the University of Florida are leading the development of a unique system designed to alert boaters to the presence of manatees.[12] An array of underwater hydrophones is deployed on posts in an area known to be frequented by manatees (fig. 10.1). If one of the hydrophones detects manatee vocalizations, a light on the above-water end of the pole lights up, cautioning boaters in the area to slow down. While manatees vocalize seldom under normal conditions and the sounds they produce aren't loud, they *do* frequently respond to recorded manatee calls by vocalizing. Perhaps the Beusse-Niezrecki system could periodically broadcast manatee calls in order to elicit response vocalizations by any manatees nearby. On the other hand, we don't yet know how manatees will interpret broadcast calls. Besides returning a vocalization, they might also approach the call source, inadvertently putting themselves in harm's way. Field testing in a controlled environment will be necessary to determine the feasibility of implementing this system.

A slightly different approach suggested by Ed Gerstein involves attaching an acoustic alerting device to the bow of all boats traveling in manatee habitat. By designing the output signal so that it is optimized for manatee detection and localization, the number of collisions could be minimized. In this case, there is some concern that manatees will become habituated to the sound and ignore it over time. Humans recognize car horns as signals of potential danger. If these horns blasted continuously, we would come to block them out as irritating noise. Because their world has grown increasingly noisy, manatees may be blocking noise already. As with the vocalization detection system, field testing will be used to assess the practicability of the acoustic warning device.

Technological approaches certainly hold promise, but they still rely on the boater compliance that has already proven problematic where slow speed

Figure 10.1. A warning system, based on listening for manatee vocalizations, is being tested by scientists at the University of Florida to alert boaters to the presence of manatees. (Cartoon by Michael Meyer and Gabe Trinity.)

zones are concerned.[13] Manatees have evolved over millions of years to be able to detect and localize biologically significant sounds in their natural environment. Boats are a very recent addition to that environment.

It may be that improved technologies of the soul are our best hope. Responsibility has always been the other side of freedom. Rather than erring by satisfying our desires, why not act conservatively to protect natural wonders that have taken millions of years to evolve? We are on this earth but briefly, and we owe it to our descendants to leave them as rich a world as possible. Every day, hardworking people make sacrifices so that their children can have an easier time of it. Perhaps we can sacrifice some of our old patterns, cultivating new forms of excitement and fulfillment that do not degrade pristine habitat—other animals' living quarters. As Henry Beston wrote many years ago:

> We need another and a wiser and perhaps a more mystical concept of animals. Remote from universal nature, and living by complicated artifice, man in civilization surveys the creature through the glass of his knowledge and sees thereby a feather magnified and the whole image in distortion. We patronize them for their incompleteness, for their tragic fate of having taken form so far

below ourselves. And therein we err, and greatly err. For the animal shall not be measured by man. In a world older and more complete than ours they move finished and complete, gifted with extensions of the senses we have lost or never attained, living by voices we shall never hear. They are not brethren, they are not underlings; they are other nations, caught with ourselves in the net of life and time, fellow prisoners of the splendor and travail of the earth.[14]

Years ago, Woodie Hartman used a bucket with a glass bottom to look through the water's mirrored surface and observe the manatees (plate 19). Today we look toward a future that offers challenges, but also the hope that we may live in harmony with manatees in Florida.

Notes

Chapter 1. Manatees in Florida

1. O'Shea 1988; Reynolds and Odell 1991.
2. Garcia-Rodriguez et al. 1998.
3. O'Shea 1988.
4. Reynolds and Odell 1991.
5. O'Shea 1988.
6. Ibid.
7. Ibid.
8. Ibid.
9. Moore 1951.
10. Gerstein 1994.
11. Behrendt 1993.

Chapter 2. Origins

1. Domning 2001a.
2. Domning 1994.
3. Ibid.
4. Domning 2001b.
5. Ibid.
6. Domning and Gingerich 1994.
7. Webb 1995.
8. Domning 1982.
9. Garcia-Rodriguez et al. 1998.
10. Reep et al. 2001, 2002.
11. Murie 1872, 1880.
12. Reep et al. 1998.
13. Marshall et al. 1998a, 2000, 2003.
14. Marshall et al. 1998b.

15. Marshall et al. 1998a.
16. Marsh et al. 1999.
17. Peterson and Bartholomew 1967.
18. Kier and Smith 1985; Marshall et al. 1998b.

Chapter 3. The Manatee Lifestyle

1. Eisenberg 1981.
2. Beck and Forrester 1988.
3. Worthy 2001; Bossart et al. 2003.
4. Hartman 1979; Best 1981; Packard 1981; Bengtson 1983; Packard 1984; Etheridge et al. 1985; Ledder 1986; Hurst and Beck 1988; Provancha and Hall 1991.
5. Thayer et al. 1984.
6. Etheridge et al. 1985.
7. Walsh and Grow 1973; Dawes and Lawrence 1980; Vicente et al. 1980.
8. Packard 1984.
9. Thayer et al. 1984; Lefebvre et al. 2000.
10. Dawes and Lawrence 1983.
11. Thayer et al. 1984.
12. Hartman 1979; Packard 1984; Lefebvre et al. 2000.
13. Reynolds and Rommel 1996.
14. Beck and Forrester 1988; Forrester 1992.
15. Beck and Barros 1991.

16. Kenworthy and Haunert 1991.
17. Ibid.
18. Langtimm and Beck 2003.
19. Mangel and Tier 1994.
20. Langer 1988; Reynolds and Rommel 1996.
21. Snipes 1984; Burn 1986; Burn and Odell 1987; Reynolds and Rommel 1996.
22. Lomolino and Ewel 1984.
23. Larkin 2000.
24. Warner 1981.
25. Lomolino and Ewel 1984; Burn 1986; Reynolds and Rommel 1996.
26. Domning and Hayek 1984.
27. Domning 1982.
28. Marsh et al. 1999.
29. Scholander and Irving 1941; Gallivan and Best 1980; Irvine 1983.
30. McNab 2002.
31. Gallivan et al.1983; Irvine 1983; Bossart et al. 2003.
32. Costa and Williams 1999.
33. Worthy 2001.
34. Ortiz et al. 2000.
35. Ibid.
36. Ortiz et al. 1998, 1999.
37. Ibid.
38. Hill and Reynolds 1989; Maluf 1989.
39. Worthy 2001.
40. Domning and de Buffrenil 1991.
41. Pabst et al. 1999.
42. Domning and de Buffrenil 1991.
43. Hartman 1979.
44. Kipps et al. 2002.
45. Bonde et al. 1983; Domning and de Buffrenil 1991.
46. Bonde et al. 1983; Rommel and Reynolds 2000.
47. Rommel and Reynolds 2000; Dearolf et al. 2001.
48. Rommel and Reynolds 2000.
49. Ibid.

Chapter 4. Endangered!

1. Hartman 1971, 1979.
2. Steller 1751.
3. Stejneger 1883; Stejneger 1887.
4. Reynolds and Odell 1991.
5. Allen 1910; O'Donnell 1981; Grabowski 1994.
6. Domning 1982.
7. Lucas 1916.
8. U.S. Fish and Wildlife Service 2001.
9. Reynolds and Wells 2003.
10. U.S. Fish and Wildlife Service 2001.
11. Marmontel et al. 1997; Runge 2003.

Chapter 5. How Many Are There?

1. Ackerman et al. 1995.
2. Irvine and Campbell 1978.
3. Brownell and Ralls 1981.
4. Reynolds and Wilcox 1994.
5. Ackerman et al. 1995.
6. Craig et al. 1997; Craig and Reynolds 2004.
7. Florida Fish and Wildlife Conservation Commission, press release 2001.
8. Packard et al. 1985; Marsh and Sinclair 1989.
9. Miller et al. 1998; Lefebvre et al. 1995.
10. Packard et al. 1986; Lefebvre and Kochman 1991; Lefebvre et al. 1995.
11. O'Shea et al. 2001.
12. Thompson et al. 1998.
13. Bossart et al. 1998.
14. O'Shea et al. 1995; Langtimm et al. 1998; Langtimm et al. 2004.

15. Hartman 1979.
16. O'Shea et al. 1995; U.S. Fish and Wildlife Service 2001.
17. Hartman 1974, 1979.
18. Ibid.
19. Beck and Reid 1995.
20. Langtimm et al. 1998.
21. Eberhardt and O'Shea 1995; Runge 2003; Runge et al. 2004.
22. Eberhardt and O'Shea 1995; Marmontel et al. 1997.
23. Marmontel et al. 1997.
24. Eberhardt and O'Shea 1995.
25. Runge et al. 2004.
26. U.S. Fish and Wildlife Service 2001.
27. O'Shea et al. 1995; Marmontel et al. 1997.
28. Reynolds 1981; Odell et al. 1995; Rathbun et al. 1995.
29. Reynolds 1981; Odell et al. 1995; Reid et al. 1995.
30. Marmontel 1995; Larkin 2000.
31. Rathbun et al. 1995; Odell et al. 1995; Larkin 2000.
32. Bengtson 1981; Gomendio et al. 1998; Reynolds et al. 2004.
33. Reynolds et al. 2004.
34. Wells et al. 1999.
35. Alcock 1983.
36. Rathbun et al. 1995.
37. Tyack and Whitehead 1982; O'Shea et al. 1985; Hernandez et al. 1995; O'Shea and Hartley 1995; Odell et al. 1995; Rathbun et al. 1995; Reid et al. 1995.
38. Rommel et al. 2001.
39. Bonde et al. 1983; O'Shea et al. 1985; S. D. Wright et al. 1995.
40. Bonde et al. 1983.
41. Bonde et al. 1983; O'Shea et al. 1985; Ackerman et al. 1995.
42. Forrester et al. 1975; Odell and Reynolds 1979; O'Shea et al. 1984, 1985; Beck and Barros 1991.
43. Marmontel et al. 1996.
44. Beck et al. 1982; Bonde et al. 1983; Ackerman et al. 1995; S. D. Wright et al. 1995.
45. Domning and de Buffrenil 1991.
46. Fawcett 1942; de Buffrenil and Schoevaert 1989; Domning and de Buffrenil 1991.
47. Wainwright et al. 1982.
48. Domning and de Buffrenil 1991.
49. Yan et al. 2005.

Chapter 6. Where Do They Go?

1. U.S. Geological Survey (National Biological Survey), Sirenia Project 1995.
2. Baugh et al. 1989.
3. Irvine and Scott 1984.
4. Bengtson 1981.
5. Rathbun et al. 1987; Reid and O'Shea 1989.
6. Reid et al. 1995; Deutsch et al. 2003.
7. Lander et al. 2001; Deutsch et al. 1998.
8. Shane 1983; Irvine 1983.
9. Hartman 1974.
10. Bell 2000.
11. Moore 1951.
12. Deutsch et al. 2003.
13. Reid et al. 1995.
14. Weigle et al. 2001; Deutsch et al. 2003.
15. Buergelt and Bonde 1983.
16. Deutsch et al. 2003.
17. Bengtson 1981.
18. Koelsch 2001.
19. Reid et al. 1995.

20. Bengtson 1981.
21. Deutsch et al. 1998, 2003.
22. Weigle et al. 2001.
23. Hartman 1979.
24. I. E. Wright et al. 2002.
25. Weigle et al. 2001.
26. I. E. Wright et al. 2002.
27. Reid et al. 1995.
28. Garcia-Rodriguez 2000.
29. Garcia-Rodriguez et al. 1998.
30. Garcia-Rodriguez et al. 2000.

Chapter 7. Brains

1. O'Shea and Reep 1990.
2. Edinger 1933, 1939; O'Shea and Reep 1990; Gingerich et al. 1994.
3. Eisenberg and Wilson 1978.
4. van Dongen 1998.
5. O'Shea and Reep 1990.
6. Ibid.
7. Marino 1998.
8. Reep and O'Shea 1990.
9. Elliot Smith 1902; Edinger 1933, 1939; Friant 1954.
10. Welker 1990.
11. Elliot Smith 1902, 344.
12. Finlay and Darlington 1995.
13. Reep et al. 1989; Marshall and Reep 1995.
14. Dexler 1912.
15. Reep et al. 1989; Loerzel and Reep 1991; Marshall and Reep 1995.

Chapter 8. Perception and Behavior

1. Ling 1977.
2. Layne and Caldwell 1964.
3. Carvell and Simons 1990; Brecht et al. 1997.

4. Peterson and Bartholomew 1967; Miller 1975.
5. Kastelein and Van Gaalen 1988; Dehnhardt and Kaminski 1995; Dehnhardt and Ducker 1996; Dehnhardt et al. 2001.
6. Rice et al. 1986, 1997.
7. Dykes 1975; Gottschaldt et al. 1973.
8. Rice 1995.
9. Burrows 1996.
10. Marshall et al. 1998a; Reep et al. 1998.
11. Reep et al. 2001.
12. Reep et al. 1989; Marshall and Reep 1995.
13. Kastelein and Van Gaalen 1988.
14. Fay 1982; Marshall 1997.
15. Marshall et al. 1998a.
16. Bachteler and Dehnhardt 1999.
17. Dehnhardt and Ducker 1996.
18. Dehnhardt et al. 1997.
19. Dehnhardt and Kaminski 1995.
20. Lamb 1983.
21. Dosch 1915.
22. Reep et al. 1998.
23. Reep et al. 2002.
24. Best 1981; Bengtson 1983; Etheridge et al. 1985; O'Shea and Reep 1990.
25. Hartman 1979; Reynolds 1979.
26. Gerstein et al. 1999.
27. Dijkgraaf 1963.
28. Montgomery et al. 1997.
29. Hassan 1989.
30. Dehnhardt et al. 2001.
31. Bryden et al. 1978; Kamiya and Yamasaki 1981.
32. Hartman 1979.
33. Supin et al. 2001.
34. Ibid.
35. Bauer et al. 2003.
36. Ibid.

37. Mass et al. 1997.
38. Harper et al. 2005.
39. J. L. Cohen et al. 1982
40. Griebel and Schmid 1996.
41. Ibid.
42. Griebel and Schmid 1997.
43. Hartman 1979.
44. Gerstein et al. 1999; Gerstein 2002.
45. Ketten et al. 1992; Wartzok and Ketten 1999.
46. Ketten et al. 1992.
47. Klishin et al. 1990.
48. Bullock et al. 1982.
49. Gerstein 2002.
50. Nowacek et al. 2004.
51. Hartman 1979.
52. Nowacek et al. 2003.
53. Sousa-Lima et al. 2002.
54. Ibid.
55. O'Shea, T.J. and J. Hermanson, personal conversations, May 2004.
56. Mackay-Sim et al. 1985.
57. Switzer et al. 1980.
58. Yamasaki et al. 1980; Levin and Pfeiffer 2002.

Chapter 9. Rehabilitation and Release

1. Murie 1880; True 1884.
2. Dimmock 1908, 1909.
3. O'Shea 1992.
4. Phillips 1964; Zeiller 1992.
5. Beck et al. 1982; S. D. Wright et al. 1995.
6. Moore 1956; Beck and Reid 1995.
7. Beck et al. 1982; S. D. Wright et al. 1995.
8. Bossart et al. 2003.
9. Walsh and Bossart 1999; Bossart 2001.
10. U.S. Fish and Wildlife Service, 2001.
11. Walsh and Bossart 1999; Bossart 2001; Walsh and Gaynor, 2001.
12. Bailey et al. 1998.
13. Bossart 2001.
14. Walsh and Bossart 1999.
15. Bailey et al. 1998.
16. Beck and Lefebvre 1995.
17. Bossart 2001; Bossart et al. 2002, 2003.
18. Worthy 2001.
19. Bossart et al. 2002.
20. U.S. Marine Mammal Commission 1996.
21. O'Shea et al. 1991.
22. Steidinger and Haddad 1981.
23. Tester and Steidinger 1997.
24. See http://research.myfwc.com.
25. Steidinger and Baden 1984.
26. Anderson 1994.
27. Tester and Steidinger 1997.
28. Lenes et al. 2001; Walsh and Steidinger 2001.
29. Pierce et al. 1990.
30. Walsh and Steidinger 2001.
31. Garrison et al. 2003.
32. Bossart et al. 1998.
33. Pierce 1986; Anderson 1994.
34. Steidinger and Baden 1984.
35. O'Shea et al. 1991.
36. Tester and Steidinger 1997.
37. Doering et al. 2002.
38. Deutsch et al. 1998.
39. I. E. Wright et al. 1998.
40. Colbert et al. 2001.

Chapter 10. The Future

1. O'Shea 1994; O'Shea et al. 2001.
2. Powell 2002.
3. Glaser and Reynolds 2003.

4. Lefebvre et al. 2001.
5. J. E. Cohen 1995.
6. Runge 2003.
7. Johansson and Greening 2000.
8. Associated Press 2003.
9. Ibid.

10. Ibid.
11. Clayton 2004.
12. Niezrecki et al. 2003.
13. Aipanjiguly et al. 2003; Futerfas 2003; Gorzelany 2004.
14. Beston 1928.

Bibliography

Ackerman, B. B., S. D. Wright, R. K. Bonde, D. K. Odell, and D. J. Banowetz. 1995. "Trends and patterns in mortality of manatees in Florida, 1974–1991." In *Population Biology of the Florida Manatee*, edited by T. J. O'Shea, B. B. Ackerman, and H. F. Percival, 223–58.

Aipanjiguly, S., S. K. Jacobson, and R. Flamm. 2003. "Conserving manatees: knowledge, attitudes, and intentions of boaters in Tampa Bay, Florida." *Conservation Biology* 17, no. 4: 1098–105.

Alcock, J. 1983. "Male mating systems." In *The Evolution of Insect Mating Systems*, edited by R. Thornhill and J. Alcock, 230–68. Cambridge: Harvard University Press.

Allen, J. A. 1910. "Additional mammals from Nicaragua." *Bulletin of the American Museum of Natural History* 28: 87–115.

Anderson, D. M. 1994. "Red Tides." *Scientific American* 271: 62–68.

Associated Press. 2003. "Hundreds of boaters protest manatee slow-speed zone." *Florida Times-Union*, May 27.

Bachteler, D., and G. Dehnhardt. 1999. "Active touch performance in the Antillean manatee: evidence for a functional differentiation of facial tactile hairs." *Zoology* 102, no. 1: 61–69.

Bailey, J. E., M. T. Walsh, A. I. Webb, T. W. Campbell, S. Dover, and L. Pablo. 1998. "Anesthesia of the Florida manatee (*Trichechus manatus*)." In *Proceedings of the 23rd Annual Meeting of the American College of Veterinary Anesthesiologists*, Orlando Fla., 21.

Bauer, G. B., D. E. Colbert, W. Fellner, J. C. Gaspard, and B. Littlefield. 2003. "Underwater visual acuity of two Florida manatees (*Trichechus manatus latirostris*)." *International Journal of Comparative Psychology* 16, nos. 2–3: 130–42.

Baugh, T. M., J. A. Valade, and B. J. Zoodsma. 1989. "Manatee use of *Spartina alterniflora* in Cumberland Sound." *Marine Mammal Science* 5, no. 1: 88–90.

Beck, C. A., R. K. Bonde, and G. B. Rathbun. 1982. "Analyses of propeller wounds on manatees in Florida." *Journal of Wildlife Management* 46, no. 2: 531–35.

Beck, C. A., and D. J. Forrester. 1988. "Helminths of the Florida manatee, *Trichechus manatus latirostris*, with a discussion and summary of the parasites of sirenians." *Journal of Parasitology* 74, no. 4: 628–37.

Beck, C. A., and N. B. Barros. 1991. "The impact of debris on the Florida manatee." *Marine Pollution Bulletin* 22, no. 10: 508–10.

Beck, C. A., and L. W. Lefebvre. 1995. "Are Female Manatees More Vulnerable to Entanglement in Crab Trap Lines?" Abstract. Eleventh Biennial Conference on the Biology of Marine Mammals, Orlando, Florida, December 14–18.

Beck, C. A., and J. P. Reid. 1995. "An automated photo-identification catalog for studies of the life history of the Florida manatee." In *Population Biology of the Florida Manatee*, edited by T. J. O'Shea, B. B. Ackerman, and H. F. Percival, 120–34.

Behrendt, B. 1993. "Boater ropes manatee, witness says." *St. Petersburg Times*. February 26.

Bell, J. T. 2000. "Characterization and analysis of artificial warm-water refugia and their use by the Florida manatee, *Trichechus manatus latirostris*, on the East Coast of Florida." Master's thesis, Duke University.

Bengtson, J. L. 1981. "Ecology of manatees (*Trichechus manatus*) in the St. Johns River, Florida." PhD diss., University of Minnesota.

———. 1983. "Estimating food consumption of free ranging manatees in Florida." *Journal of Wildlife Management* 47, no. 4: 1186–192.

Best, R. C. 1981. "Foods and feeding habits of wild and captive Sirenia." *Mammal Review* 11, no. 1: 3–29.

Beston, H. 1928. *The Outermost House:*

A Year of Life on the Great Beach of Cape Cod. Garden City, N.Y.: Doubleday, Doran, and Co. Reprint, New York: Owl Books, Henry Holt and Company, 2003.

Bonde, R. K., T. J. O'Shea, and C. A. Beck. 1983. *A Manual of Procedures for the Salvage and Necropsy of Carcasses of the West Indian Manatee (Trichechus manatus)*. National Technical Information Service, #PB83-255273. Springfield, Va.: U.S. Department of Commerce.

Bossart, G. D. 2001. "Manatees." In *Handbook of Marine Mammal Medicine*, 2nd ed., edited by L. A. Dierauf and F.M.D. Gulland, 939–60.

Bossart, G. D., D. G. Baden, R. Y. Ewing, B. Roberts, and S. D. Wright. 1998. "Brevetoxicosis in manatees (*Trichechus manatus latirostris*) from the 1996 epizootic: gross, histologic, and immunohistochemical features." *Toxicolgic Pathology* 26, no. 2: 276–82.

Bossart, G. D., R. Y. Ewing, M. Lowe, M. Sweat, S. J. Decker, C. J. Walsh, S. G. Ghim, and A. B. Jenson. 2002. "Viral papillomatosis in Florida manatees (*Trichechus manatus latirostris*)." *Experimental and Molecular Pathology* 72, no. 1: 37–48.

Bossart, G. D., R. A. Meisner, S. A. Rommel, S. G. Ghim, and A. B. Jenson. 2003. "Pathological features of the Florida manatee cold stress syndrome." *Aquatic Mammals* 29, no. 1: 9–17.

Brecht, M., B. Preilowski, and M. M. Merzenich. 1997. "Functional architecture of the mystacial vibrissae."

Behavioural Brain Research 84, nos.
1–2: 81–97.

Brownell, R. L., Jr., and K. Ralls, eds.
1981. "The West Indian manatee in
Florida." Proceedings of a workshop
held in Orlando, Florida, March 27–
29, 1978. Tallahassee, Fla.: Florida
Department of Natural Resources.

Bryden, M. M., H. Marsh, and B. W.
MacDonald. 1978. "The skin and hair
of the dugong, *Dugong dugon*."
Journal of Anatomy 126, no. 3: 637–38.

Buergelt, C. D., and R. K. Bonde. 1983.
"Toxoplasmic meningoencephalitis
in a West Indian manatee." *Journal of
the American Veterinary Medical
Association* 183, no. 11: 1294–96.

de Buffrenil, V., and D. Schoevaert.
1989. "Données quantitatives et
observations histologiques sur la
pachyostose du squelette du dugong,
Dugong dugon (Muller) (Sirenia,
Dugongidae)." *Canadian Journal of
Zoology* 67, no. 9: 2107–119.

Bullock, T. H., T. J. O'Shea, and M. C.
McClune. 1982. "Auditory evoked
potentials in the West Indian manatee (Sirenia: *Trichechus manatus*)."
Journal of Comparative Physiology
148A, no. 4: 547–54.

Burn, D. M. 1986. "The digestive strategy and efficiency of the West Indian
manatee, *Trichechus manatus*." *Comparative Biochemistry and Physiology*
85A, no. 1: 139–42.

Burn, D. M., and D. K. Odell. 1987.
"Volatile fatty acid concentrations in
the digestive tract of the West Indian
manatee, *Trichechus manatus*." *Comparative Biochemistry and Physiology*
88B, no. 1: 47–49.

Burrows, M. 1996. *The Neurobiology of
an Insect Brain*. Oxford, England:
Oxford University Press.

Carvell, G. E., and D. J. Simons. 1990.
"Biometric analyses of vibrissal
tactile discrimination in the rat."
Journal of Neuroscience 10, no. 8:
2638–48.

Chapman, H. C. 1875. "Observations on
the structure of the manatee." *Proceedings of the Academy of Natural
Sciences*, Philadelphia, 452–62.

Clayton, B. 2004. "Manatee speed
zones." *News-Press*, January 24,
national section.

Cohen, J. E. 1995. *How Many People
Can the Earth Support?* New York:
W. W. Norton.

Cohen, J. L., G. S. Tucker, and D. K.
Odell. 1982. "The photoreceptors of
the West Indian manatee." *Journal of
Morphology* 173, no. 2: 197–202.

Colbert, D. E., W. Fellner, G. B. Bauer,
C. A. Manire, and H. L. Rhinehart.
2001. "Husbandry and research
training of two Florida manatees
(*Trichechus manatus latirostris*)."
Aquatic Mammals 27, no. 1: 16–23.

Costa, D. P., and T. M. Williams. 1999.
"Marine mammal energetics." In
Biology of Marine Mammals, edited
by J. E. Reynolds, III, and S. A.
Rommel, 176–217.

Craig, B. A., M. A. Newton, R. A.
Garrott, J. E. Reynolds, III, and J. R.
Wilcox. 1997. "Analysis of aerial
survey data on the Florida manatee
using Markov chain Monte Carlo."
Biometrics 53, no. 2: 524–41.

Craig, B. A., and J. E. Reynolds, III.
2004. "Determination of manatee

population trends along the Atlantic coast of Florida using a Bayesian approach with temperature-adjusted aerial survey data." *Marine Mammal Science* 20, no. 3: 386–400.

Dawes, C. J., and J. M. Lawrence. 1980. "Seasonal changes in the proximate constituents of the seagrasses *Thalassia testudinum, Halodule wrightii,* and *Syringodium filiforme.*" *Aquatic Botany* 8, no. 4: 371–80.

———. 1983. "Proximate composition and caloric content of seagrasses." *Marine Technology Society Journal* 17, no. 2: 53–58.

Dearolf, J. L., S. A. Rommel, and J. W. Hermanson. 2001. "Compartmentalization of the Florida manatee (*Trichechus manatus latirostris*) diaphragm." *American Zoologist* 41, no. 6: 1425.

Dehnhardt, G., and A. Kaminski. 1995. "Sensitivity of the mystacial vibrissae of harbour seals (*Phoca vitulina*) for size differences of actively touched objects." *Journal of Experimental Biology* 198, no. 11: 2317–323.

Dehnhardt, G., and G. Ducker. 1996. "Tactual discrimination of size and shape by a California sea lion (*Zalophus californianus*)." *Animal Learning and Behavior* 24, no. 4: 366–74.

Dehnhardt, G., C. Friese, and N. Sachser. 1997. "Sensitivity of the trunk of Asian elephants for textural differences of actively touched objects." *Zeitschrift fur Saugetierkunde* 62, suppl. 2: 37–39.

Dehnhardt, G., B. Mauck, W. Hanke, and H. Bleckmann. 2001. "Hydrodynamic trail-following in harbor seals (*Phoca vitulina*)." *Science* 293, no. 5527: 102–104.

Deutsch, C. J., R. K. Bonde, and J. P. Reid. 1998. "Radio-tracking manatees from land and space: Tag design, implementation, and lessons learned from long-term study." *Marine Technology Society Journal* 32, no. 1: 18–29.

Deutsch, C. J., J. P. Reid, R. K. Bonde, D. E. Easton, H. I. Kochman, and T. J. O'Shea. 2003."Seasonal movements, migratory behavior, and site fidelity of West Indian manatees along the Atlantic coast of the United States." *Wildlife Monographs,* no. 151. Tucson, Ariz.: Wildlife Society.

Dexler, H. 1912. "Das Hirn von Halicore dugong Erxl." *Morphologisches Jahrbuch* 45, no. 1: 97–190.

Dierauf, L. A., and F.M.D. Gulland, eds. *CRC Handbook of Marine Mammal Medicine.* 2nd ed. Boca Raton: CRC Press.

Dijkgraaf, A. S. 1963. "The functioning and significance of the lateral-line organs." *Biological Reviews of the Cambridge Philosophical Society* 38, no. 1: 51–105.

Dimmock, A. W. 1908. "Big game hunting at sea: hunting the manatee." *Illustrated London News* 11: 333–34.

———. 1909. "Capturing a manatee." *Recreation* 29: 163–68.

Doering, P. H., R. H. Chamberlain, and D. E. Haunert. 2002. "Using submerged aquatic vegetation to establish minimum and maximum freshwater inflows to the Caloosahatchee estuary, Florida." *Estuaries* 25, no. 6B: 1343–354.

Domning, D. P. 1982. "Evolution of manatees: a speculative history." *Journal of Paleontology* 56, no. 3: 599–619.

———. 1994. "A phylogenetic analysis of the Sirenia." *Proceedings of the San Diego Society of Natural History* 29: 177–89.

———. 2001a. "The earliest known fully quadrupedal sirenian." *Nature* 413, no. 6856: 625–27.

———. 2001b. "Sirenians, seagrasses, and Cenozoic ecological change in the Caribbean." *Palaeogeography, Palaeoclimatology, Palaeoecology* 166, nos. 1–2: 27–50.

Domning, D. P., and L.-A. Hayek. 1984. "Horizontal tooth replacement in the Amazonian manatee (*Trichechus inunguis*)." *Mammalia* 48, no. 1: 105–27.

Domning, D. P., and V. de Buffrenil. 1991. "Hydrostasis in the sirenia: quantitative data and functional interpretations." *Marine Mammal Science* 7, no. 4: 331–68.

Domning, D. P., and P. D. Gingerich. 1994. "*Protosiren smithae*, new species (Mammalia, Sirenia), from the Middle Eocene of Wadi Hitan, Egypt." *Contributions from the Museum of Paleontology, University of Michigan* 29, no. 3: 69–87.

Dosch, F. 1915. "Bau und Entwicklung des Integuments der Sirenen." *Jenaische Zeitschrift* 53 (1914–1915): 805–54. Translated by D. A. Sinclair as "Structure and development of the integument of Sirenia," Technical Translation no. 1626. Ottawa: National Research Council of Canada, 1973.

Dykes, R. W. 1975. "Afferent fibers from mystacial vibrissae of cats and seals." *Journal of Neurophysiology* 38, no. 3: 650–62.

Eberhardt, L. L., and T. J. O'Shea. 1995. "Integration of manatee life-history data and population modeling." In *Population Biology of the Florida Manatee*, edited by T. J. O'Shea, B. B. Ackerman, and H. F. Percival, 269–79.

Edinger, T. 1933. "Uber Gehirne tertiarer Sirenia Agyptens und Mitteleuropas sowie der rezenten Seekuhe." *Abhandlungen der Mathematisch-naturwissenschaftlichen* (Akademie der Wissenschaften und der Literatur) 20: 5–36.

———. 1939. "Two notes on the central nervous system of fossil Sirenia." *Bulletin of the Faculty of Science, Fouad I University* 19: 41–57.

Eisenberg, J. F. 1981. *The Mammalian Radiations*. Chicago: University of Chicago Press.

Eisenberg, J. F., and D. E. Wilson. 1978. "Relative brain size and feeding strategies in the Chiroptera." *Evolution* 32, no. 4: 740–51.

Elliot Smith, G. 1902. *Descriptive and illustrated catalogue of the physiological series of comparative anatomy contained in the Museum of the Royal College of Surgeons of England*. Vol. 2. London: Taylor and Francis.

Etheridge, K., G. B. Rathbun, J. A. Powell, and H. I. Kochman. 1985. "Consumption of aquatic plants by the West Indian manatee." *Journal of Aquatic Plant Management* 23 (January): 21–25.

Fawcett, D. W. 1942. "The amedullary bones of the Florida manatee (*Trichechus latirostris*)." *American Journal of Anatomy* 71: 271–309.

Fay, F. H. 1982. "Ecology and biology of the Pacific Walrus, *Odobenus rosmarus divergens* Illiger." *U.S. Fish and Wildlife Service North American Fauna* 74: 1–279.

Finlay, B. L., and R. B. Darlington. 1995. "Linked regularities in the development and evolution of mammalian brains." *Science* 268 (June): 1578–584.

Florida Fish and Wildlife Conservation Commission. 2001. "Record number of manatees counted in 2001." Press release. June 10.

Forrester, D. J. 1992. *Parasites and Diseases of Wild Mammals in Florida.* Gainesville: University Press of Florida.

Forrester, D. J., F. H. White, J. C. Woodard, and N. P. Thompson. 1975. "Intussusception in a Florida manatee." *Journal of Wildlife Diseases* 11, no. 4: 566–68.

Friant, M. 1954. "Le cerveau du lamantin (*Manatus inunguis* Natterer)." *Vierteljahresschrift Naturforschenden Gesellschaft in Zurich* 99: 129–35.

Futerfas, J. 2003. "Correlates of boater knowledge and views regarding the Florida manatee and manatee related issues." Master's thesis, Florida International University.

Gallivan, G. J., and R. C. Best. 1980. "Metabolism and respiration of the Amazonian manatee *Trichechus inunguis*." *Physiological Zoology* 53, no.3: 245–53.

Gallivan, G. J., R. C. Best, and J. W. Kanwisher. 1983. "Temperature regu-

lation in the Amazonian manatee *Trichechus inunguis*." *Physiological Zoology* 56, no. 2: 255–62.

Garcia-Rodriguez, A. I., B. W. Bowen, D. Domning, A. A. Mignucci-Giannoni, M. Marmontel, R. A. Montoya-Ospina, B. Morales-Vela, M. Rudin, R. K. Bonde, and P. M. McGuire. 1998. "Phylogeography of the West Indian manatee (*Trichechus manatus*): How many populations and how many taxa?" *Molecular Ecology* 7, no. 9: 1137–149.

Garcia-Rodriguez, A. I., D. Moraga-Amador, W. Farmerie, P. McGuire, and T. L. King. 2000. "Isolation and characterization of microsatellite DNA markers in the Florida manatee (*Trichechus manatus latirostris*) and their application in selected sirenian species." *Molecular Ecology* 9, no. 12: 2161–163.

Garrison, V. H., E. A. Shinn, W. T. Foreman, D. W. Griffin, C. W. Holmes, C. A. Kellogg, M. S. Majewski, L. L. Richardson, K. B. Ritchie, and G. W. Smith. 2003. "African and Asian dust: from desert soils to coral reefs." *Bioscience* 53, no. 5: 469–80.

Garrod, A. H. 1877. "Notes on the manatee (*Manatus americanus*) recently living in the society's gardens." *Transactions of the Zoological Society of London* 10: 137–45.

Gerstein, E. R. 1994. "The manatee mind: discrimination training for sensory perception testing of West Indian manatees (*Trichechus manatus*)." *Marine Mammals* 1, no. 1: 10–21.

———. 2002. "Manatees, bioacoustics

and boats." *American Scientist* 90, no. 2: 154–63.

Gerstein, E. R., L. Gerstein, S. E. Forsythe, and J. E. Blue. 1999. "The underwater audiogram of the West Indian manatee (*Trichechus manatus*)." *Journal of the Acoustic Society of America* 105, no. 6: 3575–583.

Gingerich, P. D., D. P. Domning, C. E. Blane, and M. D. Uhen. 1994. "Cranial morphology of *Protosiren fraasi* (Mammalia, Sirenia) from the middle Eocene of Egypt: A new study using computed tomography." *Contributions from the Museum of Paleontology, University of Michigan* 29, no. 3: 41–67.

Glaser, K., and J. E. Reynolds, III. 2003. *Mysterious Manatees*. Gainesville: University Press of Florida.

Gomendio, M., A. H. Harcourt, and E.R.S. Roldan. 1998. "Sperm competition in mammals." In *Sperm Competition and Sexual Selection*, edited by T. R. Birkhead and A. P. Moller, 667–755. San Diego: Academic Press.

Gorzelany, J. F. 2004. "Evaluation of boater compliance with manatee speed zones along the Gulf Coast of Florida." *Coastal Management* 32, no. 3: 215–26.

Gottschaldt, K.-M., A. Iggo, and D. W. Young. 1973. "Functional characteristics of mechanoreceptors in sinus hair follicles of the cat." *Journal of Physiology (London)* 235, no. 2: 287–315.

Grabowski, S. M. 1994. *Following in the Wake of the Buccaneers*. Islamorada, Fla.: Islamorada Press.

Griebel, U., and A. Schmid. 1996. "Color vision in the manatee (*Trichechus manatus*)." *Vision Research* 36, no. 17: 2747–757.

———. 1997. "Brightness discrimination ability in the West Indian manatee (*Trichechus manatus*)." *Journal of Experimental Biology* 200, no. 11: 1587–592.

Harper, J. Y., D. A. Samuelson, and R. L. Reep. 2005. "Corneal vascularization in the Florida manatee (*Trichechus manatus latirostris*) and three-dimensional reconstruction of vessels." *Veterinary Ophthalmology* 8, no. 2: 89–99.

Hartman, D. S. 1971. "Ecology and behavior of the American manatee, *Trichechus manatus* Linnaeus, at Crystal River, Florida." PhD diss., Cornell University.

———. 1974. *Distribution, Status and Conservation of the Manatee in the United States*. Report prepared for the U.S. Fish and Wildlife Service, National Fish and Wildlife Laboratory, contract no. 14-16-0008-748; NTIS #PB81-140725.

———. 1979. "Ecology and behavior of the manatee (*Trichechus manatus*) in Florida." Special publication, *American Society of Mammalogists* 5: 1–153.

Hassan, E. S. 1989. "Hydrodynamic imaging of the surroundings by the lateral line of the blind cave fish *Anoptichthys jordani*." In *The Mechanosensory Lateral Line, Neurobiology and Evolution*, edited by S. Coombs, P. Gorner, and H. Munz, 217–27. New York: Springer-Verlag.

Hernandez, P., J. E. Reynolds, III, H. Marsh, and M. Marmontel. 1995. "Age and seasonality in spermatogenesis of Florida manatees." In *Popu-*

lation Biology of the Florida Manatee, edited by T. J. O'Shea, B. B. Ackerman, and H. F. Percival, 84–97.

Hill, D. A., and J. E. Reynolds, III. 1989. "Gross and microscopic anatomy of the kidney of the West Indian manatee, *Trichechus manatus* (Mammalia: Sirenia)." *Acta Anatomica* 135, no. 1: 53–56.

Hurst, L. A., and C. A. Beck. 1988. *Microhistological Characteristics of Selected Aquatic Plants in Florida, with Techniques for the Study of Manatee Food Habits*. U.S. Fish and Wildlife Service Biological Report 88, no. 18.

Irvine, A. B. 1983. "Manatee metabolism and its influence on distribution in Florida." *Biological Conservation* 25, no. 4: 315–34.

Irvine, A. B., and H. W. Campbell. 1978. "Aerial census of the West Indian manatee, *Trichechus manatus*, in the southeastern United States." *Journal of Mammalogy* 59, no. 3: 613–17.

Irvine, A. B., and M. D. Scott. 1984. "Development and use of marking techniques to study manatees in Florida." *Florida Scientist* 47, no. 1: 12–26.

Johansson, J.O.R., and H. S. Greening. 2000. "Seagrass restoration in Tampa Bay: A resource-based approach to estuarine management." In *Seagrasses: Monitoring, Ecology, Physiology, and Management*, edited by S. Barton, 279–93. Boca Raton: CRC Press.

Kamiya, T., and F. Yamasaki. 1981. "A morphological note on the sinus hair of the dugong." In *The Dugong*, edited by H. Marsh, 111–13. North Queensland, Australia: Zoology Department, James Cook University.

Kastelein, R. A., and M. A. Van Gaalen. 1988. "The tactile sensitivity of the mystacial vibrissae of a Pacific Walrus (*Odobenus rosmarus divergens*). Part 1." *Aquatic Mammals* 14, no. 3: 123–33.

Kenworthy, W. J., and D. E. Haunert. 1991. "The light requirements of seagrasses: proceedings of a workshop to examine the capability of water quality criteria, standards and monitoring programs to protect seagrasses." NOAA Technical Memorandum NMFS-SEFC-287.

Ketten, D. R., D. K. Odell, and D. P. Domning. 1992. "Structure, function and adaptation of the manatee ear." In *Marine Mammal Sensory Systems*, edited by J. A. Thomas, R. A. Kastelein, and A. Y. Supin, 77–95. New York: Plenum Press.

Kier, W. M., and K. K. Smith. 1985. "Tongues, tentacles and trunks: the biomechanics of movement in muscular hydrostats." *Zoological Journal of the Linnean Society* 83, no. 4: 307–24.

Kipps, E. K., W. A. McLellan, S. A. Rommel, and D. A. Pabst. 2002. "Skin density and its influence on buoyancy in the manatee (*Trichechus manatus latirostris*), harbor porpoise (*Phocoena phocoena*), and bottlenose dolphin (*Tursiops truncatus*)." *Marine Mammal Science* 18, no. 3: 765–78.

Klishin, V. O., R. P. Diaz, V. V. Popov, and A. Y. Supin. 1990. "Some characteristics of hearing of the Brazilian manatee (*Trichechus inunguis*)." *Aquatic Mammals* 16, no. 3: 140–44.

Koelsch, J. K. 2001. "Reproduction in female manatees observed in Sarasota Bay, Florida." *Marine Mammal Science* 17, no. 2: 331–42.

Lamb, G. D. 1983. "Tactile discrimination of textured surfaces: psychophysical performance measurements in humans." *Journal of Physiology (London)* 338 (May): 551–65.

Lander, M., A. Westgate, R. K. Bonde, and M. Murray. 2001. "Tagging and telemetry." In *Handbook of Marine Mammal Medicine*, 2nd ed., edited by L. A. Dierauf and F.M.D. Gulland, 851–80.

Langer, P. 1988. *The Mammalian Herbivore Stomach.* New York: Gustav Fischer.

Langtimm, C. A., T. J. O'Shea, R. Pradel, and C. A. Beck. 1998. "Estimates of annual survival probabilities for adult Florida manatees (*Trichechus manatus latirostris*)." *Ecology* 79, no. 3: 981–97.

Langtimm, C. A., and C. A. Beck. 2003. "Lower survival probabilities for adult Florida manatees in years with intense coastal storms." *Ecological Applications* 13, no. 1: 257–68.

Langtimm, C. A., C. A. Beck, H. H. Edwards, K. J. Fick-Child, B. B. Ackerman, S. L. Barton, and W. C. Hartley. 2004. "Survival estimates for Florida manatees from the photo-identification of individuals." *Marine Mammal Science* 20, no. 3: 438–63.

Larkin, I. V. 2000. "Reproductive endocrinology of the Florida manatee (*Trichechus manatus latirostris*): Estrous cycles, seasonal patterns and behavior." PhD diss., University of Florida.

Layne, J. N., and D. K. Caldwell. 1964. "Behavior of the Amazon dolphin, *Inia geoffrensis* (Blainville), in captivity." *Zoologica* 49, no. 1: 81–108.

Ledder, D. A. 1986. "Food habits of the West Indian manatee, *Trichechus manatus latirostris*, in South Florida." Master's thesis, University of Miami.

Lefebvre, L. W., and H. I. Kochman. 1991. "An evaluation of aerial survey replicate count methodology to determine trends in manatee abundance." *Wildlife Society Bulletin* 19, no. 3: 298–309.

Lefebvre, L. W., B. B. Ackerman, K. M. Portier, and K. H. Pollock. 1995. "Aerial survey as a technique for estimating manatee population size and trend—problems and prospects." In *Population Biology of the Florida Manatee*, edited by T. J. O'Shea, B. B. Ackerman, and H. F. Percival, 63–74.

Lefebvre, L. W., J. P. Reid, W. J. Kenworthy, and J. A. Powell. 2000. "Characterizing manatee habitat use and seagrass grazing in Florida and Puerto Rico: implications for conservation and management." *Pacific Conservation Biology* 5, no. 4: 289–98.

Lefebvre, L. W., M. Marmontel, J. P. Reid, G. B. Rathbun, and D. P. Domning. 2001. "Status and biogeography of the West Indian manatee." In *Biogeography of the West*

Indies, 2nd ed., edited by C. A. Woods and F. E. Sergile, 425–74. Boca Raton: CRC Press.

Lenes, J. M., B. P. Darrow, and C. Cattrall. 2001. "Iron fertilization and the Trichodesmium response on the West Florida shelf." Limnology and Oceanography 46, no. 6: 1261–277.

Levin, M. J., and C. J. Pfeiffer. 2002. "Gross and microscopic observations on the lingual structure of the Florida manatee Trichechus manatus latirostris." Anatomy, Histology and Embryology: Journal of Veterinary Medicine Series C 31, no. 5: 278–86.

Ling, J. K. 1977. "Vibrissae of marine mammals." In Functional Anatomy of Marine Mammals, vol. 3, edited by J. B. Harrison, 387–415. London: Academic Press.

Loerzel, S., and R. L. Reep. 1991. "Rindenkerne: unusual neuron aggregates in manatee cerebral cortex." International Association of Aquatic Animal Medicine Proceedings 22: 166–71.

Lomolino, M. V., and K. C. Ewel. 1984. "Digestive efficiencies of the West Indian manatee (Trichechus manatus)." Florida Scientist 47, no. 3: 176–79.

Lucas, F. A. 1916. "Sea cows, past and present." American Museum Journal (New York) 16: 315–18.

Mackay-Sim, A., D. Duvall, and B. M. Graves. 1985. "The West Indian manatee (Trichechus manatus) lacks a vomeronasal organ." Brain, Behavior and Evolution 27, no. 4: 186–94.

Maluf, N.S.R. 1989. "Renal anatomy of the manatee, Trichechus manatus (Linnaeus)." American Journal of Anatomy 184, no. 4: 269–86.

Mangel, M., and C. Tier. 1994. "Four facts every conservation biologist should know about persistence." Ecology 75, no. 3: 607–14.

Marino, L. 1998. "A comparison of encephalization between odontocete cetaceans and anthropoid primates." Brain, Behavior and Evolution 51, no. 4: 230–38.

Marmontel, M. 1995. "Age and reproduction in female Florida manatees." In Population Biology of the Florida Manatee, edited by T. J. O'Shea, B. B. Ackerman, and H. F. Percival, 98–119.

Marmontel, M., T. J. O'Shea, H. I. Kochman, and S. R. Humphrey. 1996. "Age determination in manatees using growth-layer-group counts in bone." Marine Mammal Science 12, no. 1: 54–88.

Marmontel, M., S. R. Humphrey, and T.J. O'Shea. 1997. "Population viability analysis of the Florida manatee (Trichechus manatus latriostris), 1976–1991." Conservation Biology 11, no. 2: 467–81.

Marsh, H., and D.F. Sinclair. 1989. "Correcting for visibility bias in strip transect aerial surveys of aquatic fauna." Journal of Wildlife Management 53, no. 4: 1017–1024.

Marsh, H., C. A. Beck, and T. Vargo. 1999. "Comparison of the capabilities of dugongs and West Indian manatees to masticate seagrasses." Marine Mammal Science 15, no. 1: 250–55.

Marshall, C. D. 1997. "The sirenian feeding apparatus: functional morphology of feeding involving perioral bristles and associated structures." PhD diss., University of Florida.

Marshall, C. D., and R. L. Reep. 1995. "Manatee cerebral cortex: cytoarchitecture of the caudal region in *Trichechus manatus latirostris.*" *Brain, Behavior and Evolution* 45, no. 1: 1–18.

Marshall, C. D., L. A. Clark, and R. L. Reep. 1998a. "The muscular hydrostat of the Florida manatee (*Trichechus manatus latirostris*) and its role in the use of perioral bristles." *Marine Mammal Science* 14, no. 2: 290–303.

Marshall, C. D., G. D. Huth, V. M. Edmonds, D. L. Halin, and R. L. Reep. 1998b. "Prehensile use of perioral bristles during feeding and associated behaviors of the Florida manatee (*Trichechus manatus latirostris*)." *Marine Mammal Science* 14, no. 2: 274–89.

Marshall, C. D., P. S. Kubilis, G. D. Huth, V. M. Edmonds, D. L. Halin, and R. L. Reep. 2000. "Food-handling ability and feeding-cycle length of manatees feeding upon several species of aquatic vegetation." *Journal of Mammalogy* 81, no. 3: 649–58.

Marshall, C. D., H. Maeda, M. Iwata, M. Furuta, A. Asano, F. Rosas, and R. L. Reep. 2003. "Orofacial morphology and feeding behavior of the dugong, Amazonian, West African, and Antillean manatees (Mammalia: Sirenia): functional morphology of the muscular-vibrissal complex." *Journal of Zoology* 259, no. 3: 245–60.

Mass, A. M., D. K. Odell, D. R. Ketten, and A. Y. Supin. 1997. "Retinal topography and visual acuity in the Florida manatee *Trichechus manatus latirostris.*" *Doklady Akademii Nauk* 355, no. 3: 427–30.

McNab, B. K. 2002. *The Physiological Ecology of Vertebrates : A View from Energetics.* Ithaca, N.Y.: Cornell University Press.

Miller, E. H. 1975. "Comparative study of facial expressions of two species of pinnipeds." *Behaviour* 53, nos. 3–4: 268–84.

Miller, K. E., B. B. Ackerman, L. W. Lefebvre, and K. B. Clifton. 1998. "An evaluation of strip-transect aerial survey methods for monitoring manatee populations in Florida." *Wildlife Society Bulletin* 26, no. 3: 561–70.

Montgomery, J. C., C. F. Baker, and A. G. Carton. 1997. "The lateral line can mediate rheotaxis in fish." *Nature* 389: 960–63.

Moore, J. C. 1951. "The range of the Florida manatee." *Quarterly Journal of the Florida Academy of Sciences* 14, no. 1: 1–19.

———. 1956. *Observations of Manatees in Aggregations.* American Museum Novitates, no. 1811. New York: American Museum of Natural History.

Murie, J. 1872. "On the form and structure of the manatee (*Manatus americanus*)." *Transactions of the Zoological Society of London* 8: 127–202.

———. 1880. "Further observations on the manatee." *Transactions of the*

Zoological Society of London 11: 19–48.

Niezrecki, C., R. Phillips, M. Meyer, and D. O. Beusse. 2003. "Acoustic detection of manatee vocalizations." *Journal of the Acoustic Society of America* 114, no. 3: 1640–647.

Nowacek, D. P., B. M. Casper, R. S. Wells, S. M. Nowacek, and D. A. Mann. 2003. "Intraspecific and geographic variation of West Indian manatee (*Trichechus manatus spp.*) vocalizations." *Journal of the Acoustic Society of America* 114, no. 1: 66–69.

Nowacek, S. M., R. S. Wells, E.C.G. Owen, T. R. Speakman, R. O. Flamm, and D. P. Nowacek. 2004. "Florida manatees, *Trichechus manatus latirostris*, respond to approaching vessels." *Biological Conservation* 119, no. 4: 517–23.

Odell, D. K., and J. E. Reynolds, III. 1979. "Observations of manatee mortality in south Florida." *Journal of Wildlife Management* 43, no. 2: 572–77.

Odell, D. K., G. D. Bossart, M. K. Lowe, and T. D. Hopkins. 1995. "Reproduction of the West Indian manatee in captivity." In *Population Biology of the Florida Manatee*, edited by T. J. O'Shea, B. B. Ackerman, and H. F. Percival, 192–93.

O'Donnell, D. J. 1981. "Manatees and man in Central America." PhD diss., University of California, Los Angeles.

Ortiz, R. M., G.A.J. Worthy, and D. S. MacKenzie. 1998. "Osmoregulation in wild and captive West Indian manatees (*Trichechus manatus*)."

Physiological Zoology 71, no. 4: 449–57.

Ortiz, R. M., G.A.J. Worthy, and F. M. Byers. 1999. "Estimation of water turnover rates of captive West Indian manatees (*Trichechus manatus*) held in fresh and salt water." *Journal of Experimental Biology* 202 (January): 33–38.

Ortiz, R. M., D. S. MacKenzie, and G.A.J. Worthy. 2000. "Thyroid hormone concentrations in captive and free-ranging West Indian manatees (*Trichechus manatus*)." *Journal of Experimental Biology* 203, no. 23: 3631–637.

O'Shea, T. J. 1988. "The past, present, and future of manatees in the southeastern United States: realities, misunderstandings and enigmas." In *Proceedings of the 3rd Southeastern Nongame and Endangered Wildlife Symposium*, edited by R. R. Odom, K. A. Riddleberger, and J. C. Ozier, 184–204. Social Circle, Ga.: Georgia Department of Natural Resources.

———. 1992. "Florida manatee, *Trichechus manatus latirostris*." In *Rare and Endangered Biota of Florida*, vol. 1, *Mammals*, edited by S. R. Humphrey, 190–200. Gainesville, University Press of Florida.

———. 1994. "Manatees." *Scientific American* 271: 66–72.

O'Shea, T. J., J. F. Moore, and H. I. Kochman. 1984. "Contaminant concentrations in manatees in Florida." *Journal of Wildlife Management* 48, no. 3: 741–48.

O'Shea T. J., C. A. Beck, R. K. Bonde, H. I. Kochman, and D. K. Odell. 1985.

"An analysis of manatee mortality patterns in Florida, 1976–81." *Journal of Wildlife Management* 49, no. 1: 1–11.

O'Shea, T. J., and R. L. Reep. 1990. "Encephalization quotients and life-history traits in the Sirenia." *Journal of Mammalogy* 71, no. 4: 534–43.

O'Shea, T. J., G. B. Rathbun, R. K. Bonde, C. D. Buergelt, and D. K. Odell. 1991. "An epizootic of Florida manatees associated with a dinoflagellate bloom." *Marine Mammal Science* 7, no. 2: 165–79.

O'Shea, T. J., and B. B. Ackerman. 1995. "Population biology of the Florida manatee: an overview." In *Population Biology of the Florida Manatee*, edited by T. J. O'Shea, B. B. Ackerman, and H. F. Percival, 280–88.

O'Shea, T. J., and W. C. Hartley. 1995. "Reproduction and early-age survival of manatees at Blue Spring, Upper St. Johns River, Florida." In *Population Biology of the Florida Manatee*, edited by T. J. O'Shea, B. B. Ackerman, and H. F. Percival, 157–76.

O'Shea, T. J., and C. A. Langtimm. 1995. "Estimation of survival of adult Florida manatees in the Crystal River, at Blue Spring, and on the Atlantic Coast." In *Population Biology of the Florida Manatee*, edited by T. J. O'Shea, B. B. Ackerman, and H. F. Percival, 194–222.

O'Shea, T. J., B. B. Ackerman, and H. F. Percival. 1995. "Introduction." In *Population Biology of the Florida Manatee*, edited by T. J. O'Shea, B. B. Ackerman, and H. F. Percival, 1–5.

O'Shea, T. J., L. W. Lefebvre, and C. A. Beck. 2001. "Florida manatees: per-spectives on populations, pain, and protection." In *CRC Handbook of Marine Mammal Medicine*, 2nd ed., edited by L. A. Dierauf and F.M.D. Gulland, 31–43.

O'Shea, T. J., B. B. Ackerman, and H. F. Percival, eds. 1995. *Population Biology of the Florida Manatee (Trichechus manatus latirostris).* Washington, D.C.: U.S. Department of the Interior, National Biological Service.

Pabst, D. A., S. A. Rommel, and W. A. McLellan. 1999. "The functional morphology of marine mammals." In *Biology of Marine Mammals*, edited by J. E. Reynolds, III, and S. A. Rommel, 15–72.

Packard, J. M. 1981. *Abundance, Distribution and Feeding Habits of Manatees (Trichechus manatus) Wintering between St. Lucie and Palm Beach Inlets, Florida.* Report prepared for the U.S. Fish and Wildlife Service, contract no. 14-16-0004-80-105.

———. 1984. "Impact of manatees *Trichechus manatus* on seagrass communities in eastern Florida." *Acta Zoologica Fennica* 172, no. 1: 21–22.

Packard, J. M., R. C. Summers, and L. B. Barnes. 1985. "Variation of visibility bias during aerial surveys of manatees." *Journal of Wildlife Management* 49, no. 2: 347–51.

Packard, J. M., D. B. Siniff, and J. A. Cornell. 1986. "Use of replicate counts to improve indices of trends in manatee abundance." *Wildlife Society Bulletin* 14, no. 3: 265–75.

Peterson, R. S., and G. A. Bartholomew.

1967. "The natural history and behavior of the California sea lion." Special publication, *American Society of Mammalogists* 1: 1–79.

Phillips, C. 1964. *The Captive Sea: Life Behind the Scenes of the Great Oceanariums.* Philadelphia: Chilton Books.

Pierce, R. H. 1986. "Red tide (*Ptychodiscus brevis*) toxin aerosols: a review." *Toxicon* 24, no. 10: 955–65.

Pierce, R. H., M. S. Henry, L. S. Proffitt, and P. A. Hasbrouck. 1990. "Red tide (Brevetoxin) enrichment in marine aerosol." In *Toxic Marine Phytoplankton*, edited by E. Graneli, 397–402. New York: Elsevier.

Powell, J. A. 2002. *Manatees: Natural History and Conservation.* Stillwater, Minn.: Voyageur Press.

Provancha, J. A., and C. R. Hall. 1991. "Observations on associations between seagrass beds and manatees in east central Florida." *Florida Scientist* 54, no. 2: 87–98.

Rathbun, G. B., J. P. Reid, and J. B. Bourassa. 1987. "Design and construction of a tethered, floating radiotag assembly for manatees." National Technical Information Service, #PB87-161345/AS. Springfield, Va.: U.S. Department of Commerce.

Rathbun, G. B., J. P. Reid, R. K. Bonde, and J. A. Powell. 1995. "Reproduction in free-ranging Florida manatees." In *Population Biology of the Florida Manatee*, edited by T. J. O'Shea, B. B. Ackerman, and H. F. Percival, 135–56.

Reep, R. L., J. I. Johnson, R. C. Switzer, and W. I. Welker. 1989. "Manatee cerebral cortex: cytoarchitecture of the frontal region in *Trichechus*

manatus latirostris." *Brain, Behavior and Evolution* 34, no. 6: 365–86.

Reep, R. L., and T. J. O'Shea. 1990. "Regional brain morphometry and lissencephaly in the Sirenia." *Brain, Behavior and Evolution* 35, no. 4: 185–94.

Reep, R. L., C. D. Marshall, M. L. Stoll, and D. M. Whitaker. 1998. "Distribution and innervation of facial bristles and hairs in the Florida manatee (*Trichechus manatus latirostris*)." *Marine Mammal Science* 14, no. 2: 257–73.

Reep, R. L., C. D. Marshall, M. L. Stoll, B. L. Homer, and D. A. Samuelson. 2001. "Microanatomy of perioral bristles in the Florida manatee, *Trichechus manatus latirostris.*" *Brain, Behavior and Evolution* 58, no. 1: 1–14.

Reep, R. L., C. D. Marshall, and M. L. Stoll. 2002. "Tactile hairs on the postcranial body in Florida manatees: a mammalian lateral line?" *Brain, Behavior and Evolution* 59, no. 3: 141–54.

Reid, J. P., and T. J. O'Shea. 1989. "Three years operational use of satellite transmitters on Florida manatees: Tag improvements based on challenges from the field." In *Proceedings of the 1989 North American Argos Users Conference and Exhibit*, 217–32. Landover, Md.: Service Argos.

Reid, J. P., R. K. Bonde, and T. J. O'Shea. 1995. "Reproduction and mortality of radio-tagged and recognizable manatees on the Atlantic Coast of Florida." In *Population Biology of the Florida Manatee*, edited by T. J.

O'Shea, B. B. Ackerman, and H. F. Percival, 171–91.

Reynolds, J. E., III. 1979. "The semisocial manatee." *Natural History* 88, no. 2: 44–53.

———. 1981. "Aspects of the social behavior and herd structure of a semi-isolated colony of West Indian manatees, *Trichechus manatus.*" *Mammalia* 45, no. 4: 431–51.

Reynolds, J. E., III, and D. K. Odell. 1991. *Manatees and Dugongs.* New York: Facts on File.

Reynolds, J. E., III, and J. R. Wilcox. 1994. "Observations of Florida manatees (*Trichechus manatus latirostris*) around selected power plants in winter." *Marine Mammal Science* 10, no. 2: 163–77.

Reynolds, J. E., III, and S. A. Rommel. 1996. "Structure and function of the gastrointestinal tract of the Florida manatee, *Trichechus manatus latirostris.*" *Anatomical Record* 245, no. 3: 539–58.

Reynolds, J. E., III, and R. S. Wells. 2003. *Dolphins, Whales, and Manatees of Florida: A Guide to Sharing their World.* Gainesville: University Press of Florida.

Reynolds, J. E., III, S. A. Rommel, and M. E. Pitchford. 2004. "The likelihood of sperm competition in manatees—explaining an apparent paradox." *Marine Mammal Science* 20, no. 3: 464–76.

Reynolds, J. E., III, and S. A. Rommel, eds. *Biology of Marine Mammals.* Washington, D.C.: Smithsonian Institution.

Rice, F. L. 1995. "Comparative aspects of barrel structure and development."

In *Cerebral Cortex,* vol. 11, *The Barrel Cortex in Rodents,* edited by E. G. Jones and I. T. Diamond, 1–75. New York: Plenum Press.

Rice, F. L., A. Mance, and B. L. Munger. 1986. "A comparative light microscopic analysis of the innervation of the mystacial pad. I. Vibrissal follicles." *Journal of Comparative Neurology* 252, no. 2: 154–74.

Rice, F. L., B. T. Fundin, J. Arviddson, H. Aldskogius, and O. Johansson. 1997. "Comprehensive immunofluorescence and lectin binding analysis of vibrissal follicle sinus complex innervation in the mystacial pad of the rat." *Journal of Comparative Neurology* 385, no. 2: 149–84.

Rommel, S. A., and Reynolds, J. E., III. 2000. "Diaphragm structure and function in the Florida manatee (*Trichechus manatus latirostris*)." *Anatomical Record* 259, no. 1: 41 51.

Rommel, S. A., D. A. Pabst, and W. A. McLellan. 2001. "Functional morphology of venous structures associated with the male and female reproductive systems in Florida manatees (*Trichechus manatus latirostris*)." *Anatomical Record* 264, no. 4: 339–47.

Runge, M. C. 2003. "A model for assessing incidental take of manatees due to watercraft-related activities." Appendix I to *Final Environmental Impact Statement: Rulemaking for the Incidental Take of Small Numbers of Florida Manatees (Trichechus manatus latirostris) Resulting from Government Programs Related to Watercraft Access and Watercraft Operation in the State of Florida.* Jacksonville,

Fla.: U.S. Fish and Wildlife Service, March.

Runge, M. C., C. A. Langtimm, and W. L. Kendall. 2004. "A stage-based model of manatee population dynamics." *Marine Mammal Science* 20, no. 3: 361–85.

Scholander, P. F., and L. Irving. 1941. "Experimental investigations on the respiration and diving of the Florida manatee." *Journal of Cellular and Comparative Physiology* 17, no. 2: 169–91.

Shane, S. H. 1983. "Abundance, distribution, and movements of manatees (*Trichechus manatus*) in Brevard County, Florida." *Bulletin of Marine Science* 33: 1–9.

Snipes, R. L. 1984. "Anatomy of the cecum of the West Indian manatee, *Trichechus manatus* (Mammalia, Sirenia)." *Zoomorphology* 104, no. 2: 67–78.

Sousa-Lima, R. S., A. P. Paglia, G.A.B. Da Fonseca. 2002. "Signature information and individual recognition in the isolation cells of Amazonian manatees, *Trichechus inunguis* (Mammalia: Sirenia)." *Animal Behavior* 63, no. 2: 301–10.

Steidinger, K. A., and K. Haddad. 1981. "Biologic and hydrographic aspects of red tides." *Bioscience* 31, no. 11: 814–19.

Steidinger, K. A., and D. G. Baden. 1984. "Toxic marine dinoflagellates." In *Dinoflagellates*, edited by D. L. Spector, 201–61. New York: Academic Press.

Stejneger, L. 1883. "Contributions to the history of the Commander Islands 1.

Notes on the natural history, including descriptions of new cetaceans." *Proceedings of the United States National Museum* 6: 58–89.

———. 1887. "How the great northern sea-cow (*Rytina*) became exterminated." *American Naturalist* 21: 1047–1056.

Steller, G. W. 1751. "De bestiis marinis." *Novi Commentarii Academiae Scientarum Petropolitanae* 2: 289–398.

Supin, A. Y., V. V. Popov, and A. M. Mass. 2001. *The Sensory Physiology of Aquatic Mammals*. Boston: Kluwer Academic.

Switzer, R. C., J. I. Johnson, and J.A.W. Kirsch. 1980. "Phylogeny through brain traits: relation of lateral olfactory tract fibers to the accessory olfactory formation as a palimpsest of mammalian descent." *Brain, Behavior and Evolution* 17, no. 5: 339–63.

Tester, P. A., and K. A. Steidinger. 1997. "*Gymnodinium breve* red tide blooms: Initiation, transport, and consequences of surface circulation." *Limnology and Oceanography* 42, no. 5: 1039–1051.

Thayer, G. W., K. A. Bjorndal, J. C. Ogden, S. C. Williams, and J. C. Zieman. 1984. "Role of larger herbivores in seagrass communities." *Estuaries* 7, no. 4: 351–76.

Thompson, W. L., G. C. White, and C. Gowan. 1998. *Monitoring Vertebrate Populations*. San Diego: Academic Press.

True, F. W. 1884. "The sirenian or sea-cows." In *The Fisheries and Fishery*

Industries of the United States, edited by G. B. Goode et al., sec. 1, "Natural history of useful aquatic animals," 114–136. Washington, D.C.: Government Printing Office.

Tyack, P., and H. Whitehead. 1982. "Male competition in large groups of wintering humpback whales." *Behaviour* 83, nos. 1–2: 132–54.

U.S. Fish and Wildlife Service. 2001. *Florida Manatee Recovery Plan, (Trichechus manatus latirostris)*. 3rd revision. Atlanta: U.S. Fish and Wildlife Service.

U.S. Geological Survey. 1995. "Summary on the movements of the manatee Chessie during 1995." Fact sheet. National Biological Survey, Sirenia Project. December 31.

U.S. Marine Mammal Commission. 1996. *Annual Report to Congress*. Bethesda, Md.: U.S. Marine Mammal Commission.

van Dongen, P.A.M. 1998. "Brain size in vertebrates." In *The Central Nervous System of Vertebrates*, edited by R. Nieuwenhuys, H. J. ten Donkelaar, and C. Nicholson, 2099–134. Berlin: Springer.

Vicente, V. P., J. A. Arroyo-Aguilu, and J. A. Rivera. 1980. "*Thalassia* as a food source: importance and potential in the marine and terrestrial environments." *Journal of the Agricultural University of Puerto Rico* 64: 107–20.

Wainwright, S. A., W. D. Biggs, J. D. Currey, and J. M. Gosline. 1982. *Mechanical Design in Organisms*. Princeton: Princeton University Press.

Walsh, G. E., and T. F. Grow. 1973. "Composition of *Thalassia testudinum* and *Ruppia maritima*." *Quarterly Journal of the Florida Academy of Sciences* 35, nos. 2–3: 97–108.

Walsh, J. J., and K. A. Steidinger. 2001. "Saharan dust and Florida red tides: The cyanophyte connection." *Journal of Geophysical Research—Oceans* 106, no. C6: 11597–612.

Walsh, M. T., and G. D. Bossart. 1999. "Manatee medicine." In *Zoo and Wildlife Medicine*, edited by M. E. Fowler and R. E. Miller, 507–16. Philadelphia: W. B. Saunders.

Walsh, M. T., and E. V. Gaynor. 2001. "Thermal imaging of marine mammals." In *CRC Handbook of Marine Mammal Medicine*, 2nd ed., edited by L. A. Dierauf and F.M.D. Gulland, 643–54.

Warner, A.C.I. 1981. "Rate of passage of digesta through the gut of mammals and birds." *Nutritional Abstracts and Reviews Series B* 51: 789–820.

Wartzok, D., and D. R. Ketten. 1999. "Marine mammal sensory systems." In *Biology of Marine Mammals*, edited by J. E. Reynolds, III, and S. A. Rommel, 117–75.

Webb, S. D. 1995. "Biological implications of the Middle Miocene Amazon seaway." *Science* 269, no. 5222: 361–62.

Weigle, B. L., I. E. Wright, M. Ross, and R. Flamm. 2001. *Movements of Radio-tagged Manatees in Tampa Bay and Along Florida's West Coast 1991–1996*. Florida Marine Research Institute, Technical Report 7.

Welker, W. I. 1990. "Explaining the morphology of cerebral convolutions: a review of determinants of gyri and sulci." In *Cerebral Cortex*, vol. 8, edited by E. G. Jones and A. Peters, 3–136. New York: Plenum Press.

Wells, R. S., D. J. Boness, and G. B. Rathbun. 1999. "Behavior." In *Biology of Marine Mammals*, edited by J. E. Reynolds, III, and S. A. Rommel, 324–422.

Worthy, G. 2001. "Nutrition and energetics." In *CRC Handbook of Marine Mammal Medicine*, 2nd ed., edited by L. A. Dierauf and F.M.D. Gulland, 791–828.

Wright, I. E., S. D. Wright, and J. M. Sweat. 1998. "Use of passive integrated transponder (PIT) tags to identify manatees (*Trichechus manatus latirostris*)." *Marine Mammal Science* 14, no. 1: 641–45.

Wright, I. E., J. E. Reynolds, III, B. B. Ackerman, L. I. Ward, B. L. Weigle, and W. A. Szelistowski. 2002. "Trends in manatee (*Trichechus manatus latirostris*) counts and habitat use in Tampa Bay, 1987–1994: implications for conservation." *Marine Mammal Science* 18, no. 1: 259–74.

Wright, S. D., B. B. Ackerman, R. K. Bonde, C. A. Beck, and D. J. Banowetz. 1995. "Analysis of watercraft-related mortality of manatees in Florida, 1979–1991." In *Population Biology of the Florida Manatee*, edited by T. J. O'Shea, B. B. Ackerman, and H. F. Percival, 259–68.

Yamasaki, F. S., S. Komatsu, and T. Kamiya. 1980. "A comparative morphological study on the tongues of manatee and dugong (Sirenia)." *Scientific Reports of the Whales Research Institute (Tokyo)* 32: 127–44.

Yan, J., K. B. Clifton, J. J. Mecholsky, and R. L. Reep. 2006. "Application of fracture mechanics to failure in manatee rib bone." *Journal of Biomechanics* (forthcoming).

Zeiller, W. 1992. *Introducing the Manatee*. Gainesville: University Press of Florida.

Index

Pages in **boldface** refer to plates.
Pages in *italics* refer to photographs and illustrations.

Roger Reep is a neuroscientist and professor in the College of Veterinary Medicine at the University of Florida. He has studied manatee biology for over 20 years and has published numerous papers and lectured on the organization and evolution of mammalian nervous systems. He was lead organizer for the First International Manatee and Dugong Research Conference in 1994 and for the Florida Marine Mammal Health Conferences in 2002 and 2005.

Bob Bonde is a biologist with the U.S. Geological Survey, Sirenia Project, and has been studying manatees for 25 years. He has published many scientific papers based on his study of genetics and manatee mortality and on his aerial surveys, radio tracking, and observations of animals in their natural habitat.